# BUSINESS BASICS

## Information Technology

**PUBLISHING**

First edition 1995
Third edition September 2000

ISBN 0 7517 2128 X
(previous edition 0 7517 2119 0)


British Library Cataloguing-in Publication Data

A catalogue record for this book is available from the British Library

Printed in England by

Ashford Colour Press




Published by

BPP Publishing Limited

Aldine House, Aldine Place

London W12 8AW


www.bpp.com

BPP would like to thank Genesys Editorial for editorial and production input on earlier editions of this book

# CONTENTS

# PREFACE

BUSINESS BASICS are targeted specifically at the needs of:

- Students taking business studies degrees
- Students taking business-related modules of other degrees
- Students on courses at a comparable level
- Others requiring business information at this level

This *Information Technology* text has been written with two key goals in mind.

- To present a substantial and useful body of knowledge on information technology at degree level. This is not just a set of revision notes – it explains the subject in detail and does not assume prior knowledge.

- To make learning and revision as easy as possible. Each chapter:

  - Starts with an introduction and clear objectives
  - Contains numerous activities
  - Includes a chapter roundup summarising the points made
  - Ends with a quick quiz

  And at the back of the book you will find:

  - Multiple choice questions and answers
  - Exam style questions and answers

The philosophy of the series is thus to combine techniques which actively promote learning with a no-nonsense, systematic approach to the necessary factual content of the course.

BPP Publishing have for many years been the leading providers of targeted texts for students of professional qualifications. We know that our customers need to study effectively in order to pass their exams, and that they cannot afford to waste time. They expect clear, concise and highly focused study material. As university and college education becomes more market driven, students rightly demand the same high standards of efficiency in their learning material. The BUSINESS BASICS series meets those demands.

*BPP Publishing*
*September 2000*

**Titles in this series:**

Accounting
Law
Quantitative Methods
Information Technology
Economics
Marketing
Human Resource Management
Organisational Behaviour

> You may order other titles in the series using the form at the end of this book. If you would like to send in your comments on this book, please turn to the review form following the order form.

# HOW TO USE THIS STUDY GUIDE

This book can simply be read straight through from beginning to end, but you will get far more out of it if you keep a pen and paper to hand. The most effective form of learning is *active learning*, and we have therefore filled the text with exercises for you to try as you go along. We have also provided objectives, a chapter roundup and a quick quiz for each chapter. Here is a suggested approach to enable you to get the most out of this book.

(a)  Select a chapter to study, and read the introduction and objectives at the start of the chapter.

(b)  Next read the chapter roundup at the end of the chapter (before the quick quiz and the answers to activities). Do not expect this brief summary to mean too much at this stage, but see whether you can relate some of the points made in it to some of the objectives.

(c)  Next read the chapter itself. Do attempt each activity as you come to it. You will derive the greatest benefit from the activity if you write down your answers before checking them against the answers at the end of the chapter.

(d)  As you read, make use of the 'notes' column to add your own comments, references to other material and so on. Do try to formulate your own views. In economics, many things are matters of interpretation and there is often scope for alternative views. The more you engage in a dialogue with the book, the more you will get out of your study.

(e)  When you reach the end of the chapter, read the chapter roundup again. Then go back to the objectives at the start of the chapter, and ask yourself whether you have achieved them.

(f)  Finally, consolidate your knowledge by writing down your answers to the quick quiz. You can check your answers by going back to the text. The very act of going back and searching the text for relevant details will further improve your grasp of the subject.

(g)  You can then try the case studies at the end of most chapters, the multiple choice questions at the end of the book and the exam style questions to which you are referred at the end of the chapter. Alternatively, you could wait to do these until you have started your revision – it's up to you.

**Further reading**

While we are confident that the BUSINESS BASICS books offer excellent range and depth of subject coverage, we are aware that you will be encouraged to follow up particular points in books other than your main textbook, in order to get alternative points of view and more detail on key topics.

Information Technology is a fast- moving discipline in which books rapidly become outdated. To learn more about a specific application, the "... for Dummies" (IDG Books), and the "... for Idiots (QUE) are very good.

For a business-system orientated information technology text we recommend Graham Curtis, *Business Information Systems – Analysis, Design and Practice*, 3rd (1999) edition, Addison-Wesley Longman.

# Chapter 1 :
# INFORMATION AND INFORMATION SYSTEMS

## Introduction

Welcome to Business Basics: Information Technology. One of the main areas that technology has impacted upon business is in the design and operation of information systems. In this Chapter we introduce the concept of an information system, and in particular a management information system.

We start with the information requirements of the modern organisation.

## Your objectives

After completing this chapter you should:

(a)   Understand systems theory and its relevance to Management Information Systems (MIS).

(b)   Appreciate the information requirements of a range of organisations.

(c)   Know the main features of different types of MIS.

(d)   Be aware of how Information Technology has contributed to the more efficient use of information.

# 1 SYSTEMS THEORY

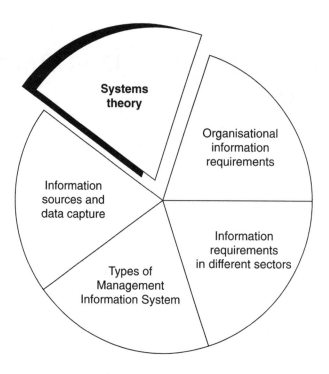

The term system is hard to define because it is so widely used. One definition of a system is given below, followed by a definition relevant in a business context.

## Definition

> A **system** is a set of interacting components that operate together to accomplish a purpose.
>
> A **business system** is a collection of people, machines and methods organised to accomplish a set of specific functions.

## 1.1 Why study systems theory?

An understanding of the concepts of systems theory is relevant to the design of Management Information Systems and it presents a particularly useful way of describing and analysing computer systems. The application of systems theory may:

(a) Create an awareness of subsystems (the different parts of an organisation), each with potentially conflicting goals which must be brought into line with each other.

(b) Help in the design and development of information systems to help decision makers ensure that decisions are made for the benefit of the organisation as a whole.

(c) Help identify the effect of the environment on systems. The external factors that affect an organisation may be wide ranging. For example, the government (in all its forms), competitors, trade unions, creditors and shareholders all have an interactive link with an organisation.

(d)    Highlight the dynamic aspects of the business organisation, and the factors which influence the growth and development of all its subsystems.

## 1.2    The component parts of a system

A system has three component parts: inputs, processes and outputs.

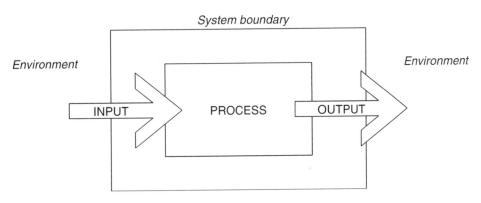

*Inputs*

Inputs provide the system with what it needs to be able to operate. Input may vary from matter, energy or human actions, to information.

(a)    Matter might include, in a manufacturing operation, adhesives or rivets.

(b)    Human input might consist of typing an instruction booklet or starting up a piece of machinery.

Inputs may be outputs from other systems. As we have seen, the output from a transactions processing system is part of the input for a management information system.

*Processes*

A process transforms an input into an output. Processes may involve tasks performed by humans, plant, computers, chemicals and a wide range of other actions. Processes may consist of assembly, for example where electronic consumer goods are being manufactured, or disassembly, for example where oil is refined. There is not necessarily a clear relationship between the number of inputs to a process and the number of outputs.

*Outputs*

Outputs are the results of the processing. They could be said to represent the purpose for which the system exists. Many outputs are used as inputs to other systems. Alternatively outputs may be discarded as waste (an input to the ecological system) or re-input to the system which has produced them, for example, in certain circumstances, defective products.

## 1.3    The system boundary

Every system has a boundary that separates it from its environment. For example, a cost accounting department's boundary can be expressed in terms of who works in it and what work it does. This boundary will separate it from other departments, such as the financial accounts department.

### 1.4 The environment

Anything which is outside the system boundary belongs to the system's environment and not to the system itself. A system accepts inputs from the environment and provides outputs into the environment.

Often, whether something is a system or a subsystem is a matter of definition, and depends on the context of the observer. For example, an organisation is a social system, and its 'environment' may be seen as society as a whole. Another way of looking at an organisation would be to regard it as a subsystem of the entire social system. Information links up the different systems and subsystems in an organisation.

### 1.5 Open systems and closed systems

In systems theory a distinction is made between open systems and closed systems.

**Definitions**

> A **closed system** is a system which is isolated from its environment and independent of it.
>
> An **open system** is a system connected to an interacting with its environment.

All business organisations, have some interaction with their environment, and so are open systems.

Open and closed systems can be described by diagram as follows.

*Closed system*

```
Shut off from
its environment
```

*Open system*

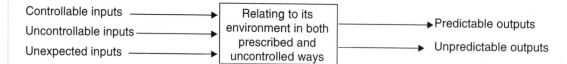

```
Controllable inputs ──────────▶   Relating to its          ──────▶ Predictable outputs
Uncontrollable inputs ────────▶   environment in both
                                  prescribed and
Unexpected inputs ────────────▶   uncontrolled ways        ──────▶ Unpredictable outputs
```

A business is an open system where management decisions are influenced by or have an influence on suppliers, customers, competitors, society as a whole and the government.

### 1.6 Control systems

A system must be controlled to keep it steady or enable it to change safely, in other words each system must have its control system. Control is required because unpredictable disturbances arise and enter the system, so that actual results (outputs of the system) deviate from the expected results.

Examples of disturbances in a business system would be the entry of a powerful new competitor into the market, an unexpected rise in labour costs, the failure of a supplier to deliver promised raw materials, or the tendency of employees to stop working in order to chatter or gossip.

A control system must ensure that the business is capable of surviving these disturbances by dealing with them in an appropriate manner.

To have a control system, there has to be a plan, standard, budget, rule book or some other guideline towards which the system as a whole should be aiming. The standard is defined by the objectives of the system.

## 1.7 Feedback

Feedback is the return of part of the output of a system to the input as a means towards improved quality or correction of errors. In a business organisation, feedback is information produced from within the organisation (for example management control reports) with the purpose of helping management and other employees and triggering control decisions.

**Definition**

> **Feedback** may be defined as modification or control of a process or system by its results or effects, by measuring differences between desired and actual results.

In a control system part of the output is fed back, so that the output can initiate control action to change either the activities of the system or the system's input.

You might like to think of a budgetary control system in a company, by which results are monitored, deviations from plan are identified and control (corrective) action taken as appropriate.

## 1.8 Filtering

**Definition**

> **Filtering** means removing 'impurities' such as excessive detail from data as it is passed up the organisation hierarchy.

Operational staff may need all the detail to do their jobs, but when they report to higher and higher subsystems the data can be progressively summarised. Unnecessary detail is filtered out leaving only the important points.

A possible problem with this is that sometimes the 'filter' may let through unimportant information and/or remove important information, with the result that the message is distorted at the next level.

Business Basics: Information Technology

## 2 ORGANISATIONAL INFORMATION REQUIREMENTS

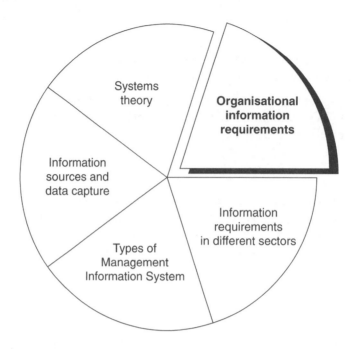

### Definitions

**Data** is the raw material for data processing. Data consists of numbers, letters and symbols and relates to facts, events, and transactions.

**Information** is data that has been processed in such a way as to be meaningful to the person who receives it.

### 2.1 What is information used for?

All organisations require information for a range of purposes. These can be categorised as follows.

- Information for planning
- Information for controlling
- Information for recording transactions
- Information for performance measurement
- Information for decision making

*Planning*

Planning requires a knowledge of the available resources, possible time-scales and the likely outcome under alternative scenarios. Information is required that helps decision making, and how to implement decisions taken.

*Controlling*

Once a plan is implemented, its actual performance must be controlled. Information is required to assess whether it is proceeding as planned or whether there is some unexpected deviation from plan. It may consequently be necessary to take some form of corrective action.

*Recording transactions*

Information about each transaction or event is required. Reasons include:

    (a)    Documentation of transactions can be used as evidence in a case of dispute.

    (b)    There may be a legal requirement to record transactions, for example for accounting and audit purposes.

    (c)    Operational information can be built up, allowing control action to be taken.

*Performance measurement*

Just as individual operations need to be controlled, so overall performance must be measured. Comparisons against budget or plan are able to be made. This may involve the collection of information on, for example, costs, revenues, volumes, time-scale and profitability.

*Decision making*

Just as decision making can be analysed into three levels, so information necessary to make decisions within an organisation can be analysed in the same way.

## 2.2    Types of information

*Strategic information*

Strategic information is used to plan the objectives of the organisation, and to assess whether the objectives are being met in practice. Such information includes overall profitability, the profitability of different segments of the business, future market prospects, the availability and cost of raising new funds, total cash needs, total manning levels and capital equipment needs.

Strategic information is:

- Derived from both internal and external sources
- Summarised at a high level
- Relevant to the long term
- Concerned with the whole organisation
- Often prepared on an 'ad hoc' basis
- Both quantitative and qualitative
- Uncertain, as the future cannot be predicted

*Tactical information*

Tactical information is used to decide how the resources of the business should be employed, and to monitor how they are being and have been employed. Such information includes productivity measurements (output per man hour or per machine hour) budgetary control or variance analysis reports, and cash flow forecasts, manning levels and profit results within a particular department of the organisation, labour turnover statistics within a department and short-term purchasing requirements.

Tactical information is:

- Primarily generated internally (but may have a limited external component)
- Summarised at a lower level
- Relevant to the short and medium term
- Concerned with activities or departments
- Prepared routinely and regularly
- Based on quantitative measures

NOTES

*Operational information*

Operational information is used to ensure that specific tasks are planned and carried out properly within a factory or office.

In the payroll office, for example, operational information relating to day-rate labour will include the hours worked each week by each employee, his rate of pay per hour, details of his deductions, and for the purpose of wages analysis, details of the time each man spent on individual jobs during the week. In this example, the information is required weekly, but more urgent operational information, such as the amount of raw materials being input to a production process, may be required daily, hourly, or in the case of automated production, second by second.

Operational information is:

- Derived from internal sources
- Detailed, being the processing of raw data
- Relevant to the immediate term
- Task-specific
- Prepared very frequently
- Largely quantitative

### 2.3 The qualities of good information

'Good' information is information that adds to the understanding of a situation. The qualities of good information are outlined in the following table.

| Quality | | Example |
|---------|---|---------|
| **A** | currate | Figures should add up, the degree of rounding should be appropriate, there should be no typos, items should be allocated to the correct category, assumptions should be stated for uncertain information. |
| **C** | omplete | Information should includes everything that it needs to include, for example external data if relevant, or comparative information. |
| **C** | ost-beneficial | It should not cost more to obtain the information than the benefit derived from having it. Providers or information should be given efficient means of collecting and analysing it. Presentation should be such that users do not waste time working out what it means. |
| **U** | ser-targeted | The needs of the user should be borne in mind, for instance senior managers need summaries, junior ones need detail. |
| **R** | elevant | Information that is not needed for a decision should be omitted, no matter how 'interesting' it may be. |
| **A** | uthoritative | The source of the information should be a reliable one (not, for instance, 'Joe Bloggs Predictions Page' on the Internet unless Joe Bloggs is known to be a reliable source for that type of information). |
| **T** | imely | The information should be available when it is needed. |
| **E** | asy to use | Information should be clearly presented, not excessively long, and sent using the right medium and communication channel (e-mail, telephone, hard-copy report etc). |

PUBLISHING

*Perfect information*

Obtaining more information first about what is likely to happen can sometimes reduce the uncertainty about the future outcome from taking a decision. We can categorise information depending upon how reliable it is likely to be for predicting what will happen in the future and hence for helping managers to make better decisions.

**Definition**

> **Perfect information** is information that is guaranteed to predict the future with 100% accuracy.
>
> **Imperfect information** is information which cannot be guaranteed to be completely accurate. Almost all information is therefore imperfect - but may still be very useful.

*Improvements to information*

The table on the following page contains suggestions as to how poor information can be improved.

| Feature | Example of possible improvements |
|---|---|
| Accurate | Use computerised systems with automatic input checks rather than manual systems. |
| | Allow sufficient time for collation and analysis of data if pinpoint accuracy is crucial. |
| | Incorporate elements of probability within projections so that the required response to different future scenarios can be assessed. |
| Complete | Include past data as a reference point for future projections. |
| | Include any planned developments, such as new products. |
| | Information about future demand would be more useful than information about past demand. |
| | Include external data. |
| Cost-beneficial | Always bear in mind whether the benefit of having the information is greater than the cost of obtaining it. |
| User-targeted | Information should be summarised and presented together with relevant ratios or percentages. |
| Relevant | The purpose of the report should be defined. It may be trying to fulfil too many purposes at once. Perhaps several shorter reports would be more effective. |
| | Information should include exception reporting, where only those items that are worthy of note - and the control actions taken by more junior managers to deal with them - are reported. |

| Feature | Example of possible improvements |
|---|---|
| Authoritative | Use reliable sources and experienced personnel. |
| | If some figures are derived from other figures the method of derivation should be explained. |
| Timely | Information collection and analysis by production managers needs to be speeded up considerably, probably by the introduction of better information systems. |
| Easy-to-use | Graphical presentation, allowing trends to be quickly assimilated and relevant action decided upon. |
| | Alternative methods of presentation should be considered, such as graphs or charts, to make it easier to review the information at a glance. Numerical information is sometimes best summarised in narrative form or vice versa. |
| | A 'house style' for reports should be devised and adhered to by all. This would cover such matters as number of decimal places to use, table headings and labels, paragraph numbering and so on. |

## 3 INFORMATION REQUIREMENTS IN DIFFERENT SECTORS

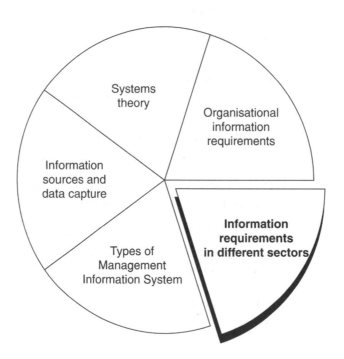

The following table provides examples of the typical information requirements of organisations operating in different sectors.

| Sector | Information type | Example(s) | General comment |
|---|---|---|---|
| **Manufacturing** | Strategic | Future demand estimates<br><br>New product development plans<br><br>Competitor analysis | The information requirements of commercial organisations are influenced by the need to make and monitor profit. Information that contributes to the following measures is important: |
| | Tactical | Variance analysis<br><br>Departmental accounts<br><br>Stock turnover | • Changeover times |
| | Operational | Production reject rate<br><br>Materials and labour used<br><br>Stock levels | • Number of common parts<br><br>• Level of product diversity<br><br>• Product and process quality |
| **Service** | Strategic | Forecast sales growth and market share<br><br>Profitability, capital structure | Organisations have become more customer and results-oriented over the last decade. As a consequence, the difference between service and other organisations information requirements has decreased. Businesses have realised that most of their activities can be measured, and many can be measured in similar ways regardless of the business sector. |
| | Tactical | Resource utilisation such as average staff time charged out, number of customers per hairdresser, number of staff per account<br><br>Customer satisfaction rating | |
| | Operational | Staff timesheets<br><br>Customer waiting time<br><br>Individual customer feedback | |

Business Basics: Information Technology

| Sector | Information type | Example(s) | General comment |
|---|---|---|---|
| **Public** | Strategic | Population demographics | Public sector (and non-profit making) organisations often don't have one overriding objective. Their information requirements depend on the objectives chosen. The information provided often requires interpretation (eg student exam results are not affected by the quality of teaching alone). |
| | | Expected government policy | |
| | Tactical | Hospital occupancy rates | |
| | | Average class sizes | |
| | | Percent of reported crimes solved | |
| | Operational | Staff timesheets | |
| | | Vehicles available | |
| | | Student daily attendance records | |
| | | | Information may compare actual performance with:<br><br>• Standards<br>• Targets<br>• Similar activities<br>• Indices<br>• Activities over time as trends |
| **Non-Profit / charities** | Strategic | Activities of other charities | Many of the comments regarding Public Sector organisations can be applied to not- for-profit organisations. |
| | | Government (and in some cases overseas government) policy | |
| | | Public attitudes | |
| | Tactical | Percent of revenue spent on admin | Information to judge performance usually aims to assess economy, efficiency and effectiveness. |
| | | Average donation | |
| | | 'Customer' satisfaction statistics | |
| | Operational | Households collected from / approached | A key measure of efficiency for charities is the percentage of revenue that is spent on the publicised cause. (eg rather than on advertising or administration). |
| | | Banking documentation | |
| | | Donations | |

# 4 TYPES OF MANAGEMENT INFORMATION SYSTEM

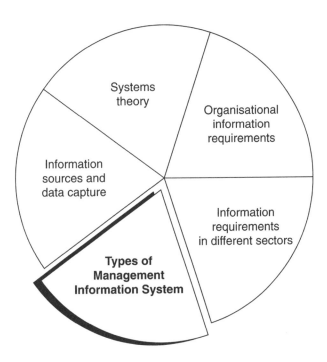

## 4.1 What is a Management Information System?

**Definition**

Two definitions of the term Management Information System (MIS) are shown below.

A **Management Information System (MIS)** converts data from internal and external sources into information, and communicates that information in an appropriate form to managers at all levels. This enables them to make timely and effective decisions for planning, directing and controlling the activities for which they are responsible.

(Lucey, *Management Information Systems*)

A computer system or related group of systems which collects and presents management information to a business in order to facilitate control.

(CIMA, *Computing Terminology*)

An MIS provides regular formal information gleaned from normal commercial data. For example, an MIS might provide information on the following.

(a) Product information. On-line, categorised information at the fingertips.

(b) Sales ledger. Information will be immediately available relating to customer turnover and payment records. Trend analysis will identify customers whose business is growing or has fallen away.

(c) Marketing. As enquiries and sales arise, the MIS can summarise this data to assist in forward planning. Customer satisfaction can be measured by post-purchase surveys and questionnaires. This information will be processed by the MIS and summarised for use by the management, both in report and graphical form.

(d) Supplier information. Information such as amount spent with each supplier, and reliability indicators (cancellations by the supplier, satisfaction of the customers) will prove useful when negotiating and making strategic decisions.

(e) Accounting. Because the transactions of the company are on the system, information will be available to trial balance stage of the nominal ledger. This will be available to the accounts department with comparable budget and prior year information, through drill down enquiry and also available in report formats.

(f) Modelling. Key data from the above areas can be combined into reports, possibly via spreadsheets, to create strategic and 'what if' models.

While an MIS may not be able to provide all the information used by management, it should be sufficiently flexible to enable management to incorporate unpredictable, informal or unstructured information into decision-making processes. For example, many decisions are made with the help of financial models (such as spreadsheets) so that the effect of new situations can be estimated easily.

A table showing typical inputs, processes and outputs at each level of a Management Information System or MIS is provided below.

|  | *Inputs* | *Processes* | *Outputs* |
|---|---|---|---|
| *Strategic* | Plans<br>Competitor information<br>Market information | Summarise<br>Investigate<br>Compare<br>Forecast | Key ratios<br>Ad hoc market analysis<br>Strategic plans |
| *Tactical* | Historical data<br>Budget data | Compare<br>Classify<br>Summarise | Variance analyses<br>Exception reports |
| *Operational* | Customer orders<br>Programmed stock<br>control levels | Update files<br>Output reports | Updated files<br>Listings<br>Invoices |

A modern organisation requires a wide range of systems to hold, process and analyse information. We will now examine the various Information Technology (IT) systems that deliver information to different levels in the organisation.

## 4.2 Transaction processing systems

Transaction processing systems, or data processing systems, are the lowest level in an organisation's use of information systems. They are used for routine tasks in which data items or transactions must be processed so that operations can continue. Handling sales orders, purchase orders, payroll items and stock records are typical examples.

Transactions processing systems provide the raw material which is often used more extensively by management information systems, databases or decision support systems. In other words:

(a) Transaction processing systems might be used to produce management information, such as reports on cumulative sales figures to date, total amounts owed to suppliers or owed by debtors and so on.

(b) However, the main purpose of transaction processing systems is as an integral part of day-to-day operations.

## 4.3 Decision support systems

Decision support systems are used by management to assist in making decisions on issues which are unstructured, with high levels of uncertainty about the true nature of the problem, the various responses which management could undertake or the likely impact of those actions.

Decision support systems are intended to provide a wide range of alternative information gathering and analytical tools with a major emphasis upon flexibility and user-friendliness.

The term decision support system is usually taken to mean computer systems which are designed to produce information in such a way as to help managers to make better decisions. They are now often associated with information 'at the touch of a button' at a manager's personal computer or workstation. DSS can describe a range of systems, from fairly simple information models based on spreadsheets to expert systems.

Decision support systems do not make decisions. The objective is to allow the manager to consider a number of alternatives and evaluate them under a variety of potential conditions. A key element in the usefulness of these systems is their ability to function interactively. This is a feature, for example, of spreadsheets. Managers using these systems often develop scenarios using earlier results to refine their understanding of the problem and their actions.

Some decision support computer systems are composed of three software elements. These subsystems then combine to provide the capabilities required for an effective decision support system.

(a) A language subsystem used by the manager to communicate interactively with the decision support system.

(b) A problem processing subsystem which provides analytical techniques and presentation capabilities.

(c) A knowledge subsystem which holds internal data and can access any needed external data. This would take the form of a database or a number of linked databases.

## 4.4 Executive Information Systems

An executive information system (EIS) is a type of DSS which gives the senior executive easy access to key internal and external data'. An EIS is likely to have the following features.

(a) Provision of summary-level data, captured from the organisation's main systems.

(b) A facility which allows the executive to drill down from higher levels of information to lower).

(c) Data manipulation facilities (for example comparison with budget or prior year data, trend analysis).

(d) Graphics, for user-friendly presentation of data.

(e) A template system. This will mean that the same type of data (eg sales figures) is presented in the same format, irrespective of changes in the volume of information required.

At the heart of an executive information system is a corporate model, which holds key information about the organisation. This model provides the interface between the database and the executive, who as a result does not have to define how information

should be displayed. The corporate model contains rules as to how the information should be presented and aggregated. The model can be amended if required.

## EXAMPLE: DRILLING DOWN

Many accounting packages still mirror manual reporting systems in that they provide details first and totals last. The format of a report from a package, whether displayed on screen or printed out, is usually a list of transactions with totals at the end of the list.

This does not fit well with the principle of management reporting by exception. For example, a sales manager monitoring sales in six different regions would first of all wish to view the sales totals for each region with a comparison of budget against actual. If totals for five regions are in line with budget, he will not immediately wish to review the underlying detail; he will be more concerned with the performance of the sixth region.

On selecting the relevant region for further investigation, he will still not wish to see an individual sales transactions listing, but will prefer to look at, for example, a report of budget against actual by product group, or perhaps by customer type. Only when he has identified the individual product group, or customer type, which is responsible for the difference between actual and budget, will he wish to look at individual products, or customers, to see where the difference lies.

An EIS will reflect the manager's real information needs. This approach has several advantages.

(a) It incorporates the principle of exception reporting.

(b) It reduces the amount of data to be reviewed (no information overload).

(c) It is screen-based, with print-outs only being required for specific matters.

The differences between an Executive Information System (EIS) and other forms of MIS are outlined below.

| Other forms of MIS | EIS |
| --- | --- |
| Many traditional information systems imitate the layout of **manual daybooks**, so that the user has to scroll through lists of individual transactions in order to find a period or category total. | An EIS starts at the summary, and then permits, but does not force, the executive to **drill down** to lower levels. |
| In traditional MIS, **exception reporting** is likely to be a strong feature. For example, if Department E is 20% off budget in a period, this will be highlighted, so that the manager can take appropriate action. | In an EIS, the user may be equally interested in Department D, which was exactly on budget. The EIS is less likely to discriminate in this way. |
| Many MIS are only designed to provide information that has been generated **within** the organisation. | An EIS is usually designed to allow **internal and external** information to be reported, although in practice the less structured and predictable nature of much external information may make this difficult. |

### 4.5 Expert systems

Expert systems allow users to benefit from expert knowledge and information. The system will consist of a database holding specialised data and rules about what to do in, or how to interpret, a given set of circumstances.

For example, many financial institutions now use expert systems to process straightforward loan applications. The user enters certain key facts into the system such as the loan applicant's name and most recent addresses, their income and monthly outgoings, and details of other loans. The system will then:

(a) Check the facts given against its database to see whether the applicant has a good previous credit record.

(b) Perform calculations to see whether the applicant can afford to repay the loan.

(c) Match up other criteria, such as whether the security offered for the loan or the purpose for which the loan is wanted is acceptable, and to what extent the loan applicant fits the lender's profile of a good risk (based on the lender's previous experience).

A decision is then suggested, based on the results of this processing. This is why it is now often possible to get a loan or arrange insurance over the telephone, whereas in the past it would have been necessary to go and speak to a bank manager or send details to an actuary and then wait for him or her to come to a decision.

There are many other business applications of expert systems.

(a) Legal advice.

(b) Tax advice.

(c) Forecasting of economic or financial developments, or of market and customer behaviour.

(d) Surveillance, for example of the number of customers entering a supermarket, to decide what shelves need restocking and when more checkouts need to be opened, or of machines in a factory, to determine when they need maintenance.

(e) Diagnostic systems, to identify causes of problems, for example in production control in a factory, or in healthcare.

(f) Project management.

(g) Education and training (diagnosing a student's or worker's weaknesses and providing or recommending extra instruction as appropriate).

An organisation can use an expert system when a number of conditions are met.

(a) The problem is reasonably well defined.

(b) The expert can define some rules by which the problem can be solved.

(c) The problem cannot be solved by conventional transaction processing or data handling.

(d) The expert could be released to more difficult problems, in the case of certain types of work. (An actuary in an insurance company is an example. Actuaries are very highly paid.)

(e) The investment in an expert system is cost justified.

This is a diagram of an expert system.

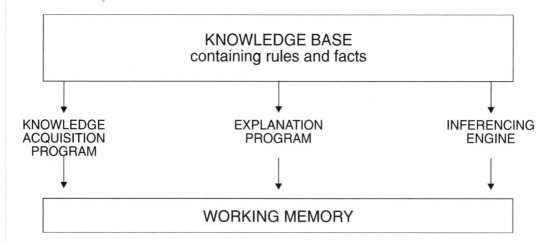

KNOWLEDGE BASE
containing rules and facts

KNOWLEDGE
ACQUISITION
PROGRAM

EXPLANATION
PROGRAM

INFERENCING
ENGINE

WORKING MEMORY

(a) The knowledge base contains facts (assertions like 'a rottweiler is a dog') and rules ('if you see a rottweiler, then run away'). Some facts contradict rules, of course, or even each other ('birds can fly' is contradicted by the existence of ostriches).

(b) The knowledge acquisition program is a program which enables the expert system to acquire new knowledge and rules.

(c) The working memory is where the expert system stores the various facts and rules used during the current enquiry, and the current information given to it by the user.

(d) The inferencing engine is the software that executes the reasoning. It needs to discern which rules apply, and allocate priorities.

**Activity 1**      **(15 minutes)**

Why do you think organisations need to automate reasoning or decision-making tasks which humans are naturally better able to perform than computers?

Advantages of expert systems include the following.

(a) The recorded information and knowledge is permanent, whereas human experts may leave the business.

(b) It is easily copied, so that one bank branch say, can have access to the same expertise as any other branch.

(c) It is consistent, whereas human experts and decision makers may not be.

(d) It can be documented. The reasoning behind an expert recommendation produced by a computer will all be recorded. Experts may have what seem to them to be inspired ideas out of the blue, not fully realising the thought processes that they have been going through while they have been mulling the problem over.

(e) Depending on the task the computer may be much faster than the human being.

The limitations of expert systems include:

(a) Systems are expensive, especially if they have to be designed from scratch, as they often would be.

(b) The technology is still in its infancy in many areas. Understanding of how the human mind works is also still fairly limited.

(c) It is very difficult to develop a system in the first place, and the system will need extensive testing and debugging before it can be trusted.

(d) People are naturally more creative. If a computer system can be creative at all, it can only be so to the extent that creativity has been programmed into it: arguably this is not creativity at all.

(e) Systems have a very narrow focus, whereas human experts can bring the whole of their experience to bear on a problem.

(f) Managers will resist being replaced by computers, or at least will sometimes be reluctant to believe the advice of an expert system.

The differences between a traditional Management Information System (MIS) and an Expert System (ES) are outlined below.

| Characteristic | Traditional MIS | ES |
|---|---|---|
| Accuracy and completeness. | The **MIS** contains purely **factual** information such as name, address and personal details, and historical information about transactions. Individual records will be updated as and when changes occur. This information will be available to users when they are dealing with customers.<br><br>Details should be totally accurate, assuming they have been **input correctly** and the most **recent changes** have been input.<br><br>The information **may not be complete** if there have been changes but there have been no recent transactions. | The **ES** will **use** some of the same information but only to collate it with an **information bank** or 'knowledge base' that includes details of types of problem and apply a set of rules, so as to provide information in the form of solutions.<br><br>The information within the system (ie the knowledge base and rule set) should accurately reflect the current state of knowledge. However it may not provide accurate solutions in an **absolute** sense, because current knowledge may be incomplete or wrong.<br><br>Moreover, it is likely to take some time for new research findings to be incorporated into the system and for rules to be amended accordingly. |
| Timeliness | Information is likely to held in a database and will be **obtainable within seconds** on demand. | The ES **may take several minutes** to perform comparisons with what is probably a very large knowledge base, and to apply rules from a very wide number of possibilities. |

| Characteristic | Traditional MIS | ES |
|---|---|---|
| User confidence | Subject to the points made above, users **should be able to rely on the information** provided by the MIS.<br><br>**The patient** can be asked to confirm address details and the like during visits, and asked about their history when seeing a doctor. Any **discrepancies or omissions** should come to light then. | **If** the ES provides information that users find **believable**, then they will be able to have confidence in it.<br><br>If, when it produces a range of possible answers, however, some of the options are **absurd**, this may undermine confidence in the system: it draws attention to the fact that the system is **not really capable of judgement** in the way a human being is.<br><br>Worse, if the system occasionally produces a **wrong solution**, then users will quickly lose confidence in it and probably **not use it at all**.<br><br>**Some users** will almost certainly be keener on using of the system than others, who prefer to use their **own judgement**. just as some people in general are keener on the use of computers than others. |
| Relevance and volume | Standard details (eg name, address) will be held in a consistent file format.<br><br>Transaction histories will **vary enormously in length**, however, and in fact it may be very difficult to read an entire history on screen. Much of what is there will **not be relevant** to the customer's current problem.<br><br>**Sorting or search facilities** if available are clearly be useful. It is also useful to **categorise** aspects of transaction history according to meaningful criteria as well as in chronological order. | It is possible that certain combinations of circumstances will give rise to a very **large number of possible solutions**.<br><br>However, they will presumably be **sorted in order of probability**, so users will not be overloaded with data and will probably ignore the least probable answers as irrelevant. |

# 5 INFORMATION SOURCES AND DATA CAPTURE

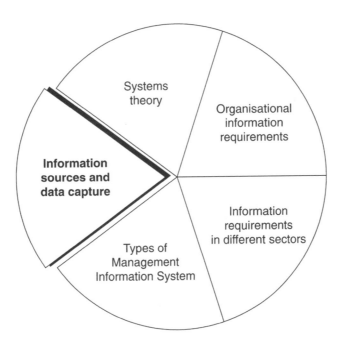

Data and information come from sources both inside and outside an organisation, and an information system should be designed so as to obtain - or capture - all the relevant data and information from whatever source.

## 5.1 Internal information

Capturing data/information from inside the organisation involves the following.

(a) A system for collecting or measuring transactions data - for example sales, purchases, stock turnover etc which sets out procedures for what data is collected, how frequently, by whom, and by what methods, and how it is processed, and filed or communicated.

(b) Informal communication of information between managers and staff (for example, by word-of-mouth or at meetings).

(c) Communication between managers.

## 5.2 Internal data sources

*The accounting records*

You should be very familiar with the idea of a system of sales ledgers and purchase ledgers, general ledgers, cash books and so on. Some of this information is of great value outside the accounts department, for example, sales information for the marketing function.

You will also be aware that to maintain the integrity of its accounting records, an organisation of any size will have systems for and controls over transactions. These also give rise to valuable information. A stock control system is the classic example: besides actually recording the monetary value of purchases and stock in hand for external financial reporting purposes, the system will include purchase orders, goods received notes, goods returned notes and so on, and these can be analysed to provide management information about speed of delivery, say, or the quality of supplies.

*Other internal sources*

Much information that is not strictly part of the accounting records nevertheless is closely tied in to the accounting system.

(a)     Information about personnel will be linked to the payroll system. Additional information may be obtained from this source if, say, a project is being costed and it is necessary to ascertain the availability and rate of pay of different levels of staff, or the need for and cost of recruiting staff from outside the organisation.

(b)     Much information will be produced by a production department about machine capacity, fuel consumption, movement of people, materials, and work in progress, set up times, maintenance requirements and so on. A large part of the traditional work of cost accounting involves ascribing costs to the physical information produced by this source.

(c)     Many service businesses, notably accountants and solicitors, need to keep detailed records of the time spent on various activities, both to justify fees to clients and to assess the efficiency and profitability of operations.

(d)     Staff themselves are one of the primary sources of internal information. Information may be obtained either informally in the course of day-to-day business or through meetings, interviews or questionnaires.

### 5.3     External information

Capturing information from outside the organisation might be entrusted to particular individuals, or might be 'informal'.

Formal collection of data from outside sources includes the following.

(a)     A company's tax specialists will be expected to gather information about changes in tax law and how this will affect the company.

(b)     Obtaining information about any new legislation on health and safety at work, or employment regulations, must be the responsibility of a particular person - for example the company's legal expert or company secretary - who must then pass on the information to other managers affected by it.

(c)     Research and development (R & D) work often relies on information about other R & D work being done by another company or by government institutions. An R & D official might be made responsible for finding out about R & D work in the company.

(d)     Marketing managers need to know about the opinions and buying attitudes of potential customers. To obtain this information, they might carry out market research exercises.

Informal gathering of information from the environment goes on all the time, consciously or unconsciously, because the employees of an organisation learn what is going on in the world around them - perhaps from newspapers, television reports, meetings with business associates or the trade press.

### 5.4     External data sources

Obviously an organisation's files are full of external information such as invoices, letters, advertisements and so on received from customers and suppliers. But there are many occasions when an active search outside the organisation is necessary.

NOTES

## Definition

> The phrase **environmental scanning** is often used to describe the process of gathering external information, which is available from a wide range of sources.

(a) The government.

(b) Advice or information bureaux.

(c) Consultancies of all sorts.

(d) Newspaper and magazine publishers.

(e) There may be specific reference works which are used in a particular line of work.

(f) Libraries and information services.

(g) Increasingly businesses can use each other's systems as sources of information, for instance via electronic data interchange (EDI).

(h) Electronic sources of information are becoming increasingly important.

    (i) For some time there have been 'viewdata' services such as Prestel offering a very large bank of information gathered from organisations such as the Office for National Statistics, newspapers and the British Library. Topic offers information on the stock market. Companies like Reuters operate primarily in the field of provision of information.

    (ii) **The Internet** is a vast network linking up millions of computers across the world via telecommunications links. We look at the Internet in detail in Chapter 5.

## 5.5 Efficient data collection

To produce meaningful information it is first necessary to capture the underlying data. The method of data collection chosen will depend on the nature of the organisation, cost and efficiency. Some common data collection methods are outlined below.

### MICR

Magnetic ink character recognition (MICR) involves the recognition by a machine of special formatted characters printed in magnetic ink. The characters are read using a specialised reading device.

The main advantage of MICR is its speed and accuracy, but MICR documents are expensive to produce. The main commercial application of MICR is in the banking industry - on cheques and deposit slips.

### Optical mark reading

Optical mark reading involves the marking of a pre-printed form with a ballpoint pen or typed line or cross in an appropriate box. The card is then read by an OMR device which senses the mark in each box using an electric current and translates it into machine code.

Applications in which OMR is used include National Lottery entry forms, and answer sheets for multiple choice questions.

*Scanners and OCR*

A scanner is device that can read text or illustrations printed on paper and translate the information into a form the computer can use. A scanner works by digitising an image, the resulting matrix of bits is called a bit map.

To edit text read by an optical scanner, you need optical character recognition (OCR) software to translate the image into ASCII characters. Most optical scanners sold today come with OCR packages. Businesses may use a scanner and OCR to obtain 'digital' versions of documents they have only paper copies of. For good results the paper copy must be of good quality.

*Bar coding and EPOS*

Bar codes are groups of marks which, by their spacing and thickness, indicate specific codes or values. Look at the back cover of this book for an example of a bar code.

Large retail stores are introducing Electronic Point of Sale (EPOS) devices, which include bar code readers. This enables the provision of immediate sales and stock level information.

*Magnetic stripe cards*

The standard magnetic stripe card contains machine-sensible data on a thin strip of magnetic recording tape stuck to the back of the card. The magnetic card reader converts this information into directly computer-sensible form. The widest application of magnetic stripe cards is as bank credit or service cards.

*EFTPOS*

Many retailers have now introduced EFTPOS systems (Electronic Funds Transfer at the Point of Sale). These are systems for the electronic transfer of funds at the point of sale. Customers in shops and at petrol stations can use a plastic card (usually a credit card or debit card) to purchase goods or services, and using an EFTPOS terminal in the shop, the customer's credit card account or bank current account will be debited automatically. EFTPOS systems combine point of sale systems with electronic funds transfer.

*Smart cards*

A smart card is a plastic card in which is embedded a microprocessor chip. A smart card would typically contain a memory and a processing capability. The information held on smart cards can therefore be updated (eg using a PC and a special device).

*Voice recognition*

Computer software has been developed that can convert speech into computer sensible form: the input device needed in this case is a microphone. Users are required to speak clearly and reasonably slowly.

---

**Activity 2**                                        **(20 minutes)**

Drawing on personal experience (if possible), give five examples of the inefficient use of information.

---

**FOR DISCUSSION**

Discuss your examples from Activity 2 with others in your group.

---

*With organisations able to collect and store ever-increasing amounts of information, the importance of managing information effectively can not be over-stated. We look at how information can be managed in the next chapter.*

**Chapter roundup**

- General system principles apply to any type of system, including information systems.

- Any system can be thought of in terms of inputs, processing and outputs.

- An environment surrounds the system but is not part of it. A systems boundary separates the system from its environment.

- An open system has a relationship with its environment which has both prescribed and uncontrolled elements.

- A closed system is shut off from its environment and has no relationship with it.

- Control in a system is needed to ensure that the system's operations go according to plan. Control cannot be applied unless there is information about the operations of the system

- Feedback is control information generated by the system itself, and involves a comparison of actual results against the target or plan.

- Organisations require information for recording transactions, measuring performance, making decisions, planning and controlling.

- 'Good' information aids understanding. ACCURATE is a handy mnemonic for the qualities of good information.

- An organisation's information requirements will be influenced by the sector they operate in.

- Information may be strategic, tactical or operational.

- A wide range of systems are available to hold, process and analyse information.

- An information system should be designed to obtain information from all relevant sources - both internal and external.

- A range of data collection methods are available - depending on the situation.

**Quick quiz**

1   List the three component parts of a system. (See section 1.2)

2   Distinguish between strategic, tactical and operational information. (See section 2.2)

3   List five qualities of 'good' information. (See section 2.3)

4   Give an example of strategic, tactical and operational information relevant to an organisation operating in the service sector. (See section 3)

5   Decision support systems are used for routine decisions. TRUE or FALSE? (See section 4.3)

NOTES

6      What is an EIS? (See section 4.4)

7      List three business applications of an expert system. (See section 4.5)

8      Briefly explain five methods of data capture. (See section 5.5)

## Answers to Activities

1      The primary reason has to do with the relative cost of information. An expert can spend a great deal of time acquiring a specialised body of knowledge, but the commercial value of this expertise ceases with the expert's retirement or departure from the labour force.

         Secondly, enshrining an expert's accumulated wisdom in a computer system means that this wisdom can be accessed by more people. Thus, the delivery of complicated services to customers, decisions whether or not to extend credit and so forth, can be made by less experienced members of staff if the expert's knowledge is available to them. If a manufacturing company has a complicated mixture of plant and machinery, then the repair engineer may accumulate a lot of knowledge over a period of time about the way it behaves: if a problem occurs, the engineer will be able to make a reasoned guess as to where the likely cause is to be found. If this accumulated expert information is made available to less experienced staff, it means that some of their learning curve is avoided.

         An expert system is advantageous because it saves time, like all computer systems (in theory at least) but it is particularly useful as it possesses both knowledge and a reasoning ability.

2      There are many possible suggestions, including those given below.

         The organisation's bankers take decisions affecting the amount of money they are prepared to lend.

         The public might have an interest in information relating to an organisation's products or services.

         The media (press, television etc) use information generated by organisations in news stories, and such information can adversely or favourably affect an organisation's relationship with its environment.

         The government (for example the Department of Trade and Industry) regularly requires organisational information.

         The Inland Revenue and HM Customs and Excise authorities require information for taxation and VAT assessments.

         An organisation's suppliers and customers take decisions whether or not to trade with the organisation.

## Further question practice

*Now try the following practice question at the end of this text.*

     Exam style question      **1**

PUBLISHING

# Chapter 2 :
# INFORMATION MANAGEMENT

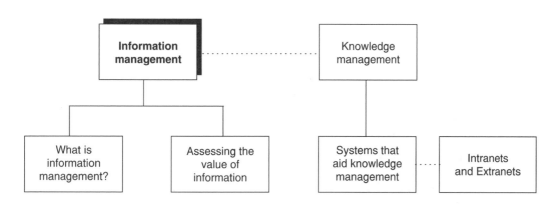

## Introduction

The modern business environment can be volatile. Businesses are increasingly reliant on good quality information and knowledge to anticipate and respond to change. As the importance of information and knowledge has increased, organisations have come to realise that, like any other valuable resource, **information and knowledge should be managed effectively.**

Many of the tools and techniques used to manage information utilise Information Technology.

## Your objectives

After completing this chapter you should:

(a)   Understand the importance of information to modern organisations.

(b)   Understand the concepts of information management and knowledge management.

(c)   Be able to describe some widely used information management tools and techniques.

# 1    WHAT IS INFORMATION MANAGEMENT?

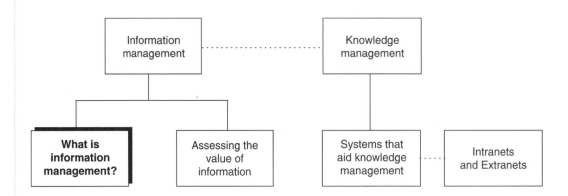

## 1.1    What is information management?

Information must be managed just like any other organisational resource. Information management entails the following tasks.

(a)    Identifying current and future information **needs**.

(b)    Identifying information **sources**.

(c)    **Collecting** the information.

(d)    **Storing** the information.

(e)    Facilitating existing methods of **using** information and identifying new ways of using it.

(f)    Ensuring that information is **communicated** to those who need it, and is **not communicated** to those who are **not** entitled to see it.

**Technology** has provided new sources of information, new ways of collecting it, storing it and processing it, and new methods of communicating and sharing it. This in turn has meant that information needs have **changed** and will continue to change as new technologies become available.

Although computing and telecommunications technology provide fabulous tools for carrying out the information management tasks listed above, they are **not always the best tools**; nor are they always even available.

## 1.2    Users of information

The information generated by an organisation may be used internally or externally. **Internal** users of information include (by status) the following.

- The board (or equivalent)
- Directors with functional responsibilities
- Divisional general managers
- Divisional heads
- Departmental heads
- Section leaders, forepeople or supervisors
- Employees

---

**Activity 1**                 **(20 minutes)**

It is important to bear in mind that information may be relevant to people outside the organisation as well as to its internal management and employees. In fact, decisions relating to an organisation can be taken by outsiders. Give four examples of decisions which may be taken by outsiders.

---

## 2    ASSESSING THE VALUE OF INFORMATION

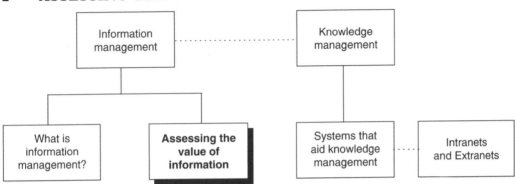

### 2.1   Factors that make information a valuable commodity

Information is now recognised as a valuable resource that can enable an organisation to establish an advantage over their competitors; a **competitive advantage.** Easy **access** to information, the **quality** of that information and **speedy methods of exchanging** the information have become essential elements of business success.

Organisations that make **good use of information** in decision-making, and which use new technologies to access, process and exchange information are likely to be **best placed to survive** in increasingly competitive world markets.

The **factors which make information valuable** are as follows.

(a)   The **source** of the information

     If the information comes from a source that is widely known and respected for quality, thoroughness and accuracy (Reuters, say, or the BBC) it will be more valuable to users than information from an unknown or untested source, because it can be relied upon with confidence.

(b)   The ease of assimilation

     Modern methods of presentation can use not only words and figures but also **colour graphics, sound and movement.** This makes the receipt of information a richer (and so more valuable) experience, and it means that information can be more easily, and therefore more quickly, understood: again a feature that people will be willing to pay for.

(c)   Accessibility

     If information can be made available in an easily accessible place (such as the **Internet**) users do not have to commit too much time and effort to retrieve it. If just a few sentences of information is required, and they can find these (for instance using an Internet search engine) without having to buy a whole book or newspaper, then they should be willing to pay for this convenience.

Information which is **obtained but not used** has no value to the person that obtains it. Also, an item of information which leads to savings of £90 is not worth having if it costs £100 to collect.

---

**Activity 2**                                                                     **(20 minutes)**

The value of information lies in the action taken as a result of receiving it. What questions might you ask in order to make an assessment of the value of information?

---

An assessment of the value of information can be derived in this way, and the cost of obtaining it should then be compared against this value. On the basis of this comparison, it can be decided whether certain items of information are worth having. It should be remembered that there may also be intangible benefits which may be harder to quantify.

Deciding whether it is worthwhile having more information should depend on the **benefits** expected from getting it and the **extra costs** of obtaining it. The benefits of more information should be measured in terms of the difference it would make to management decisions if the information were made available.

### 2.2 Assessing cost and value

The information system is used to produce a wide variety of information. The **cost** of an individual item of information is **not always easy to quantify**. For example, if a manager uses a MIS to obtain the sales history of a customer what is the cost of this enquiry? The cost is difficult to calculate because:

(a)    The information **already exists**, as it is used for a number of different purposes. It might be impossible to predict how often it will be used, and hence the economic benefits to be derived from it.

(b)    The information system which is used to process these requests has also been purchased..

Just as the costs of an item of information are hard to assess, so too the **benefits are often hard to quantify**. While nobody doubts that information is vital, it is not always easy to construct an economic assessment of the value of information. For example a monthly variance analysis report may lead to operational decisions being made but the economic consequences of this decision may not be easy to predict or **measure**.

*Traditional methods*

Traditional **investment appraisal methods** can be applied with varying degrees of success to problems of this kind. There are three principal methods of evaluating a capital project: the payback method, the accounting rate of return and discounted cashflow methods.

These methods are covered in Business Basics: Quantitative Methods.

## 2.3 The benefits of a proposed information system

The benefits from a proposed information system should be evaluated against the costs. To quantify the benefits several factors need to be considered.

(a) **Savings** generated because the old system will no longer be operated. The savings may include **staff costs** and **other operating costs**.

(b) **Extra savings** or **revenue benefits** because of the improvements or enhancements that the new system should bring:

    (i) Possibly more **sales revenue** and so additional contribution.

    (ii) Better **stock control** (with a new stock control system) and so fewer stock losses from obsolescence and deterioration.

    (iii) Savings in **staff time**, resulting perhaps in reduced future staff growth.

Some benefits might be **intangible**, or impossible to give a money value to. Even if they cannot be quantified, they must be identified and fully explained. It is arguable that the larger proportion of all computerised information systems benefits is intangible.

(a) Greater **customer satisfaction**, arising from a more prompt service (eg because of a computerised sales and delivery service).

(b) Improved **staff morale** from working with a 'better' system.

(c) **Better decision making** is hard to quantify, but may result from a better MIS, DSS or EIS.

## 3 KNOWLEDGE MANAGEMENT

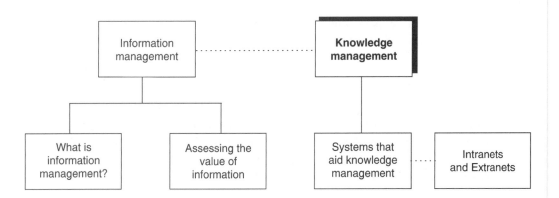

## 3.1 What is knowledge management?

Studies have indicated that 20 to 30 percent of company resources are wasted because organisations are not aware of what **knowledge they already possess**. Lew Platt, Chief executive of Hewlett Packard, has articulated this in the phrase 'If only HP knew what HP knows, we would be three times as profitable'.

**Definitions**

> **Knowledge** is information within people's minds.
>
> **Knowledge management** describes the process of collecting, storing and using the knowledge held within an organisation.

PUBLISHING

Knowledge is now commonly viewed as a sustainable source of **competitive advantage,** and one that it is essential f or companies to tap. In an era of rapid change and uncertainty, companies need to **create new knowledge, nurture it and disseminate it** throughout the organisation, and **embody it in technologies, products and services.** Several sectors – for example, the financial services industries - depend on knowledge as their principal means of value creation.

**Knowledge is valuable** because humans use it to create new ideas, insights and interpretations and apply these to information use and decision making. However knowledge, like information, is of no value unless it is applied to decisions and actions in a purposeful business context.

People in organisations are constantly **converting knowledge into various forms of information** (memos, reports, e-mails, briefings) and **acquiring information for others to improve their knowledge**.

**Knowledge management** programmes are attempts at:

(a) Designing and installing techniques and processes to create, protect and use **explicit knowledge** (that is knowledge that the company knows that it has). Explicit knowledge includes facts, transactions and events that can be clearly stated and **stored in management information systems.**

(b) Designing and creating environments and activities to discover and release **tacit knowledge** (that is, knowledge that the company does not know it has). Tacit knowledge is implied or inferred, it concerns the feelings and experiences **stored in peoples minds**.

Organisations should encourage people to share their knowledge. This can be done through **improved management of information** about **where knowledge resides,** how it can be **deployed and reused** and when it can create greater business value through **new ideas and innovations.**

A range of **technology** is available to support KM. The three main threads are information retrieval, document management and workflow processing.

### 3.2 Organisational learning

The process by which an organisation develops its store of knowledge is sometimes called organisational learning. A learning organisation is centred on the **people** that make up the organisation and the **knowledge** they hold. The organisation and employees feed off and into the central pool of knowledge. The organisation uses the knowledge pool as a tool to teach itself and its employees.

### 3.3 Knowledge management or information management?

There are dozens of **different approaches** to KM, including document management, information management, business intelligence, competence management, information systems management, intellectual asset management, innovation, business process design, and so on.

You might be forgiven for thinking, therefore, that 'knowledge management' is just a different, more up-market **label** for information management?

(a) It is true that many KM projects have a significant element of information management. After all, people need information about where knowledge resides, and to share knowledge they need to transform it into more or less transient forms of information.

(b)    But beyond that, KM does have two distinctive tasks: to facilitate the **creation** of knowledge and to **manage the way people share and apply it**. Companies that prosper with KM will be those that realise that it is as much about **managing people** as about information and technology.

## EXAMPLE: HOW TO FACILITATE KNOWLEDGE SHARING

The business trend for the new millennium might well be summed up as, 'Tradition is out, innovation is in.' World-class companies now realise that the best ideas do not necessarily come from the executive boardroom but from all levels of the company; from line workers all the way through top management.

Companies that have cultures that **encourage best practice sharing** can unlock the rich stores of knowledge within each employee: sharing promotes overall knowledge, and facilitates further creativity. World-class companies are innovatively implementing best practice sharing to shake them of out of the rut of 'the way it's always been done.' Programs such as General Electric's Work-Out sessions or Wal-Mart's Saturday meetings help employees challenge conventions and suggest creative new ideas that drive process improvement, increased efficiency, and overall, **a stronger bottom line.**

The fundamental goal of **knowledge management** is to capture and disseminate knowledge across an increasingly global enterprise, enabling individuals to avoid repeating mistakes and to operate more intelligently - striving to create an entire **learning organisation** that work as efficiently as its most seasoned experts.

*Best Practices* recently updated report, '*Knowledge Management of Internal Best Practices*', profiles innovative methods used by world-class companies to communicate best practices internally. The study provides recommendations for how to create a best practice-sharing culture through all levels of the organisation, how to use both external and internal sources to find best practices and how to capture that knowledge and communicate it to all employees.

Best Practices, LLC contacted over fifty leading companies at the vanguard of knowledge management to compile its report. Some of the vital issues these thought leaders addressed include **measurement and management of intellectual assets**, best practice identification and recognition systems, best practice prioritisation systems, communication of best practices, and **knowledge sharing through technology**. For example, in the area of best practice **communications, the report examines how General Electric spreads best practices with regular** job rotations.

*Adapted from Chapel Hill, N.C. (Business Wire) Feb 2000 via News Edge Corporation*

## 4    SYSTEMS THAT AID KNOWLEDGE MANAGEMENT

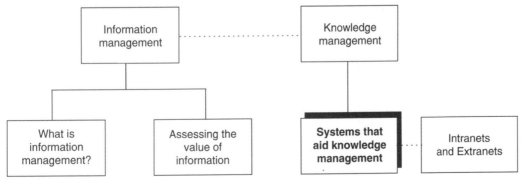

## 4.1 What type of systems aid knowledge management?

Any system that encourages people to work together and share information and knowledge will aid knowledge management (eg databases, Intranets, communication tools). We will now look at some common systems.

## 4.2 Computer Supported Co-operative Working

Organisations by their very nature rely upon people working together and co-operating with each other, and so obviously information systems should be designed to help people to do this. This is the principle behind *Computer Supported Co-operative Working* (CSCW).

**Definition**

> **Computer supported co-operative (or 'collaborative') working** is a term which combines the understanding of the way people work in groups with the enabling technologies of computer networking and associated hardware, software, services and techniques.

Internal telephone networks are perhaps the most obvious example of the use of technology to facilitate group working. Other examples, such as video-conferencing and e-mail, are described later in this chapter.

**Definition**

> **Groupware** is a term used to describe a collection of IT tools designed for the use of co-operative or collaborative work groups. Typically, these groups are small project-oriented teams that have important tasks and tight deadlines. Groupware can involve software, hardware, services, and/or group process support.

At the **individual** level groupware is similar to an electronic personal organiser. Features might include the following.

(a)  A **scheduler** (or diary or calendar), allowing users to keep track of their schedule and plan meetings with others.

(b)  An electronic **address book** to keep personal and business contact information up-to-date and easy to find. Contacts can be sorted and filed in any way.

(c)  **To do** lists. Personal and business to-do lists can be kept in one easy-to-manage place, and tasks can quickly be prioritised.

(d)  A **journal**, which is used to record interactions with important contacts, record items (such as e-mail messages) and files that are significant to the user, and record activities of all types and track them all without having to remember where each one was saved.

(e)  A **jotter** for jotting down notes as quick reminders of questions, ideas, and so on.

There are clearly advantages in having information such as this available from the desktop at the touch of a button, rather than relying on scraps of paper, address books, and corporate telephone directories. However, it is when groupware is used to **share information** with colleagues that it comes into its own. Here are some of the features that may be found.

(a) **Messaging**, comprising an **e-mail** in-box which is used to send and receive messages from the office, home, or the road and **routing** facilities, enabling users to send a message to a single person, send it sequentially to a number of people (who may add to it or comment on it before passing it on), or sending it to every one at once.

(b) Access to an **information database**, and customisable 'views' of the information held on it, which can be used to standardise the way information is viewed in a workgroup.

(c) **Group scheduling**, to keep track of colleagues' itineraries. Microsoft Exchange Server, for instance offers a 'Meeting Wizard', which can consult the diaries of everyone needed to attend a meeting and automatically work out when they will be available, which venues are free, and what resources are required.

(d) **Public folders**. These collect, organise, and share files with others on the team or across the organisation.

(e) One person (for instance a secretary or a stand-in during holidays or sickness) can be given '**delegate access**' to another's groupware folders and send mail on their behalf, or read, modify, or create items in public and private folders on their behalf.

(f) **Conferencing**. Participation in public, online discussions with others.

(g) **Assigning tasks**. A task request can be sent to a colleague who can accept, decline, or reassign the task. After the task is accepted, the groupware will keeps the task status up-to-date on a task list.

(h) **Voting** type facilities that can, say, request and tally responses to a multiple-choice question sent in a mail message (eg 'Here is a list of options for this year's Christmas party').

(i) **Hyperlinks** in mail messages. The recipient can click the hyperlink to go directly to a Web page or file server.

(j) **Workflow management** (see below) with various degrees of sophistication.

**4.3 Workflow**

**Definition**

> **Workflow** is a term used to describe the defined series of tasks within an organisation to produce a final outcome

Sophisticated workgroup computing applications allow the user to define different **workflows** for different types of jobs. For example, in a publishing setting, a document might be automatically routed from writer to editor to proofreader to production.

At **each stage** in the workflow, **one individual** or group is **responsible** for a specific task. Once the task is complete, the workflow software ensures that the individuals responsible for the **next** task are notified and receive the data they need to complete their stage of the process.

Workflow systems can be described according to the type of process they are designed to deal with. There are three common types.

(a) **Image-based workflow systems** are designed to automate the flow of paper through an organisation, by transferring the paper to digital "images". These were the first workflow systems that gained wide acceptance. These systems are closely associated with 'imaging' (or 'document image processing' (DIP)) technology, and help with the routing and processing of digitised images.

(b) **Form-based workflow systems** (formflow) are designed to route forms intelligently throughout an organisation. These forms, unlike images, are text-based and consist of editable fields. Forms are automatically routed according to the information entered on them. In addition, these form-based systems can notify or remind people when action is due.

(c) **Co-ordination-based workflow systems** are designed to help the completion of work by providing a framework for **co-ordination** of action. Such systems are intended to improve organisational productivity by addressing the issues necessary to **satisfy customers**, rather than automating procedures that are not closely related to customer satisfaction.

## 5 INTRANETS AND EXTRANETS

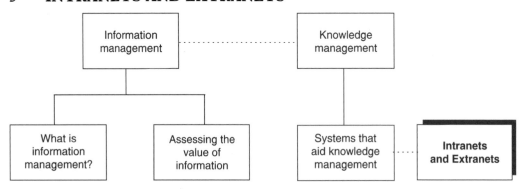

### 5.1 Intranets

**Definition**

> An **intranet** is an internal network used to share information. Intranets utilise Internet technology and protocols.

The idea behind an 'intranet' is that companies set up their own **mini version of the Internet.** Intranets use a combination of the organisation's own networked computers and Internet technology. Each employee has a browser, used to access a server computer that holds corporate information on a wide variety of topics, and in some cases also offers access to the Internet.

Potential applications include company newspapers, induction material, online procedure and policy manuals, employee web pages where individuals post up details of their activities and progress, and **internal databases** of the corporate information store.

Most of the **cost** of an intranet is the **staff time** required to set up the system.

The **benefits** of intranets are diverse.

(a)     Savings accrue from the **elimination of storage**, **printing** and **distribution** of documents that can be made available to employees on-line.

(b)     Documents on-line are often **more widely used** than those that are kept filed away, especially if the document is bulky (eg manuals) and needs to be searched. This means that there are **improvements in productivity** and **efficiency**.

(c)     It is much **easier to update** information in electronic form.

(d)     Wider access to corporate information should open the way to **more flexible working patterns**, eg material available on-line may be accessed from remote locations.

## CASE EXAMPLE: GROUPWARE AND INTRANETS

The original idea of a 'personal' computer was to allow people to work together and share information across a network through a mainframe computer. However, users became so frustrated at their inability to get what they wanted from mainframe systems that they welcomed the IBM PC, used in stand-alone mode, with open arms.

This meant in turn that groupware (software designed to let users work together and share information through computers) had to be invented. (Examples are Lotus Notes (now **Lotus Domino**), **Novell Groupwise**, and **Microsoft Exchange**.) Groupware technology has been widely used to enable people to communicate, to share information, to work together and, most importantly, to carry out business processes and execute transactions, often using unstructured data.

The current fashion for intranets has given new impetus to these ideas, and all of the major products have now adopted Internet-type standards. Such products may have an advantage over intranets built from scratch because they recognise and address the problems of bringing about the **cultural changes** needed to get better business processes and **generate competitive advantage**.

## CASE EXAMPLE: SWISS BANK CORPORATION INTRANETS

One of the biggest users of intranets is Swiss Bank Corporation. In fact it has so many - around 100 - that it has just appointed a head of intranets to co-ordinate them all.

At Swiss Bank Corporation intranets are used for:

Corporate accounting and credit information

Publishing research internally, and to a select group of 50 external clients

Trading information

Ordering information technology equipment

IT project management

Informing staff of regulatory changes

The job of Marie Adee, the company's new head of intranets, is to unify the disparate sites so that employees can find information easily. The sites will also be given a common look and feel. All the company's sites can be searched using the Netscape Navigator Web browser, but the company is also standardising on Lotus Domino software.

This software will sit on the server computers that store the intranet information. Domino incorporates Lotus Notes information sharing software. So employees will be able to input information to Web sites either through Notes or through their Web browsers. It will also be possible for SBC to set up workflow applications - which control the flow of work between users in a team.

## 5.2 Extranets

### Definition

An **extranet** is an intranet that is accessible to authorised outsiders.

Whereas an intranet resides behind a firewall and is accessible only to people who are members of the same company or organisation, an extranet provides various levels of accessibility to outsiders.

### FOR DISCUSSION

How could a college use an extranet to serve students?

Only those outsiders with a valid username and password can access an extranet, with varying levels of access rights enabling control over what people can view. Extranets are becoming a very popular means for **business partners to exchange information**.

Extranets therefore allow better use of knowledge held within an organisation - by facilitating access to that knowledge.

*Neural computing*

Neural computing is seen by some observers as the 'next step' in computing. Unlike conventional computing techniques, neural computing is modelled on the biological processes of the human brain and has many **human-like qualities**. For example, neural computers can **learn from experience**. The can analyse vast quantities of complex data and **identify patterns** from which predictions can be made. They have the ability to cope with incomplete or 'fuzzy' data , and can deal with previously unspecified or **new situations**. As such they are ideally suited to real world applications and can provide the solution to a host of currently commercially impractical problems.

Neural techniques and artificial intelligence technology have been incorporated into software applications such as **data mining** packages. Such packages enable businesses to sift through vast quantities of raw data in order to spot **hidden trends** or anomalies which may be commercially significant.

*We will be looking at the features of widely used Information Technology in Chapter 5.*

**Chapter roundup**

- **Information** is a **valuable resource** that requires efficient management.

- **Technology** has changed how information is collected, stored and processed, as well as changing the information needs of organisations

- The **cost and value** of information are often not easy to quantify - but attempts should be made to do so.

- **Knowledge management** describes the process of collecting, storing and utilising the knowledge held by people and systems within an organisation.

- There are a wide range of systems available that encourage knowledge management including:

  ° Computer supported co-operative working
  ° Groupware
  ° Workflow and workgroup applications
  ° Intranets and extranets

- **Neural computing** utilises concepts such as artificial intelligence in an attempt to enable computers to 'learn' from experience.

**Quick quiz**

1 List five tasks of information management. (See Section 1.1)

2 What factors should be considered when assessing the cost and value of information? (See Section 2.2)

3 Define knowledge and knowledge management. (See Section 3.1)

4 What is a 'learning-organisation' centred on? (See Section 3.2)

5 What is groupware? (See Section 4.2)

6 List four benefits of an intranet. (See Section 5.1)

7 What is an extranet? (See Section 5.2)

**Answers to Activities**

1 There are many possible suggestions, including those given below.

(a) The organisation's **bankers** take decisions affecting the amount of money they are prepared to lend.

(b) The **public** might have an interest in information relating to an organisation's products or services.

(c) The **media** (press, television etc) use information generated by organisations in news stories, and such information can adversely or favourably affect an organisation's relationship with its environment.

(d) The **government** (for example the Department of Trade and Industry) regularly requires organisational information.

(e) The **Inland Revenue** and **HM Customs and Excise** authorities require information for taxation and VAT assessments.

NOTES

(f)     An organisation's **suppliers** and **customers** take decisions whether or not to trade with the organisation.

2     (a)    What information is provided?

(b)    What is it used for?

(c)    Who uses it?

(d)    How often is it used?

(e)    Does the frequency with which it is used coincide with the frequency of provision?

(f)    What is achieved by using it?

(g)    What other relevant information is available which could be used instead?

**Further question practice**

*Now try the following practice question at the end of this text.*

Exam style question     **2**

# Chapter 3 :
# INFORMATION SYSTEM DESIGN

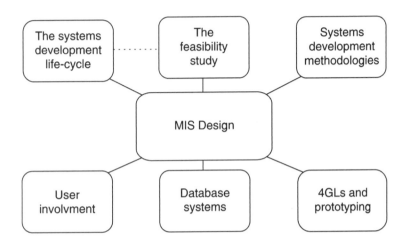

## Introduction

Even very small organisations now tend to have computerised systems. In this chapter we discuss a variety of issues relating to the design and development of computerised Management Information Systems.

## Your objectives

After completing this chapter you should understand:

(a)   The processes of system design and development.

(b)   The nature and purpose of systems maintenance and performance evaluation.

NOTES

# 1 THE SYSTEMS DEVELOPMENT LIFE-CYCLE

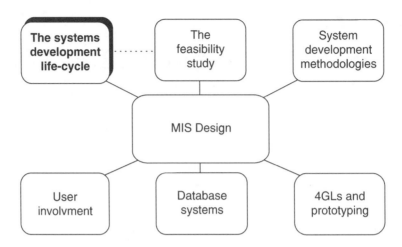

At least some elements of almost all Management Information Systems are now computerised.

**In the early days of computing**, systems were developed in a fairly haphazard fashion. Systems development usually involved the automation of existing procedures. The development of systems **was not properly planned**. The consequences were often poorly designed systems, which were not suited to users' needs. A more disciplined approach to systems development is known was developed, and became known as the **systems development life-cycle**. A six-stage **model** of the development life-cycle is explained below.

## 1.1 Stages of the systems development life-cycle

| Stage | Comment |
| --- | --- |
| **Identification of a problem** | In the case of the development of a new information system, this stage will involve an analysis of the organisation's information requirements. Such an analysis should be carried out in conjunction with users, so that their **actual** requirements can be identified, rather than their **likely** requirements. |
| **Feasibility study** | This involves a brief review of the existing system and the identification of a range of possible alternative solutions. One will usually be recommended on the basis of its costs and benefits, although it is possible for a decision not to proceed to result. |
| **Systems investigation** | This is a fact finding exercise which investigates the existing system to assess its problems and requirements and to obtain details of data volumes, response times and other key indicators. |
| **Systems analysis** | Once the workings of the existing system have been documented, they can be analysed. This process examines why current methods are used, what alternatives might achieve the same, or better, results, what restricts the effectiveness of the system and what performance criteria are required from a system. |

| Stage | Comment |
|---|---|
| **Systems design** | This is a technical phase which considers both computerised and manual procedures, addressing, in particular, inputs, outputs, program design, file design and security. A detailed specification of the new system is produced. |
| **Systems implementation** | This stage carries development through from design to operations. It involves acquisition (or writing) of software, program testing, file conversion or set-up, acquisition and installation of hardware and 'going live'. |
| **Review and maintenance** | This is an ongoing process which ensures that the system meets the objectives set during the feasibility study, that it is accepted by users and that its performance is satisfactory. |

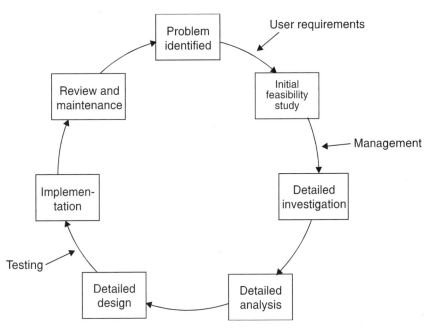

The systems development lifecycle approach to systems development was adopted by many organisations. It provided a model of how systems should be developed. It imposed a **disciplined** approach to the development process, it encouraged **communication** between systems professionals and 'ordinary' users and it recognised the importance of **analysis and design**, previously much neglected.

## 1.2 Drawbacks of the SDLC

While the basic SDLC approach has some advantages, it has a number of drawbacks **if not properly implemented**.

(a) While it was efficient at automating operational areas, the **information needs of middle and senior management were ignored**. Computerisation was a means of speeding up high-volume routine transaction processing, not providing information for decision-making.

(b) User input was obtained only early in the development process. This often resulted in the need for substantial (and costly) system modifications later.

(c) **New systems rarely lived up to users' expectations**. Even with packaged software, users may be disappointed. It becomes increasingly difficult to change system requirements the further a system is developed, and users were required to 'sign off' at an early stage.

(d) Much system documentation was **written for programmers and specialists**. It was highly technical, more of a technical manual than a guide for the user. Problems could also occur, if inadequately documented modifications led to 'bugs' elsewhere in the system.

(e) Many routine transaction processing systems **could not cope with unusual situations**, and so some complicated processing was still performed manually.

## 2    THE FEASIBILITY STUDY

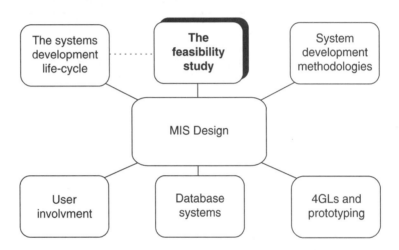

Before any system is implemented a feasibility study should be conducted. For very small systems the 'study' may involve only one individual and take less than a day. Complex systems may require a study involving a team of people and lasting months.

**Definition**

> A **feasibility study** is a formal study to decide what type of system can be developed which meets the needs of the organisation.

### 2.1 Terms of reference

The **terms of reference** for a feasibility study for a large information systems project might consist of the following items.

- To **investigate and report on an existing system**, its procedures and costs

- To define the **systems requirements**

- To establish **whether these requirements are being met** by the existing system

- To establish whether they could be met by an **alternative system**

- To specify **performance criteria** for the system

- To recommend the **most suitable system** to meet the system's objectives

- To prepare a **detailed cost budget**, within a specified budget limit

- To prepare a draft **plan for implementation** within a specified timescale

- To establish whether the hoped-for benefits could be realised

- To establish a detailed design, implementation and operating budget

- To compare the detailed budget with the **costs of the current system**

- To set the **date** by which the study group must report back

- To decide **which operational managers** should be approached by the study group

## 2.2 The feasibility study team

A feasibility study team should be appointed to carry out the study (although individuals might be given the task in the case of smaller projects).

(a) Members of the team should be drawn from the **departments affected by the project**.

(b) At least one person must have a **detailed knowledge of computers and systems design** (in a small concern it may be necessary to bring in a systems analyst from outside, or to rely on an accountant as the 'computer expert').

(c) The team must include people that have a **detailed knowledge of the organisation** and what the **information needs** of the system are

## 2.3 Areas of feasibility

The **study** itself will concentrate on **three key areas** in which a project must be feasible if it is to proceed.

- **Technical** feasibility
- **Operational** feasibility
- **Economic** feasibility

## 2.4 Technical feasibility

The requirements, as defined in the feasibility study, must be **technically achievable**. This means that any proposed solution must be capable of being implemented using available hardware, software and other equipment. The type of requirement which might depend for success on technical feasibility might be one of the following.

- **Volume** of transactions which can be processed within a given time

- **Capacity** to hold files or records of a certain size

- Response **times**

- **Number** of users which can be supported without deterioration in the other criteria

## 2.5 Operational feasibility

Operational feasibility is a key concern. If a solution makes technical sense but **conflicts with the way the organisation does business**, the solution is not feasible. Thus an organisation might reject a solution because it forces a change in management responsibilities and chains of command, or does not suit regional reporting structures, or because the costs of redundancies, retraining and reorganisation are considered too high.

## 2.6 Economic feasibility

A system which satisfies the above criteria must still be economically feasible. This means that it must be a 'good investment'. This has two strands.

(a) The project selected must be the **'best' option from those computerisation projects** under consideration.

(b) The project selected must **compete with other projects in other areas of the business** for funds. Even if it is projected to produce a positive return and satisfies all relevant criteria, it may not be chosen because a new warehouse is needed or the head office is to be relocated, and available funds are allocated to these projects instead.

## 2.7 Costs and benefits

**Cost-benefit analysis** before or during the development of information systems is complicated by the fact that many of the system cost elements are **poorly defined** (particularly for development projects) and that benefits can often be highly qualitative and subjective in nature.

### The costs of a proposed system

In general the best cost estimates will be obtained for **complete systems** bought from an **outside vendor** who provides a cost quotation against a specification. Less concrete cost estimates are generally found with development projects where the work is performed by the organisation's own employees. The costs of a new system will include costs in a number of different categories.

**Equipment costs** (capital costs/leasing costs) include the following.

- Computer and peripherals
- Ancillary equipment
- The initial system supplies (disks, tapes, paper etc)

**Installation costs** relate to the infrastructure.

- New building (if necessary)
- The computer room (wiring, air-conditioning etc)

**Development costs** include costs of measuring and analysing the existing system and costs of looking at the new system. They include software/consultancy work and systems analysis and programming as well as changeover costs.

**Personnel costs** include all those one-off and ongoing costs not related to systems professionals.

- Staff training
- Staff recruitment/relocation
- Staff salaries and pensions
- Redundancy payments
- Overheads

**Operating costs**, which may in the long-term comprise up to 70% of overall systems costs, are the ongoing running costs.

- Consumable materials (tapes, disks, stationery etc)

- Maintenance
- Accommodation costs
- Heating/power/insurance/telephone
- Standby arrangements

A distinction can be made between **capital costs** and **revenue costs**, which may be either 'one-off' costs in the first year or regular annual costs. The distinction between capital costs and revenue costs is important.

(a) To establish the **cash outflows** arising from the system, the costs/benefit analysis of a system ought to be based on cash flows and DCF.

(b) The annual **charge against profits** is usually of interest! Capital items will be capitalised and depreciated, and revenue items will be expensed as incurred as a regular annual cost. The items treated as '**one-off' revenue costs** are costs which would usually fall to be treated as revenue which, by virtue of being incurred during the period of development only and in connection with the development are one-off. In practice, accounting treatment of such items may vary widely between organisations depending on their accounting policies and on agreement with their auditors.

---

**Activity 1**                                               **(30 minutes)**

Draw up a table with three headings: capital cost items, one-off revenue cost items and regular annual costs. Identify at least three items to be included under each heading. You may wish to refer back to the preceding paragraph for examples of costs.

---

**Benefits**

Among the criteria for **justifying** the cost of a new systems development may be the following.

(a) **Reduction in the danger of loss** through error or fraud. For example, customers may be prevented from exceeding their credit limits.

(b) **Sharing of information** through international **networks**.

(c) **Improved reputation and company image**, in terms of responsiveness to customer needs and the company's standing within the industry.

(d) **Better administrative and management control systems**, possibly using fewer but more highly trained staff.

(e) **Greater confidence in decision making,** through techniques of forecasting, planning, investment and modelling.

(f) **Increased responsiveness,** with the company being better placed to respond rapidly and flexibly to changing circumstances.

(g) **Enhanced job satisfaction** for staff. Self esteem, motivation and group cohesion may rise in line with highly regarded skills.

(h) **Better presentation** of all types of printed and on-screen inputs, both those generated for internal purposes and those which are communicated externally.

(i) Ultimately the benefits should add up to **increased profit** for the organisation.

Many of the benefits here are **intangible**. Convincing executives to invest in new systems development may require a powerful argument based on a combination of tangible and intangible benefits, using wherever possible, capital investment appraisal techniques.

## 2.8 The feasibility study report

Once each area of feasibility has been investigated a number of possible projects may be put forward. The results are included in a **feasibility report**. This should contain the following items.

- **Terms of reference**
- Description of **existing system**
- **System requirements**
- Details of the **proposed system(s)**
- **Cost/benefit analysis**
- **Development** and **implementation** plans
- **Recommendations** as to the preferred option

## 3 SYSTEMS DEVELOPMENT METHODOLOGIES

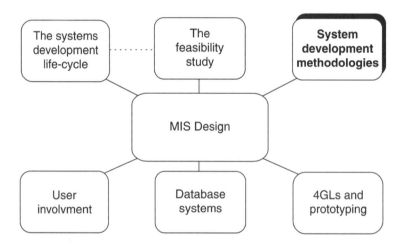

One popular approach to systems development and design is to use some kind of **methodology** such as **Structured Systems Analysis and Design**.

## 3.1 What is a systems development methodology?

**Definition**

> A systems development '**methodology**' of procedures, techniques, tools and documentation aids which will help systems developers in their efforts to implement a new information system.

When a methodology is used, hardware and software are developed or acquired that meet the demands of the information system specifications rather than developing a system acquired to fit hardware and software.

The needs of **users** are expressed in the outputs or potential outputs required of the system. The user's information requirements and potential requirements should determine the type of data collected or captured by the system.

## 3.2 Comparing and evaluating methodologies

Jayaratna (*Understanding and Evaluating Methodologies,* 1994) estimates that there are **over 1,000 brand named methodologies** in use in the world.

All methodologies seek to facilitate the '**best**' solution. But 'best' may be interpreted in a number of ways, such as **most rapid** or **least cost** systems. Some methodologies are highly **prescriptive** and require rigid adherence to stages whilst others are highly **adaptive** allowing for creative use of their components. The former may be viewed as following a recipe and the latter as selecting suitable tools from a toolkit.

In choosing the **most appropriate methodology**, an organisation must consider the following questions.

- How **open** is the system?
- To what extent does the methodology facilitate **participation**?
- Does it generate alternative solutions?
- Is it well documented, tried, tested and proven to work?
- Can **component 'tools'** be selected and used as required?
- Will it benefit from computer aided tools and prototyping?

It is **not necessary to be restricted** to the tools offered by just one methodology. For instance soft systems methodology may be useful at the outset, to get a system well-defined, and subsequently to review its performance. Elements of harder techniques and possibly prototyping might usefully be employed during development.

Ultimately it is important to remember that whilst methodologies may be valuable in the development their use is a matter of great skill and experience. They **do not, by themselves, produce good systems solutions**.

| | |
|---|---|
| **Activity 2** | **(10 minutes)** |
| Why does it matter how 'open' a system is? | |

## 3.3 Advantages of methodologies

(a) The **documentation** requirements are rigorous.

(b) **Standard methods** allow **less qualified staff** to carry out some of the analysis work, thus **cutting the cost** of the exercise.

(c) Using a standard development process leads to **improved system specifications**.

(d) Systems developed in this way are **easier to maintain and improve**.

(e) **Users are involved** with development work from an early stage and are required to sign off each stage.

(f) The emphasis on **diagramming** makes it easier for relevant parties, including users, to **understand** the system than if purely narrative descriptions were used.

(g) The structured framework of a methodology **helps with planning**. It defines the tasks to be performed and sets out when they should be done. Each step has an identifiable end product. This allows control by reference to actual achievements rather than to estimates of progress.

(h)  A logical design is produced that is **independent of hardware and software**. This logical design can then be given a physical design using whatever computer equipment and implementation language is required.

(i)  Techniques such as data flow diagrams, logical data structures and entity life histories **allow information to be cross-checked** between diagrams and ensure that the system delivers is what is required.

## 3.4 Disadvantages of methodologies

(a)  Methodologies were originally tailored to **large, complex organisations**. Only recently have they been adapted for PC-based systems.

(b)  It has been argued that methodologies are ideal for analysing and documenting processes and data items are operational level, but are perhaps **inappropriate for information of a strategic nature** that is collected on an ad hoc basis.

(c)  Some are a little **too limited in scope**, being too concerned with systems design, and not with their impact on actual work processes or social context of the system.

(d)  The conceptual basis of some is **not properly thought out**. Many methodologies grew out of diagramming conventions.

(e)  Arguably, methodologies are just as happy documenting a bad design as a good one.

## 4 FOURTH GENERATION LANGUAGES AND PROTOTYPING

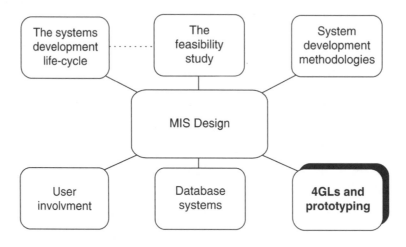

## 4.1 Fourth generation languages (4GLs)

*Background*

A **programming language** is neither the 'normal' written language of humans, nor is it usually the machine code language of computers.

(a)  A computer can only deal with data and program instructions which are in **binary form** (the 1 and 0 corresponding to the on and off states of a transistor). Every program must be in a computer's **machine code** before the computer can interpret it.

(b)     A program in a programming language, however, can be translated into **machine code**. Programming languages are **easier for humans to use**, being more condensed and displaying a logic that humans can understand.

**Assembly languages** were a subsequent development from machine code. They are also machine specific, but the task of learning and writing the language is made easier than with machine language because they are **written in symbolic form**. Instead of using machine code operation numbers, the programmer is able to use easily learned and understood operation mnemonics (for example, ADD, SUB and MULT).

Machine code and assembly languages are sometimes known collectively as **low-level languages**.

To overcome the low-level language difficulty of machine dependency, high-level (or machine independent) languages were developed. Such programming languages, with an extensive vocabulary of words and symbols are used to instruct a computer to carry out the necessary procedures, regardless of the type of machine being used. Some examples of **high-level languages,** also know as **third-generation languages** are **COBOL, Pascal, C, C++** and **Java**.

*4GLs*

A fourth generation language is a programming language that is easier to use than languages like COBOL, PASCAL and C++. Well known examples include **Informix** and **Powerhouse**.

**Definition**

> The term **fourth generation language (4GL)** loosely denotes software which enables systems designers to 'write' a program with little programming knowledge. A 4GL offers the user an English-like set of commands and simple control structures in which to specify general data processing or numerical operations. These programs are then translated into a conventional high-level language.

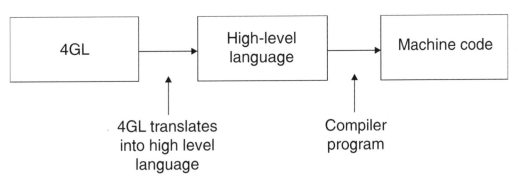

Most fourth generation systems use a mixture of text and graphics, often a **graphical user interface**. A fourth generation system should have the following features.

(a)     It should be **easy to learn** and use.

(b)     It should contain **on-line 'help'** facility for users.

(c)     It should be usable **interactively**.

(d)     It should be **'fault' tolerant** (ie any mistakes in data entry should be dealt with easily).

(e)     It should be suitable for **document design** work.

An **application generator** is a type of 4GL used to create complete **applications programs**. The user describes what needs to be done and the data and files which are to be used. The applications generator then translates this description into a program.

The basis for this process is the recognition that **many of the functions** such as data input, sorting, searching, file management, report writing and the like are **quite similar** in operation even when these program segments are found in quite different applications programs.

### 4.2 Advantages of 4GLs

(a) It enhances **end-user computing,** so limiting the work of IS/IT staff.

(b) It taps user **creativity**.

(c) It **diffuses IT** throughout the organisation.

(d) It vastly increases programmer **productivity**, even though it uses more hardware resources.

### 4.3 Disadvantages of 4GLs

(a) **Over-enthusiastic** use by users might overload the main hardware resources.

(b) The information systems department might get overloaded by **training** requirements.

(c) Programs written in a 4GL do make **less efficient use of computer processing power** and memory. This can have the effect of slowing down the execution of a program to unacceptable levels.

### 4.4 Prototyping

The use of 4GLs, together with the realisation that users need to see how a system will look and feel to assess its suitability, have contributed to the increased use of **prototyping**.

**Definition**

> A **prototype** is a model of all or part of a system, built to show users early in the design process how it will appear. As a simple example, a prototype of a formatted screen output from a system could be prepared using a graphics package, or even a spreadsheet model. This would describe how the screen output would appear to the user. The user could make suggested amendments, which would be incorporated into the next model.

Using prototyping software, the programmer can develop **a working model of application program quickly**. He or she can then **check with the data user** whether the prototype program that has been designed appears to **meet the user's needs,** and if it doesn't it can be amended

**Advantages and disadvantages of prototyping**

4.5 **Advantages of prototyping.**

(a)     It makes it possible for programmers to present a 'mock-up' version of a program to a data user, to see how it works, **before anyone has to commit substantial time and money** to the project. The data user can judge the prototype before things have gone too far to be changed.

(b)     The process facilitates the production of **'custom built' application software** rather than off-the-shelf packages which may or may not suit user needs.

(c)     It makes **efficient use of programmer time** by helping programmers to develop programs more quickly. Prototyping may speed up the 'design' stage of the systems development life-cycle.

(d)     A prototype does not necessarily have to be written in the language of what it is prototyping, so prototyping is not only a tool, but a **design technique**.

4.6 **Disadvantages of prototyping.**

(a)     Many prototyping tools are **tied** to a particular make of **hardware**, or a particular **database system**.

(c)     It is sometimes argued that prototyping tools are **inefficient** in the program codes they produce, so that programs are bigger and require more memory than a more efficiently coded program.

(d)     Prototyping may help users to steer the development of a new system towards an **existing system**.

(f)     Some believe prototyping tools encourage the production of **shoddy programs** at a high speed.

---

**FOR DISCUSSION**

Has anyone in your group been involved in , or affected by, the implementation of a new system? How were user concerns addressed?

Was user involvement encouraged?

---

## 5  DATABASE SYSTEMS

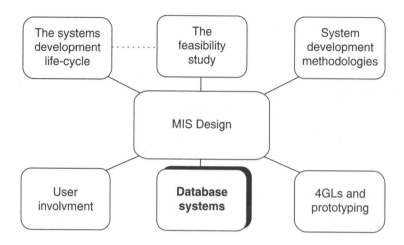

### 5.1  What is a database system?

The term 'database system' is used to describe a wide range of systems that utilise a central pool of data. In this context the term 'database system' involves much more than a single database package such as Microsoft Access. the different elements of a database system are shown in the diagram on the following page.

**Definitions**

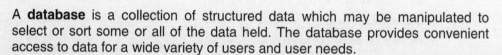

A **database** is a collection of structured data which may be manipulated to select or sort some or all of the data held. The database provides convenient access to data for a wide variety of users and user needs.

A **database management system (DBMS)** is the software that builds, manages and provides access to a database. It allows a systematic approach to the storage and retrieval of data.

The independence of logical data from physical storage, and the independence of data items from the programs which access them, is referred to as **data independence**

Duplication of data items is referred to as **data redundancy**

A database should have four major **objectives**.

(a)   It should be **shared**.

(b)   It should provide for the **needs of different users** who each have their own processing requirements and data access methods.

(c)   The database should be **capable of evolving.** It must be able to meet the **future** data processing needs of users.

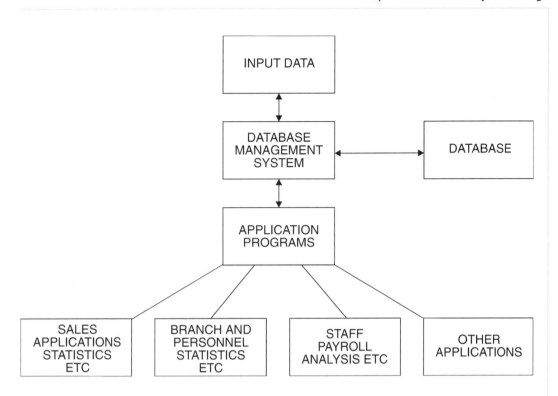

## 5.2 Advantages of a database system

(a) Avoidance of **unnecessary duplication** of data.

(b) Data is looked upon as serving the **organisation as a whole**, not just for individual departments. The database concept encourages management to regard data as a resource that must be **properly managed.**

(c) The installation of a database system encourages management to **analyse data**, relationships between data items, and how data is used in different applications.

(d) **Consistency** - because data is only held once, the possibility of departments holding conflicting data on the same subject is reduced.

(e) Data on file is independent of the user programs that access the data. This allows **greater flexibility** in the ways that data can be used. New programs can be easily introduced to make use of existing data in a different way.

(f) Developing **new application programs** with a database system is easier because the programmer is not responsible for the file organisation.

## 5.3 Disadvantages of a database system

(a) There are problems of **data security** and **data privacy**. There is potential for unauthorised access to data. Administrative procedures for data security must supplement software controls.

(b) Since there is only one set of data, it is essential that the data should be **accurate** and free from corruption.

(c) Since data is held once, but its use is widespread, the impact of **system failure** would be greater.

(d) If an organisation develops its own database system from scratch, **initial development costs** will be high.

### 5.4 Database administrator

Control over data and systems development can be facilitated by the appointment of a **database administrator**, who controls and sets standard for:

- The input of data
- Its definition, for instance the development of logical data models
- Physical storage structures
- System performance
- Security and integrity of data, eg maintenance of the data dictionary (see later)
- Back-up and recovery strategies

The principal role of a DBA can be described as ensuring that the database **functions correctly and efficiently** at all times. To achieve these aims the DBA will carry out a variety of tasks, including some or all of those discussed below. The DBA must be a person that is **technically competent** and possesses a **good understanding** of the **business and operational needs** of the organisation.

### 5.5 Data dictionary

**Definition**

> A **data dictionary** is an index of data held in a database, used to assist in maintenance and any other access to the data.

A data dictionary is a feature of many database systems and CASE tools. As the term might suggest, it provides a method for **looking up the items of data** held in the database, to establish the following.

(a) **Field names, types, lengths and default values**. For instance a 'year' field would be numeric with four digits and may have a default value of the current year.

(b) A list of the entity, attribute and relationship types.

(c) A list of the **aliases** (see below).

(d) A list of all the **processes** which use data about each entity type.

(e) **How to access** the data in whatever manner is required (a data dictionary is sometimes called a data directory).

(f) What the data codes and symbols mean.

(g) The **origin** of the data.

(h) Possible range of values.

(i) **Ownership** of the data.

(j) Other comments.

A data dictionary is a record of each **data store** in the system and each **data flow** in the system.

The data dictionary is a form of technical documentation. It is also a **control tool** and ensures that all in the organisation define data **consistently**. This is extremely important for large projects which involve several programmers.

A data dictionary helps with systems analysis, systems design and systems maintenance.

(a) During systems analysis a data dictionary helps the analyst **organise information** about the data elements in the system, where they come from, where they go to what fields are used (name, type, length).

(b) During systems design a data dictionary helps the analyst and programmers to ensure that no data elements are missed out.

(c) Defining data items (ie building the dictionary) is a major part of the process of producing the physical system, and some data dictionaries can even generate program code automatically.

(d) Once the system is operational, and an **amendment** is required to a program, a data dictionary will help the programmer to understand what each data element is used for, so the impact of any amendments can be established. This is sometimes called **impact analysis.**

(e) Future **maintenance** work on the system is unlikely to be carried out by the people who originally wrote it. A data dictionary records the original work and helps to ensure continuity.

## 5.6 Using a database

There are four main operations in using a database.

(a) Creating the database **structure**, ie the structure of files and records.
(b) **Entering data** on to the database files, and **amending/updating** it.
(c) Retrieving and manipulating the data.
(d) Producing **reports**.

## 5.7 Creating the database structure

The creation of the database structure involves carrying out an **analysis** of the data to be included. It is necessary to specify what **files** will be held in the database, what **records** (entities) and the **fields** (attributes) they will contain, and how many **characters** will be in each field. The files and fields must be named, and the characteristics of particular fields (for example **all-numeric** or **all-alphabetic** fields) should be specified.

When the database structure has been established, the data user can **input data** and create a file (or files) or **derive data** from existing records.

Possible problems in **amalgamating data** are outlined below.

(a) The **compatibility** between systems is not just a matter of whether one system's files are computer-sensible to another system. It may extend to matters such as **different systems of coding**, different formats for personal data (with/without a contact name? with/without phone or fax number, and so on), different field sizes.

(b) There is potential for **loss or corruption of data** during the conversion process. This could mean a small amount of re-keying or it could be a disastrous, permanent loss of valuable information.

Full **back-ups** should be taken at the start of the process, and back-ups of information on the old system should continue during any period of parallel running.

(c) Existing application-specific systems are unlikely to have sufficient **storage** space to accommodate the combined data. This can easily be resolved, but it must be resolved with an eye to the **future growth** of the business and future use of the database.

(d) **Access to data must not suffer**. Operational users will be attempting to extract information from a much larger pool, and the system must be designed in such a way that they do not have to wade through large amounts of data that is irrelevant.

Those developing the system must consult those users who do the processing to ensure their information needs are met by the new data architecture.

(e) As well as offering the potential for new kinds of report the system must continue to **support existing reporting**.

Once more, **extensive consultation** with users is essential.

(f) Once the data has been amalgamated the business faces the task of ensuring that it is **secure**. A systems failure will now mean that no part of the business can operate, rather than at most just one part.

## 5.8    Retrieval and manipulation of data

Data can be retrieved and manipulated in a variety of ways.

(a) By **specifying the required parameters** - for example from a database of employee records, records of all employees in the sales department who have been employed for over 10 years and are paid less than £22,000 pa could be extracted. Search and retrieve parameters that are used regularly, can be stored on a search parameters file for future use.

(b) Retrieved data can be **sorted** on any specified field (for example for employees, sorting might be according to grade, department, age, experience, salary level etc).

(c) Some **calculations** on retrieved data can be carried out - such as calculating **totals** and **average** values.

### Query languages

A database can be interrogated by a **query language**. A query language is a formalised method of constructing queries in a database system. A query language provides the ways in which you ask a database for data. Some query languages can be used to change the contents of a database.

The illustration below shows the screen from within the query building area of Microsoft Access.

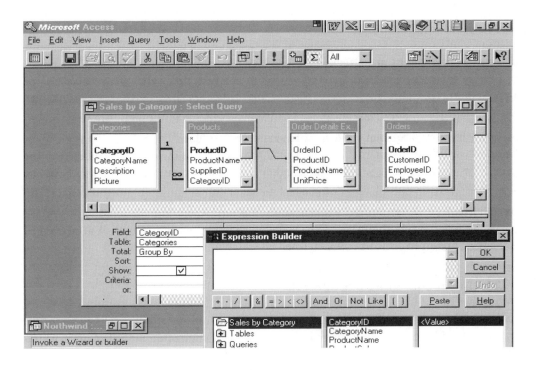

## 5.9 Report production

Most database packages include a **report generator facility** which allows the user to design report structures in a format which suits the user's requirements and preferences. Report formats can be stored on disk, if similar reports are produced periodically, and called up when required.

**We explain some of the functions of the Microsoft Access database package in Chapter 7.**

## 6 USER INVOLVEMENT

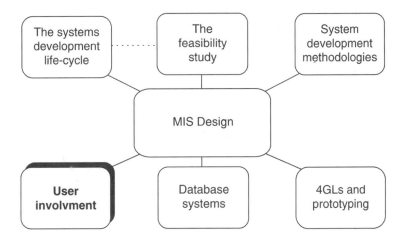

## 6.1 The importance of user involvement

The importance of user involvement in the development of a computerised Management Information System can not be over estimated. This section looks at a number of approaches intended to ensure that the required level of involvement is achieved.

## 6.2 Structured walkthroughs

Structured walkthroughs are a technique used by analysts and programmers to present their design to interested **user groups** – in other words to 'walk' them through the design. Structured walkthroughs are **formal meetings**, in which the **documentation produced during development is reviewed and checked** for errors or omissions.

These presentations are used both to **introduce and explain** the new systems to users and also to offer the users the opportunity of **making constructive criticism** of the proposed systems, and suggestions for further amendments/improvements, before the final systems specification is agreed.

Users are involved in structured walkthroughs because their knowledge of the desired system is more extensive than that of the systems development personnel. Walkthroughs are sometimes referred to as **user validation**.

## 6.3 The importance of signing off work

At the end of each stage of development, the resulting output is presented to users for their approval. There must be a **formal sign-off** of each completed stage before work on the next stage begins.

This **minimises reworking**, as if work does not meet user requirements, only the immediately preceding stage must be revisited. More importantly, it clarifies responsibilities and leaves little room for later disputes.

(a) If the systems developers fail to deliver something that both parties formally agreed to, it is the **developers' responsibility** to put it right, at their own expense, and compensate the user for the delay.

(b) If users ask for something extra or different, that was not formally agreed to, the developers cannot be blamed and **the user must pay** for further amendments and be prepared to accept some delay.

> ### Activity 3 (20 minutes)
> What, besides identification of mistakes (errors, omission, inconsistencies etc), would you expect the benefits of a walkthrough to be?

## 6.4 Joint applications development

Joint applications development is based on a **partnership between users and IT specialists**. When this was originally pioneered in the 1970s, it involved developers and users **specifying an entire application in just a few days**, right down to detailing screen layouts, by participating in day-long design sessions. Specific steps were followed to ensure that the design process was completed in those few days, and accomplished its goal, largely by bringing the decision makers together into one place at one time.

Joint Applications Development (JAD) was originally developed by **IBM** to promote a more participative approach to systems. The potential value to an organisation may be as follows.

(a) It creates a **pool of expertise** comprised of interested parties from all relevant functions.

(b) **Reduced risk of systems 'imposed'** by computer systems personnel.

(c) This **increases the corporate ownership** and responsibility for systems solutions.

(d) Emphasises the **information needs of users** and their relationship to business needs and decision making.

There are a number of possible **risks** affecting the potential value of JAD.

(a) The relative **inexperience of many users** may lead to misunderstandings and possibly unreasonable expectations/demands on the system performance.

(b) The danger of **lack of co-ordination** leading to fragmented, individual, possibly esoteric information systems.

The shift of emphasis to applications development by end-users must be well managed and controlled. An organisation may wish to set up an **information centre** to provide the necessary support and co-ordination.

## 6.5 Rapid applications development

JAD may also be used as a tool for users and IT specialists to build software using **rapid applications development (RAD)**. RAD can be described as a quick way of building software. It combines a management approach to systems development with the use of modern software tools such as **graphics-based user interfaces** and object oriented design methods. RAD also involves the **end-user** heavily in the development process.

At the start of the process, users and systems designers meet to **identify the overall business objectives** and to discuss the **technology required** to support these objectives. They produce a detailed definition of the required application, a description of the planned implementation and an indication of the flexibility required.

## 6.6 User groups

A user group is a forum for users of particular hardware or, more usually, software, so that they can **share ideas and experience** and, on occasions, acting as an arbiter in disputes with the supplier. The term is more commonly associated with users of **existing packaged software** who wish to contribute ideas for the continuing development and improvement of packages.

User groups are usually set up either by the **software manufacturers** themselves (who use them to maintain contact with customers and as a source of new product ideas) or by groups of users who were not satisfied with the level of support they were getting from suppliers of proprietary software.

Users of a particular package can meet, or more usually exchange views over the **Internet** to discuss **solutions, ideas or 'short cuts'** to improve productivity. An (electronic) **newsletter** service might be appropriate, based view exchanged by members, but also incorporating ideas culled from the wider environment by IT specialists.

Sometimes user groups are set up **within individual organisations**. Where an organisation has written its own application software, or is using tailor-made software, there will be a very small knowledge base initially, and there will obviously not be a national user group, because the application is unique.

## 6.7 Critical success factors

The use of **critical success factors** can help to determine the information requirements of managers which in turn assists in identifying the information systems required by an organisation. The critical success factors (CSF) method was developed by John Rockart in the late 1970s in order to define executive information needs.

**Definition**

> For each executive, **critical success factors** are the few key areas of the job where things must go right for the organisation to flourish.'
>
> (Sprague and McNurlin, **Information Systems Management in Practice**)

There are usually **fewer than ten** of these factors that any one executive should monitor. Furthermore, they are very time dependent, so they should be re-examined as often as necessary to keep abreast of the current business climate.

**Two separate types** of critical success factor can be identified. A **monitoring** CSF is used to keep abreast of existing activities and operations. A **building** CSF helps to measure the progress of new initiatives and is more likely to be relevant at senior executive level.

- **Monitoring** CSFs are important for **maintaining** business

- **Building** CSFs are important for **expanding** business

  'Let me stress that the CSF approach does not attempt to deal with information needs for strategic planning. Data needs for this management role are almost impossible to pre-plan. The CSF method centres, rather, on information needs for **management control** where data needed to **monitor and improve** existing areas of business can be more readily defined.'

  (Rockart, **Critical Success Factors** (Harvard Business Review))

### 6.8 Determining CSFs and performance indicators

One approach to determining the factors which are critical to success in performing a function or making a decision is as follows.

- List the organisation's corporate objectives and goals
- Determine which factors are critical for accomplishing the objectives
- Determine a small number of **performance indicators** for each factor

### EXAMPLE

One of the **objectives** of an organisation might be to maintain a high level of service direct from stock without holding uneconomic stock levels. This is first quantified in the form of a **goal,** which might be to ensure that 95% of orders for goods can be satisfied directly from stock, while minimising total stockholding costs and stock levels.

**CSFs** might then be identified as the following.

- **Supplier performance** in terms of quality and lead times
- Reliability of **stock records**
- **Forecasting** of demand variations

## 6.9 Performance indicators

The determination of **performance indicators** for each of these CSFs is not necessarily straightforward. Some measures might use **factual**, objectively verifiable, data, while others might make use of 'softer' concepts, such as opinions, perceptions and hunches.

For example, the reliability of stock records can be measured by means of physical stock counts, either at discrete intervals or on a rolling basis. Forecasting of demand variations will be much harder to measure.

Where measures use quantitative data, performance can be measured in a number of ways.

- In **physical quantities**, for example units produced or units sold
- In **money terms**, for example profit, revenues, costs or variances
- In **ratios** and **percentages**

## FOR DISCUSSION

HJK Ltd is a light engineering company which produces a range of components, machine tools and electronic devices for the motor and aircraft industry. It employs about 1,000 people in 12 main divisions.

Discuss possible CSFs for HJK Ltd.

## 6.10 Data sources for CSFs

In general terms there are four **sources** of CSFs.

(a) The **industry** that the business is in.

(b) The **company** itself and its situation within the industry.

(c) The **environment**, for example consumer trends, the economy, and political factors of the country in which the company operates.

(d) Temporal organisational factors, which are **areas of corporate activity** which are currently **unacceptable** and represent a cause of concern, for example, high stock levels.

More specifically, possible internal and external data sources for CSFs include the following.

(a) **The existing system**. The existing system can be used to generate reports showing **failures to meet CSFs.**

(b) **Customer service department**. This department will maintain details of **complaints** received, **refunds** handled, **customer enquiries** etc. These should be reviewed to ensure all failure types have been identified.

(c) **Customers**. A survey of customers, provided that it is properly designed and introduced, would reveal (or confirm) those areas where **satisfaction** is high or low.

(d) **Competitors**. Competitors' operations, pricing structures and publicity should be closely monitored.

(e) **Accounting system**. The **profitability** of various aspects of the operation is probably a key factor in any review of CSFs.

NOTES

    (f)    **Consultants**. A specialist consultancy might be able to perform a detailed review of the system in order to identify ways of satisfying CSFs.

*We look at some of the activities carried out in the implementation, maintenance and review stages of the SDLC in Chapter 4.*

**Chapter roundup**

- The **systems development life-cycle aims** to add discipline to many organisations' approach to system development. It is a model of how systems should be developed. However, in its original form it had a number of **drawbacks**, most notably that it **ignored users**' needs.

- The feasibility study is a formal study to decide what type of system can be developed which meets the needs of the organisation.

- There are three key areas in which a project must be feasible if it is to be selected. It must be justifiable on **technical, operational and economic** grounds.

- One of the most important elements of the feasibility study is the **cost-benefit analysis**. Costs may be analysed in different ways, but include equipment costs, installation costs, development costs, personnel costs and running costs. Benefits are usually more intangible, but include cost savings, revenue benefits and qualitative benefits.

- A **methodology** is a collection of procedures, techniques, tools and documentation aids which are designed to help systems developers in their efforts to implement a new system.

- A **4GL** enables programs to be constructed more quickly, as English-like commands can be taken to produce high-level code.

- **Database systems** are now common. The term 'database system' describes any system that utilises a central pool of information for a range of purposes.

- **Structured walkthroughs** are a technique used by those responsible for systems design to present their design to **users**. A structured walkthrough is a meeting in which the output from a phase or stage of development is presented to users for discussion and for formal approval.

- **Joint applications development** is an approach to development based on a partnership between users and IT specialists.

- One way of ensuring full user involvement in and commitment to design is the technique of **prototyping**. Prototyping assists programmers by helping them to write application programs much more quickly.

**Quick quiz**

    1    What are the stages of the systems development lifecycle? (See Section 1.1)

    2    What three areas must a project be feasible in? (See Section 2.3)

    3    List five types of costs that may be incurred when developing a new system and five benefits. (See Section 2.7)

    4    What is a methodology? (See Section 3.1)

5    What are the disadvantages of using a methodology? (See Section 3.4)

6    What are the advantages and disadvantages of prototyping? (See Sections 4.2 and 4.3)

7    List four approaches that may be utilised in systems development to ensure user needs are met. (See Sections 6.2 – 6.7)

## Answers to Activities

1

| Capital cost items | 'One-off' revenue cost items | Regular annual costs |
|---|---|---|
| Hardware purchase costs | Consultancy fees | Operating staff salaries/wages |
| Software purchase costs | Systems analysts' and programmers' salaries | Data transmission costs |
| Purchase of accommodation (if needed) | Costs of testing the system (staff costs, consumables) | Consumable materials |
| | | Power |
| Installation costs (new desks, cables, physical storage etc) | Costs of converting the files for the new system | Maintenance costs |
| | Staff recruitment fees | Cost of standby arrangements |
| | | Ongoing staff training |

2    An open system is much affected by unpredictable and rapidly changing environmental factors (a hospital admissions system, for instance) and it needs an approach that takes account of 'soft' problems. A highly stable system, such as a payroll system, simply needs to follow predefined rules (payroll rules change, but even the changes are relatively predictable).

3    (a)    Users become involved in the systems analysis process. Since this process is a critical appraisal of their work, they should have the opportunity to provide feedback on the appraisal itself.

(b)    The output from the development is shown to people who are not systems development personnel. This encourages its originators to prepare it to a higher quality and in user-friendly form.

(c)    Because the onus is on users to approve design, they are more likely to become committed to the new system and less likely to 'rubbish' it.

(d)    The process focuses on quality of and good practice in operations generally.

(e)    It avoids disputes about who is responsible for what.

## Further question practice

*Now try the following practice question at the end of this text.*

Exam style question    **3**

# Chapter 4 :

# SYSTEM IMPLEMENTATION, MAINTENANCE AND REVIEW

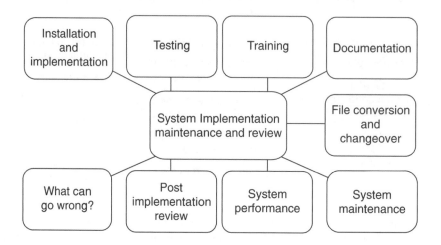

## Introduction

Even if you have designed the best system in the world things can still go wrong when you actually try to put it in place. Implementation covers a **wide range of issues**, ranging from simple things like remembering that computers need desks to sit on and cables to link them up, the approach taken when changing to a new system.

Throughout its life, a system should operate effectively and efficiently. To do this, the system needs to be **maintained. We end this chapter with a** look at the **evaluation and review of systems.** This should be an ongoing process to ensure the system continues to meet requirements.

## Your objectives

After completing this chapter you should understand:

    (a)    The nature and purpose of systems maintenance and performance evaluation.

    (b)    The main issues relating to the development of an information system, and the risks involved in implementation.

    (c)    The role of training in ensuring users are able to fully utilise a new system.

# 1 INSTALLATION AND IMPLEMENTATION

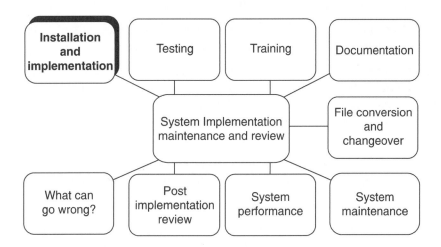

## 1.1 The stages of implementation

The main stages in the implementation of a computer system are as follows.

(a) Installation of the **hardware and software.**
(b) Testing.
(c) **Staff training** and production of documentation.
(d) **Conversion** of files and database creation.
(e) Changeover.

The items in this list do not necessarily happen in a set chronological order, and some can be done at the same time - for example staff training and system testing can be part of the same operation.

The requirements for implementation vary from system to system as we shall see throughout this chapter.

*Installation of equipment*

Installing a **mainframe** computer or a large network is a major operation that is carried out by the manufacturer/supplier.

If just a few PCs are being installed in a small network, the customer may have to install the hardware himself. This should not be difficult, provided that the manufacturer's instruction manuals are read carefully.

*Installation of a PC*

The **office accommodation** for PCs and peripheral equipment will also need a little bit of planning.

(a) PCs can be used in any office environment, but they generate **some heat** when they operate (just like any other machine) and so it is inadvisable to put them in small, hot rooms.

(b) **Large desks** may be advisable, to accommodate a screen and keyboard and leave some free desk space for the office worker to use.

(c) There should be plenty of **power sockets** - enough to meet future needs as the system grows, not just immediate needs.

(d) If noisy printers are being purchased, it may be advisable to locate these in a **separate printer room**, to cut down the noise for office workers.

(e)     There should be a **telephone** close to the computer, for communicating with the dealer or other organisation which provides **system support and advice** when the user runs into difficulties.

(f)     **Cabling** for network connections needs to take account of possible future changes in office layout or in system requirements.

When the hardware has been installed, the **software** may then need installing too. To install the software, the computer user must follow the instructions in the user's manual. Installing software used to be tedious and lengthy, taking perhaps half an hour for a package, but most new software is provided on CD-ROM and can be installed in minutes.

PCs almost invariably come with **operating software** pre-loaded these days (eg Windows). Some suppliers provide other pre-loaded software such as **Microsoft Office.**

If possible, **back-up copies** should be made of all software.

Whether or not this is done the software should be **registered** with the manufacturer, either by filling in a registration form and posting it or often, these days, by completing a form on screen and sending it in via telecommunications links.

**Insurance** should be arranged against losses due to fire or theft. It is also possible to obtain insurance against accidental loss of data. If all the data on a hard disk were lost, for example, it could be a long job to re-enter all the lost data, but with insurance cover, the cost of the clerk to do the re-inputting would be paid for by the insurance.

*Installation of a mainframe*

If a mainframe installation is to be successful it must be carefully planned. Many of the issues described above, such as furniture needs, cabling and so on, still apply. The **particular problems** of planning a large installation include the following.

***The characteristics of different types of computers are explained in Chapter 5.***

The **site selected** for the main computer might be in an existing or a new building. Factors in the choice of site are the need for the following.

(a)     Adequate **space** for computer and peripherals, including servicing room.

(b)     Room for expansion.

(c)     **Easy access** for computer equipment and supplies (it should be unnecessary to knock holes in outside walls, as has happened, in order to gain access for equipment).

(d)     **Nearness** to principal **user** departments.

(e)     Space available for a **library, stationery** store, and **systems maintenance** staff.

The **site preparation** may involve consideration of certain potential problems.

(a)     **Air conditioning** (temperature, humidity and dust).

(b)     Special electricity supplies.

(c)     **Raised floor** (or **false ceiling**) so that **cables** may pass from one piece of equipment to another.

(d)     Fire protection devices.

(e)     Furnishings.

**Standby equipment** should be arranged, to ensure **continuity of processing** in the event of power or computer failure. Such equipment may include standby **generators** and standby **computers**.

## 2 TESTING

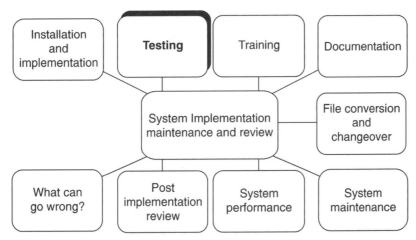

A system must be thoroughly tested before implementation, otherwise there is a danger that the new system will **go live with faults** that might prove costly. The scope of tests and trials will again **vary with the size** of the system.

Three types of testing can be identified: off-line testing, on-line testing and user-acceptance testing.

### 2.1 Off-line testing

**Definition**

> **Off-line testing** describes the testing (usually performed by the developer) of a software program carried out on machines not controlled by the central processor that will ultimately control the new program.

Off-line testing will include a **diagnostic routine**, or debugging routine, provides for outline program testing and error correction during program development. When a programmer is testing a program, and the program does not operate correctly, he must locate the cause of the error. Diagnostic routines enable him to find out what the program was doing at the time it failed.

Test data will be prepared of the type that the program will be required to process. This test data will deliberately include **invalid/exceptional items** to test whether the program reacts in the right way and generates the required management reports.

The anticipated results of processing will be worked out in advance and then after processing the test program, there will be **item for item checking** against the actual computer output to test whether the program has operated as required.

Business Basics: Information Technology

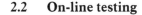

### 2.2 On-line testing

There will then be an overall systems test - to test that all elements of the system operate and interact correctly.

**Definition**

> **On-line testing** is that carried out (usually by the developer) under the control of the principal central processor. On-line testing usually tests the full program.

Various personnel will be involved in system tests.

(a) The **IS project manager** will have overall responsibility for the project, and must ensure that the tests are planned and executed properly, and the system is fully documented.

(b) **Systems analysts** must check with their tests that the system achieves the objectives set for it, and do not contain any errors.

(c) **Programmers** must be on hand to de-bug any faults which the earlier program tests had not spotted.

(d) The **computer operations manager** will be in charge of data preparation work and operations in the computer room.

Test data should be constructed to test **all conditions**. For example, dummy data records and transactions should be input which are designed to test all the data validation routines and the **links** between different parts of the system in the system.

Unusual, but feasible, transactions could be tested, to see how the system handles them - for example two wage packets in the same week for the same employee.

Many managers prefer to use **historical data** in trials, because it is then possible to check the output of the new system against the output that the old system produced.

### 2.3 Acceptance testing

**Definition**

> **Acceptance testing** is testing of a system by the user department, after the system has passed its systems test.

The purposes of having trials conducted by the user department's managers are to:

- Find **software errors** which exist but have not yet been detected
- Find out exactly what the **demands of the new system** are
- Find out whether any **major changes in operating procedures** will be necessary

Another aspect of the user department trials (or a subsequent stage of trials) might be to test the system with **large volumes of data,** and at the same time use the tests as an opportunity to **train staff** in the new system and the new procedures.

These 'bulk' tests on the system involve a range of checks.

(a) **Error correction** procedures (ie user department routines).
(b) The inter-relationship between **clerical and computer procedures**.
(c) The **timing** of computer runs.
(d) The **capacity** of files, file handling, updating and amendment.
(e) Systems **controls**, including auditing requirements.
(f) Procedures for **data capture**, **preparation** and **input** and the distribution of **output**.

# 3 TRAINING

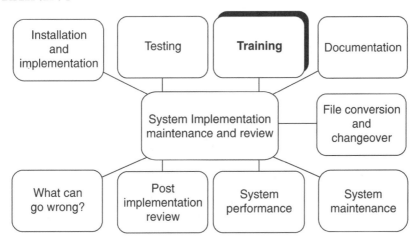

## 3.1 IT training

Staff training in the use of information technology is as important as the technology itself as **without effective operation** at all levels computer systems can be an expensive **waste of resources** in any business.

The issue of training raises the wider matter of how to make personnel at all levels competent and willing to use IT. If organisations wish to encourage end-user computing then a training program can be part of a wider **'propaganda' exercise** by information systems professionals.

Training is not simply an issue that affects operational staff. As PCs are used more and more as management tools, training in information technology **affects all levels** in an organisation, from senior managers learning how to use an executive information system for example, to accounts clerks learning how to use an accounts management system.

A **systematic approach** to training can be illustrated in a flowchart as follows.

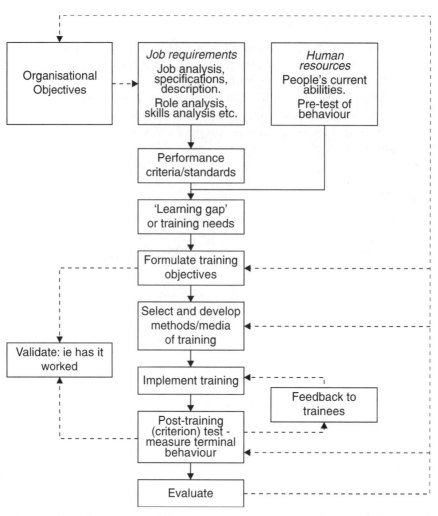

Note the following points in particular.

(a) Training is provided primarily to help the **organisation** achieve its **objectives,** not just for the benefit of staff.

(b) An individual's **training need** is generally defined as follows.

| | |
|---|---|
| Required level of competence | X |
| Current level of competence | (Y) |
| Training need | Z |

(c) Training should be **evaluated** to make sure that it has worked. If not the method may have been wrong. Whatever the cause, the training need still exists.

### 3.2 Training for senior management

Senior management can be 'trained' in a number of ways of varying degrees of formality. The completely **informal** approach might include the provision of information from the following sources.

(a) **Newspapers** (most of the quality press run regular articles on IT and computing).

(b) **Subordinates** (getting subordinate members of staff to demonstrate a system).

(c) **Individual demonstrations** of computer systems for senior executives.

**Semi-formal** training is of greater value.

    (a)    Executive **briefings** (for example presentation before or after board meetings).

    (b)    Video **demonstrations** (for example during lunchtime).

    (c)    **Short seminars**, designed around an issue that is narrowly defined.

**Formal sessions** such as day **courses** are necessary if managers are to learn how to use a particular system, for example an EIS or a spreadsheet package.

Some commentators have argued that senior managers who are knowledgeable about computers and related technologies **make wiser decisions** in the following areas.

    (a)    **Allocation of resources** to information systems (especially if the information system gives an organisation competitive advantage).

    (b)    **Planning** for information systems.

    (c)    Establishing an appropriate **corporate culture** for technological development.

    (d)    The establishment of an informed scepticism when dealing with IT professionals means that managers **won't be blinded by science**, and will be able to communicate their needs more effectively.

    (e)    Informed managers will have a better understanding of their subordinates' work.

### 3.3    Training middle management

The type of training middle management receives is likely to be **more structured** and **more tailored** to the particular applications within their remit.

Middle management is responsible for the **correct use of systems** in an age of distributed processing and end-user computing. Middle management is also responsible for implementing in detail the organisation's computer **security policy**.

The accent is also on the **business issues**. Managers do not necessarily need to know **how** computers work. They need to know **what** computing can do for them.

### 3.4    Training users

Users need a number of different types of computer and systems training.

    (a)    **Basic literacy** in computers such as the concept of a file, updating, maintenance and so forth, might be needed. This might help users relate the workings of a manual system to its computer replacement. Also, some basic ideas as to how to use a computer efficiently can be usefully taught.

    (b)    Users also need to get up and running with particular applications **quickly**, even if they do not go into the finer points of it. If the system is complex, such training gives users an **overall view** of the system, commands and procedures.

    (c)    Users might sometimes need a **refresher course**, especially if they do not use a particular application regularly.

    (d)    Users need training while operating the application (**on-the-job training**).

Some of these facilities are provided by the computer system itself. For example, many software packages have a **Help facility** which enables a user to learn facts about the system while they are using it.

**Computer based training** has the advantage of encouraging users to become acquainted with the technology they will be using, and to develop their skills at their own pace. **Multimedia training packages** exist for many widely-used software packages.

Training can also be provided by:

- Reading the **user manuals**
- Attending **courses** that the dealer or employer provides
- Attending **courses** on a leading software package

With large computer systems, extensive training of large numbers of staff will probably be necessary, and so further training measures may include other media.

(a) **Lectures** on general or specific aspects of the system - possibly with the use of films, video, tape-recordings, slides, overhead projectors etc.

(b) **Discussion meetings**, possibly following on from lectures, which allow the staff to ask questions and sort out problems.

(c) **Internal company magazines**, to explain the new system in outline.

(d) **Handbooks**, detailing in precise terms the new documentation and procedures. Different handbooks for each function will often be prepared by different persons.

(e) Using **trials/tests** on the new system to give staff direct experience before the system 'goes live'.

# 4 DOCUMENTATION

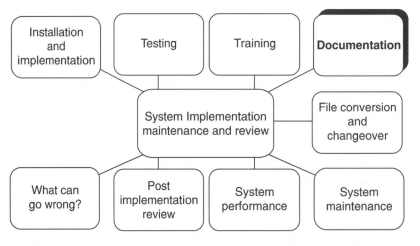

**Definition**

**Documentation** includes a wide range of technical and non-technical books, manuals, descriptions and diagrams relating to the use and operation of a computer system. Examples include user manuals, hardware and operating software manuals, system specifications and program documentation.

## 4.1 The systems specification

The systems specification is a **complete documentation of the whole system** and must always be properly maintained (ie kept up to date) as parts of the system are changed or added to.

Many of the problems in computer installations arise because of **inadequate** systems and program documentation and controls must be set up to ensure that **updating procedures** are always carried out.

### 4.2 Program specifications

A program specification, or program documentation, is the complete description of a program, usually including **notes, flowcharts**, a listing of all the **codes,** and perhaps test data and expected results. There should be a program specification for every individual program in the system.

**Initial specifications** are drawn up by the systems analyst and the programmer then uses the specification as the **basis of writing and testing the required program**.

When the program has been written and tested, one copy of the **final specification** will form part of the overall systems specification, and a second copy will be retained by the programmer to form part of the programmer's own documentation for the program.

### 4.3 Computer operations manual

This manual provides full documentation of the **operational procedures** necessary for the 'hands-on' running of the system. Amongst the matters to be covered by this documentation would be the following.

(a) **Systems set-up procedures**. Full details should be given for each application of the necessary file handling and stationery requirements etc.

(b) **Security procedures**. Particular stress should be placed on the need for checking that proper authorisation has been given for processing operations and the need to restrict use of machine(s) to authorised operators.

(c) **Reconstruction control procedures**. Precise instructions should be given in relation to matters such as file dumping and also the recovery procedures to be adopted in the event of a systems failure.

(d) **System messages**. A listing of all messages likely to appear on the operator's screen should be given together with an indication of the responses which they should evoke.

### 4.4 User manual

At some stage **before staff training** takes place, the system must be fully documented for the computer **user**. Matters to be dealt with should include the following.

(a) **Input**. Responsibilities and procedures for preparation of input including requirements for establishment of batch control totals, authorisation etc.

(b) **Error reports**. Full explanation of nature and form of error reports (eg exception reports for items rejected by data validation checks) and instructions as to the necessary action to be taken.

(c) **File amendment procedures**. Full explanation of necessary authorisation and documentation required for file amendment.

(d) **Output.** What this is, what form it takes, what should be done with it etc.

The user documentation is used to **explain** the system to the user and to help to train staff. Additionally, it provides a **point of reference** should the user have some problems with the system in the future - eg an error condition or a screen message that he or she does not understand.

When a system is developed in-house, the user documentation might be written by a systems analyst. However, it might be considered preferable for the user documentation to be **written by** a member of the **user's department's staff**, possibly a junior manager who has spent some time with the project development team, learning about the system.

### 4.5 System changes manual

Amendments to the original systems specification will almost inevitably occur, in addition to the computerisation of additional company activities. The objective of the system changes manual is to ensure that such changes are just as **strictly controlled** as was the case with the original systems development and introduction. Four matters to be covered in this respect would be as follows.

(a) Recording of the request and **reason** for a change.

(b) Procedures for the **authorisation** of changes.

(c) Procedures for the **documentation** of changes.

(d) Procedures for the **testing** of changes.

## 5 FILE CONVERSION AND CHANGEOVER

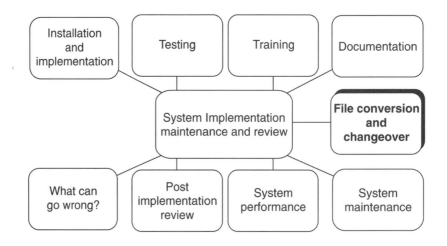

### 5.1 File conversion

### Definition

> **File conversion**, means converting existing files into a format suitable for the new system.

File conversion may be a **major part** of the systems implementation or it may be largely painless, if upgrading say, from version 1 of a standard package to version 2. If it means the conversion of existing manual file records into a medium used by the **computer** it may be very expensive. It may involve the transcription of records, or parts of them, on to specially designed forms before they are keyed on to the appropriate computer medium.

Because of the volume of data that must be copied on to the new files, the problem of **input errors** is a serious one, whatever data validation checks may be operating.

Once the file has been created, **extensive checking** for accuracy is essential, otherwise considerable problems may arise when the system becomes operational.

Before starting to load live data about customers, suppliers or employees etc, management should check whether the system must be registered under **data protection legislation** – eg in the UK the **Data Protection Act 1998**.

*Existing computer files*

If the system is already computerised on a system that the organisation now wishes to abandon, the difficulties of file conversion will usually (though not always) be reduced. When it comes to the actual transcription from the old files to the new computer files the use of a special **conversion program** or **translation program** will speed up the whole process.

The problem of conversion has reduced significantly as major **software manufacturers** have realised that it may be a barrier to people using their products. Thus an Excel spreadsheet can be saved in Lotus 1-2-3 format, if this is what the user wants.

*Existing manual files*

The stages in file conversion from manual files to computer files, where this is a very complex process, are normally as follows.

(a)   Ensuring that the **original** record files are **accurate and up to date**.

(b)   Recording the old file data on **specially designed input documents**.

This will usually be done by the user department personnel (with temporary staff if required) following instructions laid down by the designer or software supplier.

The instructions will include the procedures for allocating **new code numbers** (a coding system, including check digits if necessary, may have to be designed by this stage) and for checking **the accuracy and completeness** of the data selected and entered on the input documents (usually verification by another person and the establishment of control totals).

(c)   **Transcribing** the completed input documents on to the **computer media**.

(d)   Data entry programs would include **validation checks** on the input data. The contents of the file must then be printed out and **completely checked** back to the data input forms (or even the original file if possible).

(e)   **Correcting any errors** that this checking reveals.

Other problems of file conversion which must be considered include the following.

(a)   The possible provision of **additional staff,** or the use of a computer bureau, to cope with the file conversion and prevent bottlenecks.

(b)   The establishment of **cut-off dates** where live files are being converted (should the conversion be during slack times, for example, during holidays, weekends?).

(c)   The decision as to whether files should be converted **all at once,** or whether the conversion should be **file by file** or record group by record group (with subsequent amalgamation).

Once the new system has been fully and satisfactorily tested the **changeover** can be made. This may be according to one of four approaches.

- Direct changeover
- Parallel running

- Pilot tests
- Phased or 'staged' implementation

## 5.2 Direct changeover

This is the method of changeover in which the old system is **completely replaced** by the new system **in one move**.

This may be unavoidable where the two systems are substantially different, or where extra staff to oversee parallel running are unobtainable.

While this method is comparatively **cheap** it is **risky** (system or program corrections are difficult while the system has to remain operational): management must have complete confidence that the new system will work.

The new system should be introduced during **slack periods,** for example over a bank holiday weekend or during an office closure such as a factory's summer shutdown or in the period between Christmas and the New Year.

## 5.3 Parallel running

This is a form of changeover whereby the **old and new** systems are **run in parallel** for a period of time, both processing current data and enabling cross checking to be made.

This method provides a **degree of safety** should there be problems with the new system. However, if there are differences between the two systems cross-checking may be difficult or impossible.

Furthermore, there is a **delay** in the actual implementation of the new system, a possible indication of **lack of confidence** in the new system, and a need for **more staff** to cope with both systems running in parallel.

This cautious approach, if adopted, should be properly planned, and the plan should include the following.

(a) A firm **time limit** on parallel running.

(b) Details of **which data** should be **cross-checked** - all of it? - some of it on a sample basis?

(c) Instructions on how **errors** are to be dealt with - they could be errors in the old system.

(d) Instructions on how to cope with **major problems** in the new system.

## 5.4 Pilot operation

This is **cheaper** and **easier to control** than parallel running, and provides a **greater degree of safety** than does a direct changeover. There are two types of pilot operation.

(a) Retrospective parallel running

This is an approach in which the new system operates on **data already processed** by the old system. The existing results are available for cross-checking and the system can be tested without the problems of staffing and disruption caused by parallel running.

(b) Restricted data running

This involves a **complete logical part** of the system being chosen and run as a unit on the new system. If that is shown to be working well, one or more of the remaining parts are then transferred, until eventually all parts are operating on the new system.

For example, one group of customer accounts from the sales ledger might be run on the new system. Again, the planning should involve the setting of strict time limits for each phase and instructions on how problems are to be dealt with. It must be remembered that two systems have to be controlled and additional staff, as well as a longer period for implementation, may be required.

## 5.5 Phased implementation

Phased implementation takes two possible forms

(a)   It can on the one hand resemble **parallel running**, the difference being that only a portion of the data is run in parallel, for example for **one branch** only.

(b)   Alternatively, phased implementation may consist of a number of **separate direct changeovers**, for example where a large system is to be replaced and the criteria for direct changeover apply.

The use of this method of implementation is best suited to very **large projects** and/or those where distinct parts of the system are **geographically dispersed**.

Where this approach is adopted care must be taken to control any **system amendments** incorporated in the later phases to ensure the overall system remains totally compatible.

## FOR DISCUSSION

Has anyone in your group been involved in a system changeover? What method was used? Did the changeover proceed smoothly?

# 6    SYSTEM MAINTENANCE

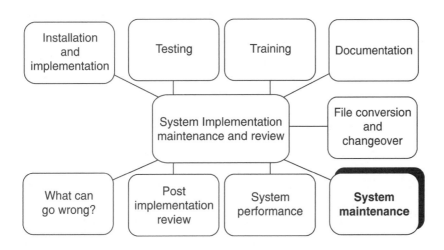

### 6.1 Types of maintenance

There are three types of maintenance activity.

- Corrective maintenance
- Perfective maintenance
- Adaptive maintenance

### Definition

**Corrective maintenance** is carried out in reaction to a system failure, for example in processing or in an implementation procedure. Its objective is to ensure that systems remain operational.

**Perfective maintenance** is carried out in order to perfect the software, or to improve software so that the processing inefficiencies are eliminated and performance is enhanced.

**Adaptive maintenance** is carried out to take account of anticipated changes in the processing environment. For example new taxation legislation might require change to be made to payroll software.

**Corrective** maintenance usually consists of action in response to a **problem**. Much **perfective** maintenance consists of making enhancements requested by **users** to improve or extend the facilities available. The user interface may be amended to make software more user friendly.

The key features of system maintenance ought to be **flexibility** and **adaptability**.

(a) The system, perhaps with minor modifications, should cope with changes in the computer user's procedures or volume of business.

(b) The computer user should benefit from advances in computer hardware technology without having to switch to another system altogether.

### 6.2 The causes of system maintenance

Besides environmental changes, three factors contribute to the need for maintenance.

| Factor | Comment |
|---|---|
| **Errors** | However carefully and diligently the systems development staff carry out systems testing and program testing, it is likely that **bugs** will exist in a newly implemented system. Most should be identified during the first few runs of a system. The effect of errors can obviously vary enormously. |
| **Changes in requirements** | Although users should be consulted at all stages of systems development, problems may arise after a system is implemented because users may have found it difficult to express their requirements, or may have been concerned about the future of their jobs and not participated fully in development. |
| | Cost constraints may have meant that certain requested features were not incorporated. Time constraints may have meant that requirements suggested during development were ignored in the interest of prompt completion. |

| Factor | Comment |
|---|---|
| **Poor documentation** | If old systems are accompanied by poor documentation, or even a complete lack of documentation, it may be very difficult to understand their programs. It will be hard to update or maintain such programs. Programmers may opt instead to patch up the system with new applications using newer technology. |

Corrective and adaptive maintenance should be carried out **as and when** problems occur, but perfective maintenance may be carried out on a more scheduled system-by-system basis (Sales system in January, Purchases in February, etc).

Assuming the system is intended to reflect business needs, it ought to be possible to predict with reasonable certainty when business **growth** will make maintenance necessary. It is possible to contend with increasing volumes and communication needs by enhancing the existing computer system on site, on a modular basis.

- Installing **disks** of **greater capacity** and **higher speed**
- Installing a **more powerful processor**
- Changing to **faster printers**
- Installing **additional terminals** or **network facilities**

As mentioned, systems analysts will always try to design **flexibility** into computer systems, so that the system can **adapt** to change.

However, there will come a point at which **redevelopment** is necessary, for example where hardware upgrades or the availability of new software make radical change necessary, or following a company restructuring.

# 7    SYSTEMS PERFORMANCE

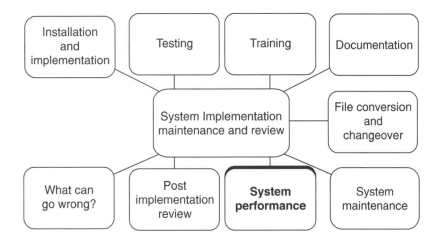

## 7.1    Performance measurement

It is not possible to identify and isolate every consequence of an implementation project and the impact of each on organisational effectiveness. To achieve some approximation to a complete evaluation, therefore, certain **indirect measures** must be used.

(a)    **Significant task relevance** attempts to observe the results of system use.

For example, document turnaround times might have improved following the acquisition of a document image processing system, or minutes of meetings might be made available and distributed faster following the addition of a company secretarial function to a local area network.

(b) The **willingness to pay** of users might give an indication of value.

Users can be asked how much they (their department) would be prepared to pay in order to gain the benefit of a certain upgrade, for example the availability of a particular report. Inter-departmental pricing will be a critical factor in the success of this approach.

(c) **Systems logs** may give an indication of the value of the system if it is a 'voluntary use' system, such as an external database.

(d) **User information satisfaction** is a concept which attempts to find out, by asking users, how they rate their satisfaction with a system. They may be asked for their views on timeliness, quality of output, response times, processing and their overall confidence in the system.

(e) The adequacy of system **documentation** may be measurable in terms of how often manuals are actually used and the number of errors found or amendments made. However, low usage of a user manual, for instance, may mean either that the manual is useless or that the system is so good that it is self-explanatory.

---

**Activity 1** (15 minutes)

Operational evaluation should consider, among other issues, whether input data is properly provided and output is useful. Output documents are often considered by users to be of marginal value, perhaps of use for background information only. In spite of this there is a tendency to continue producing existing reports.

How might you identify whether a report is being used?

---

Performance reviews will vary in content from organisation to organisation, but the matters which will probably be looked at are as follows.

(a) The **growth** rates in file sizes and the number of transactions processed by the system. Trends should be analysed and projected to assess whether there are likely to be problems with lengthy processing time or an inefficient file structure due to the volume of processing.

(b) The clerical **manpower** needs for the system, and deciding whether they are more or less than estimated.

(c) The identification of any **delays** in processing and an assessment of the consequences of any such delays.

(d) An assessment of the efficiency of **security** procedures, in terms of number of breaches, number of viruses encountered.

(e) A check of the **error rates** for input data. High error rates may indicate inefficient preparation of input documents, an inappropriate method of data capture or poor design of input media.

(f) An examination of whether **output** from the computer is being used to good purpose. (Is it used? Is it timely? Does it go to the right people?)

(g)   Operational **running costs**, examined to discover any inefficient programs or processes. This examination may reveal excessive costs for certain items although in total, costs may be acceptable.

## 7.2   Improving performance

**Computer systems efficiency audits** are concerned with improving **outputs** from the system and their use, or reducing the costs of system **inputs**. With falling costs of computer hardware and software, and continual technological advances there should often be **scope for improvements** in computer systems, which an audit ought to be able to identify.

*Outputs from a computer system*

With regard to outputs, the efficiency of a computer system would be enhanced in any of the following ways.

(a)   **More outputs** of some value could be produced by the **same input** resources.

For example:

(i)   If the system could process **more transactions**.

(ii)   If the system could produce **more management information** (eg sensitivity analysis).

(iii)   If the system could make information **available to more people** who might need it.

(b)   **Outputs of little value** could be **eliminated** from the system, thus making savings in the cost of inputs.

For example:

(i)   If reports are produced **too frequently**, should they be produced less often?

(ii)   If reports are **distributed too widely**, should the distribution list be shortened?

(iii)   If reports are **too bulky**, can they be reduced in size?

(c)   The **timing** of outputs could be better.

Information should be available in good time for the information-user to be able to make good use of it. Reports that are issued late might lose their value. Computer systems could give managers **immediate** access to the information they require, by means of file enquiry or special software (such as databases or spreadsheet modelling packages).

(d)   It might be found that outputs are not as satisfactory as they should be, perhaps because:

(i)   **Access** to information from the system is limited, and could be improved by the use of a **database** and a **network** system.

(ii)   Available outputs are **restricted** because of the **method of data processing** used (eg batch processing instead of real-time processing) or the **type of equipment** used (eg stand-alone PCs compared with client/server systems).

NOTES

*Depending on your current level of knowledge, you may need to refer to some parts of Chapter 5 before attempting the following activity.*

---

**Activity 2** **(15 minutes)**

What elements of hardware and software might restrict the capabilities of a system?

---

*Inputs to a computer system*

The efficiency of a computer system could be improved if the same volume (and frequency) of output could be achieved with **fewer input** resources, and at **less cost**.

Some of the ways in which this could be done include the following.

(a)   **Multi-user** or **network** systems might be more efficient than stand-alone systems.

   Multi-user systems allow several input operators to work on the same files at the same time, so that if one person has a heavy workload and another is currently short of work, the person who has some free time can help his or her busy colleague - thus improving operator efficiency.

(b)   **Real-time** systems might be more efficient than batch processing.

(c)   Using computers and external storage media with **bigger storage** capacity.

   A frequent complaint is that '**waiting time**' for the operator can be very long and tedious. Computer systems with better backing storage facilities can reduce this operator waiting time, and so be more efficient.

(d)   Using more up to date software.

Management might also wish to consider whether time spent **checking and correcting** input data can be eliminated. An **alternative method of input** might be chosen. For example bar codes and scanners should eliminate the need to check for input errors.

*Multi-user and network systems are explained in Chapter 5.*

# 8 POST-IMPLEMENTATION REVIEW

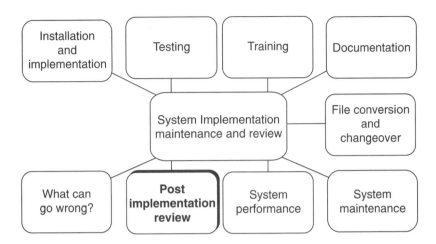

## 8.1 The post-implementation review

**The post-implementation review** should establish whether the objectives and targeted performance criteria have been met, and if not, why not, and what should be done about it.

In appraising the operation of the new system immediately after the changeover, comparison should be made between **actual and predicted performance**. This will include (amongst other items):

- Consideration of **throughput speed** (time between input and output)
- Use of computer **storage** (both internal and external)
- The number and type of **errors/queries**
- The **cost** of processing (data capture, preparation, storage and output media, etc)

If the implementation has involved a **steering committee**, the committee may also be responsible for overseeing the post-implementation review. The **internal audit** department may be required to do much of the work involved in the review.

The post-implementation measurements should **not be made too soon** after the system goes live, or else results will be abnormally affected by 'teething' problems, lack of user familiarity and resistance to change.

### The post-implementation review report

The findings of a post-implementation review team should be formalised in a **report**.

(a) A **summary** of their findings should be provided, emphasising any areas where the system has been found to be **unsatisfactory**.

(b) A review of **system performance** should be provided. This will address the matters outlined above, such as run times and error rates.

(c) A **cost-benefit review** should be included, comparing the forecast costs and benefits identified at the time of the feasibility study with actual costs and benefits.

(d) **Recommendations** should be made as to any **further action** or steps which should be taken to improve performance.

## 9 INFORMATION SYSTEMS PROJECTS – WHAT CAN GO WRONG?

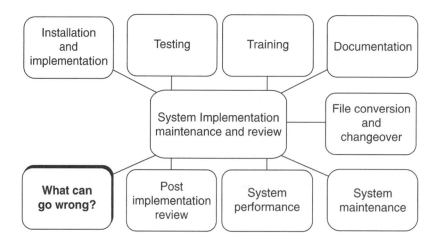

### 9.1 Conflicting demands

A systems development project is **affected by a number of factors, often in conflict with each other**. The requirement to keep to a specified **time** might for example increase **costs**, if there are delays and new staff have to be employed, or reduce **quality** if corners are cut. It is with these aims in mind that **management** of the project must be conducted.

(a)   **Quality** of the system required, in terms of basic system requirements.

(b)   The **resources**, both in terms of staff recruitment and work scheduling, and technology.

(c)   **Time,** both to complete the project, and in terms of the opportunity cost of time spent on this project which could be spent on others.

(d)   **Costs,** which are monitored and controlled, in accordance with the budget set for the project.

Perhaps the best way of understanding why active management of information systems projects is **necessary** is by seeing **what happens when they go wrong**. It is not uncommon for a systems development project to be late and over budget, and for the system produced still not to deliver what was expected. A number of factors can combine to produce these expensive disasters, as explained in the following paragraphs.

### 9.2 Project managers

The person appointed project manager in an Information Systems project is often an Information Technology specialist. Such an individual might be a highly proficient analyst or programmer, but **not a good manager**.

The project manager has a number of conflicting requirements.

(a)   The **systems manager,** usually the project manager's boss, wants the project delivered on time, to specification and within budget.

(b)   **Users,** and the **management** of the function to which they belong, want a system which does everything they require - but they are not always certain what they want. User input is vital to a project, but user management and staff may not be able to take time off from their normal duties to help out. If the project is late, over budget, and does not do all which is required of it, then users will be vocal critics.

(c)     The project manager has to plan and supervise the work of **analysts** and **programmers**.

The project manager needs to develop an **appropriate management style**. As the project manager needs to encourage participation from users, an excessively authoritarian style is not suitable.

### 9.3    Other factors

Other factors can be identified.

(a)     The project manager accepts an **unrealistic deadline** for having the system up and running. The timescale is fixed too early on in the planning process: the user's idea of when the system would be needed is taken as the deadline, before sufficient consideration is given to the realism of this timescale.

(b)     **Poor or non-existent planning** is a recipe for disaster. Ludicrous deadlines would appear much earlier if a proper planning process was undertaken.

(c)     **Control is non-existent** (ie no performance reviews).

(d)     **Users change their requirements,** resulting in costly changes to the system as it is being developed.

(e)     **Poor timetabling and resourcing** is a cause of problems. It is no use being presented on day 1 with a team of programmers, when there is systems analysis and design work to do. As the development and implementation of a computer project may take a considerable length of time (perhaps 18 months from initial decision to operational running for a medium-sized installation) a proper **plan** and time **schedule** for the various activities must be drawn up.

### 9.4    Steering committees

One tool used to reduce the likelihood of a poor system being developed is the steering committee. Some organisations set up a steering committee to oversee the development of information systems within the organisation. The steering committee's tasks are as follows.

(a)     To **approve (or reject) projects** whose total budgeted cost is below a certain limit and so within their authorisation limit.

(b)     To **recommend projects** to the board of directors for acceptance when their cost is high enough to call for approval at board level.

(c)     To establish **company guidelines** within the framework of the IT strategy for the development of computer based processing and management information systems.

(d)     The **co-ordination and control** of the work of the study group(s) and project development groups, in respect of the development time, the cost and the technical quality of the investigations.

(e)     The **evaluation** of the feasibility study reports and system specifications. The steering committee must be satisfied that each new system has been properly justified.

(f)     To monitor and **review each new system after implementation** to check whether the system has met its objectives. If it hasn't, to investigate the reasons for the system's failure, and take any suitable control or remedial measures.

(g)   In an organisation which has a continuing programme of new DP projects, assessing the contribution of each project to the long term **corporate objectives** of the organisation, ranking projects in order of **priority** and assigning resources to the most important projects first, and taking decisions to defer projects when insufficient resources are available.

The steering committee might include the following.

- The **information director** or a senior IS staff member
- **Accountants** for technical financial advice relating to costs and benefits
- Senior **user management**

**Chapter roundup**

- The main stages in the systems **implementation** process are installation of hardware and software, staff training, system testing, file creation and changeover.

- **Installation** of equipment requires careful planning. The **user** may install a small number of PCs, but larger computers will be installed by the **supplier**. Considerations include site selection, site preparation and delivery itself.

- **Training** is a key part of the implementation of a new system. The approach adopted and the medium through which training is given will vary depending on the target audience. **Senior** management are more likely to be interested in the **overall capabilities** and limitations of systems, while **junior** staff need to be taught the **functional** aspects.

- A system must be thoroughly **tested** before implementation, otherwise there is a danger that it may not function properly when it goes live. The nature and scope of testing will vary depending on the size of the system.

- There are four possible approaches to system changeover: direct changeover, parallel running, pilot tests and phased implementation. These vary in terms of time required, cost and risk

- There are three types of systems maintenance. **Corrective** maintenance is carried out to correct an error, **perfective** maintenance aims to make enhancements to systems and **adaptive** maintenance takes account of anticipated changes in the processing environment.

- **Performance reviews** can be carried out to look at a wide range of systems functions and characteristics. Technological change often gives scope to **improve** the quality of outputs or reduce the extent or cost of inputs.

- During the **post-implementation review**, an evaluation of the system is carried out to see whether the targeted performance criteria have been met and to carry out a review of costs and benefits. The review should culminate in the production of a report and recommendations.

- Some organisations use steering committees to oversee the development of information systems.

## Quick quiz

1   List the main stages in the implementation of a computer system (See section 1.1)

2   Name three types of testing. (See sections 2.1-2.3)

3   What different types of training do operational users need? (See section 3.4)

4   What does the system changes manual contain? (See section 4.5)

5   What is parallel running? (See section 5.3)

6   When might phased implementation be appropriate? (See section 5.5)

7   List three types of maintenance. (See section 5.5)

8   What factors contribute to the need for maintenance? (See section 6.2)

9   What is a computer system efficiency audit concerned with? (See section 7.2)

10   What should the post-implementation review establish? (See section 8.1)

## Answers to Activities

1   The method chosen depends on how imaginative you are.

You could simply cease production of the report and see if anyone asks for it when it fails to appear. (If they ask for it simply in order to add it to a file, you can draw your own conclusions.)

A study could be carried out to see what each recipient of the report does with it and assess its importance.

A report pricing structure could be implemented - this would be a strong incentive to functional management to cancel requests for unnecessary output.

2   A system's capabilities might be limited by the following restrictions.

   (a)   The size of the computer's memory.
   (b)   The power of the processor.
   (c)   The capacity of the computer's backing storage.
   (d)   The number of printers linked to the computer.
   (e)   The number of terminals.
   (f)   The software's capabilities.

## Further question practice

*Now try the following practice question at the end of this text.*

Exam style question   **4**

# Chapter 5 :

# SELECTING AND MANAGING INFORMATION TECHNOLOGY

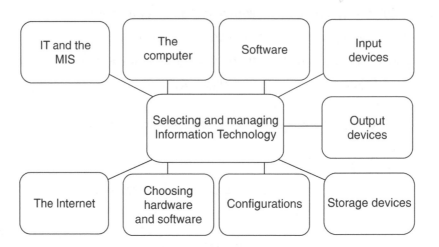

## Introduction

In this chapter we look at the features of Information Technology hardware and software in common use.

We start with a look at the computer. Computers were first used in business in the 1960s. Since the development of the integrated circuit (incorporating a number of circuits in a single chip) in the 1970s, their use has become widespread.

Compared with manual data processing, computers have the advantages of speed, accuracy, the ability to process large volumes of data and to perform complex operations.

Initially, their main commercial use was to process large volumes of transactions data, but over time they have been used increasingly to provide management information.

Later in the chapter we look at the Internet - potentially the most significant business and social development since the advent of the telephone. As with any new technology the Internet provides both opportunities and risks.

## Your objectives

After completing this chapter you should have an understanding of:

    (a)    The various types of Information Technology hardware and software.

    (b)    The need for back-up routines.

    (c)    The main issues relating to the Internet.

# 1 INFORMATION TECHNOLOGY AND THE MIS

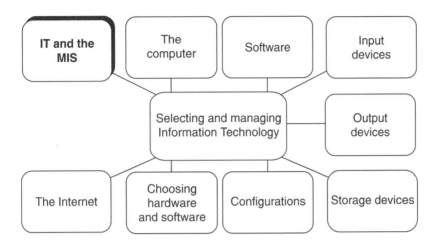

Most organisation's Management Information Systems use **information technology**.

**Definition**

**Information Technology** is a term used to describe the coming together of computer technology with data transmission technology, to revolutionise information systems. Computer hardware, based on microchip technology with ever-increasing power and capacity, has been harnessed to an extensive telecommunications network.

There are a number of reasons why **manual** information systems are **less beneficial** than **computerised** systems.

(a) Labour **productivity** is usually lower, particularly in routine and operational applications.

(b) Processing is **slower** where large volumes of data need to be dealt with.

(c) Besides taking up more time and requiring more staff, slower processing means that **information that could be provided**, such as statistical analyses of data or lists (of customers or products or whatever) categorised in a variety of ways, **will not be provided** at all, because there is not time.

(d) The **risk of errors** is greater, especially in repetitive work like payroll calculations.

(e) Information is generally **less accessible**. Unless there is a great deal of duplication of records access to information is restricted to one user at a time. Paper files can easily be mislaid or buried in in-trays, in which case the information they contain is not available at all. This can mean inconvenience and wasted time internally and may prevent the organisation from providing its services to customers.

(f) It is difficult to make **corrections or alterations**. If a document contains errors or needs updating it is often necessary to recreate the **whole** document from scratch, rather than just a new version with the relevant details changed. If several copies of a paper record are stored in different places each of them will need to be changed: this can easily be overlooked and so some parts of the system will be using out of date or inaccurate data. Unless changes are dated, it may not be clear which is the correct version.

(g) **Quality of output** is less consistent and not as high as well-designed computer output. At worst, handwritten records may be illegible and so completely useless. Badly presented information may fail to communicate because key points will not have their intended impact.

(h) Paper based systems are generally very **bulky** both to handle and to store, and office space is expensive.

# 2 THE COMPUTER

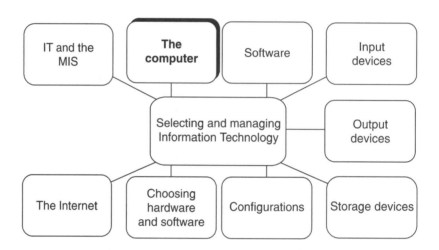

The definition of a 'computer' given in CIMA's *Computing Terminology* is as follows.

'A *device* which will accept input data, process it according to programmed logical and arithmetic rules, store and output data and/or calculate results. The ability to store programmed instructions and to take decisions which vary the way in which a program executes (although within the defined logic of the program) are the principal distinguishing features of a computer. ...'

A **computer** is a mixture of physical, **tangible** things like keyboards, mice, screens, circuits and cables (**hardware**), and **intangible** arithmetic and logic (**software**). Using electrical impulses, the two are connected and communicate with each other.

## 2.1 Types of computer

Computers can be classified as follows, although the differences between these categories are becoming increasingly vague.

- Supercomputers
- Mainframe computers
- Minicomputers
- Microcomputers, now commonly called PCs

A **supercomputer** is used to process **very large amounts of data very quickly**. They are particularly useful for occasions where high volumes of calculations need to be performed, for example in **meteorological or astronomical applications**.

A **mainframe** computer system is one that has at its heart a very powerful central computer, linked by cable or telecommunications to many (in some cases hundreds or thousands) terminals. A mainframe has **many times more processing power than a PC** and offers **extensive data storage** facilities.

Mainframes are used by organisations such as **banks** that have very large volumes of processing to perform and have special security needs. Many organisations have now replaced their old mainframes with **networked** 'client-server' systems of mid-range computers and PCs because this approach is thought to be cheaper and offer more flexibility.

Nevertheless, mainframes are considered to offer greater **reliability, functionality and data security** than networked systems. Proponents claim that for organisations with 200 or more users they are cheaper to run in the medium term than other alternatives.

A **minicomputer** is a computer whose size, speed and capabilities lie somewhere **between those of a mainframe and a PC**. The term was originally used before PCs were developed, to describe computers which were cheaper but less well-equipped than mainframe computers.

With the advent of PCs, and with mainframes now being physically smaller than in the past, **the definition of a minicomputer has become rather vague**. There is really no definition which distinguishes adequately between a PC and a minicomputer.

A key event in the development of the **PC** was the launch of the IBM PC in 1981. In the early years of the development of personal computers, the Apple Macintosh (technically not a PC) became the standard for graphics-based applications and IBM compatibles, or clones, were chosen for text-based (business) applications. However, as chips have become more powerful, the difference in emphasis has become far less important.

PCs are now the norm for **small to medium-sized business** computing and for home computing, and **most larger businesses** now use them for day-to-day needs such as word-processing. Often they are linked together in a **network** to enable sharing of information between users.

*PCs*

The original portable computers were heavy, weighing around five kilograms, and could only be run from the mains electricity supply. Subsequent developments allow true portability.

(a) The **laptop** or **notebook** is powered either from the electricity supply or using a rechargeable battery and can include all the features and functionality of desktop PCs. A typical **notebook** is now about the size of an A4 pad of paper.

(b) The **pocket computer** (or palmtop, or handheld) is increasingly compatible with true PCs. Devices range from basic models which are little more than electronic organisers to relatively powerful processors running 'cut-down' versions of Windows and Microsoft Office, and including communications features.

---

**Activity 1**                                                  **(10 minutes)**

Is a laptop or notebook computer cheaper or more expensive than an equivalent specification desktop PC? Why do you think this is?

---

*A typical PC specification*

Here is the specification for a **fairly powerful PC**, from an advertisement that appeared in Summer 2000. This PC cost around £800.

| PC SPECIFICATION | |
| --- | --- |
| Intel 650 MHz Pentium III Processor | 3.5" (1.44MB) Floppy Disk Drive |
| 10GB hard disk drive | 15" SVGA Monitor |
| 56 kpbs internal fax modem | 105 Key Windows Keyboard |
| 512K CPU Cache | Logitech 2 button mouse |
| 128MB RAM<br>High speed 64-bit data path to memory | Midi Tower Case 3 × 5.25"& 3 × 3.5"<br>drive bays, 2 serial ports, 1 parallel port |
| 32 Speed CD ROM | Windows 98 pre-loaded |

*The processor*

2.14    The processor is the '**brain**' of the computer. The processor may be defined as follows. The processor (sometimes referred to as the central processing unit or CPU) is divided into three areas:

- Arithmetic and logic unit
- Control unit
- Main store or memory

The processing unit may have all its elements - arithmetic and logic unit, control unit, and the input/output interface-on a single '**chip**'. A chip is a small piece of silicon upon which is etched an integrated circuit, which consists of transistors and their interconnecting patterns on an extremely small scale.

The chip is mounted on a carrier unit which in turn is 'plugged' on to a circuit board - called the **motherboard** - with other chips, each with their own functions.

The most common chips are those made by the Intel company. Each generation of Intel CPU chip has been **able to perform operations in fewer clock cycles** than the previous generation, and therefore works more quickly. The latest generation is Pentium III.

*MHz and clock speed*

The processor receives program instructions and sends signals to peripheral devices. The number of cycles produced per second is usually measured in **MegaHertz** (MHz). 1 MHz = one **million** cycles per **second**. A typical modern business PC might have a specification of 450 MHz, but models with higher clock speeds (eg 700 MHz) are now common.

*Memory*

The computer's memory is also known as main store or internal store The memory will hold the following.

- **Program instructions**
- The **input data** that will be processed next
- The **data** that is **ready for output** to an output device

*Bits and bytes*

Each individual storage element in the computer's memory consists of a simple circuit which can be switched **on** or **off**. These two states can be conveniently expressed by the numbers 1 and 0 respectively.

Each 1 or 0 is a **bit**. Bits are grouped together in groups of eight to form **bytes**. A byte may be used to represent a **character**, for example a letter, a number or another symbol.

Business PCs now make use of **32 bit** processors. Put simply, this means that data travels around from one place to another in groups of 16 or 32 bits, and so modern PCs operate considerably faster than the original 8 bit models.

The processing capacity of a computer is in part dictated by the capacity of its memory. Capacity is calculated in kilobytes (1 kilobyte $= 2^{10}$ (1,024) bytes) and megabytes (1 megabyte $= 2^{20}$ bytes) and gigabytes ($2^{30}$). These are abbreviated to Kb, Mb and Gb.

*RAM*

RAM (random access memory) is **memory that is directly available to the processing unit**. It holds the data and programs in current use. RAM in microcomputers is 'volatile' which means that the contents of the memory are erased when the computer's power is switched off.

The RAM on a typical business PC is likely to have a capacity of **32 to 128 megabytes**. The size of the RAM is **extremely** important. A computer with a 400 MHz clock speed but only 16 Mb of RAM will not be as efficient as a 200 MHz PC with 64 Mb of RAM.

*Cache*

The **cache** is a small capacity but **extremely fast** part of the memory which saves a second copy of the pieces of data most recently read from or written to main memory. When the cache is full, older entries are 'flushed out' to make room for new ones.

*ROM*

ROM (read-only memory) is **a memory chip into which fixed data is written permanently** at the time of its manufacture. New data cannot be written into the memory, and so the data on the memory chip is unchangeable and irremovable. ROM is 'non-volatile' memory, which means that its contents do not disappear when the computer's power source is switched off. A computer's start-up program, known as a 'bootstrap' program, is always held in a form of a ROM.

When you turn on a PC you will usually see a reference to **BIOS** (basic input/output system). This is part of the ROM chip containing all the programs needed to control the keyboard, screen, disk drives and so on.

Business Basics: Information Technology

# 3    SOFTWARE

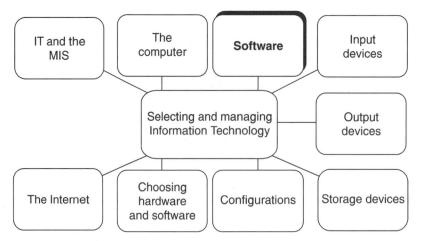

## 3.1    The operating system

The **operating system** provides the interface between the computer hardware and both the user and the other software.

Operating software can be defined as a program or suite of programs which provide the 'bridge' between **applications** software (such as word processing packages, spreadsheet or accounting packages) and the hardware.

An operating system will typically perform the following tasks.

(a)    Initial **set-up** of the computer, when it is switched on.

(b)    Checking that the **hardware** (including peripheral devices such as printers) is functioning properly.

(c)    Calling up of **program files and data files** from external storage into memory.

(d)    **Opening and closing** of files, checking of file labels etc.

(e)    Maintenance of **directories** in external storage.

(f)    Controlling **input and output devices**, including the interaction with the user.

(g)    Controlling system **security** (for example monitoring the use of passwords).

(h)    Handling of **interruptions** (for example program abnormalities or machine failure).

(i)    Managing **multitasking**.

**Multitasking** means doing more than one task at once, for example printing out a Word document while you work in Excel.

*UNIX*

The UNIX operating system was developed as a **non-proprietary** (ie not specific to one manufacturer) operating system that could be portable to different computer architectures. UNIX works equally well in a PC network environment as in a **mainframe** or **minicomputer** system, though it is more common in the latter.

*Windows*

Early incarnations of Windows, culminating in **Windows 3.1** and **Windows for Workgroups 3.11,** were not genuine operating systems in their own right, but were an operating environment for an older Microsoft system called **MS-DOS**. This meant that MS-DOS was always running underneath any applications and users were therefore still constrained by, for example, **eight-character file names** and various problems relating to the conventional memory of a PC.

In 1993, Microsoft launched **Windows NT**, a complete operating system in its own right, designed for **networks.** Today Windows NT provides strong competition for other network operating systems like Novell Netware. For PCs and smaller networks there is **Windows 95** and **Windows 98.**

*Windows 98*

Features of Windows 98 include the following.

| Feature | Comment |
|---|---|
| **Easy to use** | User interface enhancements include easier navigation, such as **single-click launching** of applications, icon highlighting, forward/backward buttons, and an easy to customise Start Menu. |
| | A 'desktop', from which everything in the system branches out. Disk drives, folders (directories), applications and files can all be placed on the desktop. |
| | A 'taskbar' which is always on top and which includes a **Start** button (featured in advertising around the time of the release) and buttons representing every open application. |
| | **Long file names** are supported (up to 256 characters). |
| **Faster** | **Application loading**, **system start-up**, and **shut down** time are **faster**. A technology called 'OnNow' simply 'suspends' the computer when it is not needed, avoiding the normal shut down and boot up procedures. |
| | **Multitasking** is more stable than previous versions. |
| | A **Tune-Up Wizard** helps the PC to maintain itself automatically and provide the best possible performance. File storage is more efficient, freeing up hard drive space. |
| **Web integration** | The Microsoft Web browser **Microsoft Internet Explorer** is included in Windows 98. There are a variety of features designed to enhance **Internet access** and use of Internet facilities and technologies, and integrate them with the users system. For instance it is possible to access a website directly from the 'Explorer' file management system. |
| **More entertaining** | Windows 98 has better **graphics** and **video capabilities**. It supports **Digital Versatile Disks** (DVD). |
| **More manageable for businesses** | Tools such as Dr. Watson and System Information Utility make it easier for IT support staff to **diagnose and correct problems**. |
| | There is a **Recycle Bin** for easy deletion and recovery of files. |
| | Easy integration with **networking** software |

Although it has bugs and irritations for the experienced user, Microsoft Windows provides a **comprehensive working environment,** enabling a wide range of programs written by many software companies to look and feel similar to other programs.

*Windows 2000*

At the time of publication, **Windows 2000** was not in common use. It is essentially an upgrade to Windows 98, and includes many of the existing features explained in this section.

There are four editions of Windows 2000.

(a)    **Windows 2000 Professional** – for business desktops and laptops.

(b)    **Windows 2000 Server** – a network operating systems.

(c)    **Windows 2000 Advanced Server** – an operating system for commerce and business critical operations.

(d)    **Windows 2000 Datacenter Server** – for large scale enterprises with business critical operations.

*Apple Macs*

There are some computer users, particularly those working in design and graphics, who prefer the **Apple Macintosh** system. For an organisation that already has many Apple Macs and many staff familiar with them the best option may be to continue to use them.

*Other operating systems*

Other competitors to Windows exist, such as **IBM's OS/2** but, since the majority of PC manufacturers send out their products with Windows pre-loaded, this is the system that is likely to predominate.

*Applications software*

Applications software consists of **programs which carry out a task for the user** as opposed to programs which control the workings of a computer.

*Application packages*

Application **packages** are ready-made programs written to perform **a particular job**. The job will be common to many potential users, so that the package could be adopted by all of them for their data processing operations. The package should be fully documented and the documentation should include specifications of input and output formats and file layouts, user instruction manuals, hardware requirements and details of how the package may be varied to suit the user's individual needs.

*General purpose packages*

A distinction can be made between application packages and more general purpose packages.

(a)    As we have seen, an **application package** is a program or set of programs that will carry out a **specific** processing application - for example, a **payroll** package would be specific to payroll processing.

(b)    A **general purpose** package is an off-the-shelf program that can be used **for processing of a general type:** the computer user can apply the package to a variety of uses of his own choice. **Spreadsheet** packages and **desktop publishing** packages are examples of general purpose packages.

*Integrated software*

Integrated software refers to programs, or packages of programs, that perform a **variety of different processing operations**, using **data which is compatible** with whatever operation is being carried out.

**Accounts packages** often consist of program '**modules**' that can be integrated into a larger accounting system. There will be a module for each of the sales ledger system, the purchase ledger system, the nominal ledger, and so on. Output from one 'module' in an integrated system can be used as input to another, without the need for re-entry of data.

**'Office'** software allows the user to carry out a *variety* of processing operations, such as word processing, using spreadsheets and creating and using a database. The best known example is Microsoft Office, which includes word processing (Word), spreadsheet (Excel), database (Access) and a presentation package (PowerPoint).

## 4    INPUT DEVICES

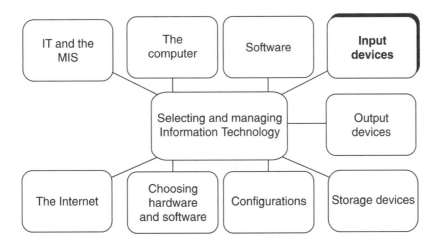

Input is a labour-intensive process, typically involving the keying in of data using a keyboard. The process of inputting data can also be achieved through a variety of **data capture** techniques.

### 4.1    The keyboard

Computer keyboards are derived from the basic 'QWERTY' typewriter keyboard.

### 4.2    The VDU

A VDU (visual display unit) or **'monitor'** displays text and graphics. The screen's **resolution** is the number of pixels that are lit up. More and smaller pixels enable detailed high-resolution display. Super VGA, or **SVGA**, is the standard for newer monitors and offers resolutions up to $1,280 \times 1,024$.

**Touch-sensitive** screens have been developed but they are expensive and not widely used.

### 4.3    Mouse

A **mouse** is generally used in conjunction with a keyboard. A mouse is a handheld device with a rubber or metal ball protruding from a small hole in its base used to instruct the cursor on screen.

*The material in the next section has already been covered (in the context of efficient data collection) in Chapter 1. We repeat the material here to refresh your memory.*

### 4.4 Document reading methods

**Document reading methods** save time and money and also **reduce errors.** Some common document reading methods are described below.

*Magnetic ink character recognition*

**MICR** is the recognition by a machine of special formatted characters printed in magnetic ink (such as those as on a cheque). The characters are read using a specialised reading device. The main advantage of MICR is its accuracy, but MICR documents are expensive to produce, and so MICR has only limited application in practice.

*Optical mark reading*

**Optical mark reading** involves the marking of a pre-printed form with a ballpoint pen or typed line or cross in an appropriate box. The card is then read by an OMR device which senses the mark in each box using an electric current and translates it into machine code. Applications in which OMR is used include **National Lottery** entry forms, and answer sheets for multiple choice questions.

*Scanners and OCR*

A scanner is device that can **read text or illustrations printed on paper** and translate the information into a **form the computer can use**. A scanner works by digitising an image, the resulting matrix of bits is called a **bit map.**

To edit text read by an optical scanner, you need **optical character recognition (OCR)** software to translate the image into ASCII characters. Most optical scanners sold today come with OCR packages.

### 4.5 Bar coding and EPOS

**Bar codes** are groups of marks which, by their spacing and thickness, indicate specific codes or values. Look at the back cover of this book for an example of a bar code.

Large retail stores are introducing **Electronic Point of Sale (EPOS)** devices, which include bar code readers. This enables the provision of immediate sales and stock level information.

### 4.6 Magnetic stripe cards

The **standard magnetic stripe card** contains machine-sensible data on a **thin strip of magnetic recording tape** stuck to the back of the card. The magnetic card reader converts this information into directly computer-sensible form. The widest application of magnetic stripe cards is as **bank credit or service cards.**

### 4.7 EFTPOS

Many retailers have now introduced **EFTPOS systems (Electronic Funds Transfer at the Point of Sale)**. These are systems for the electronic transfer of funds at the point of sale. Customers in shops and at petrol stations can use a plastic card (usually a credit card or debit card) to purchase goods or services, and using an EFTPOS terminal in the shop, the customer's credit card account or bank current account will be debited automatically. EFTPOS systems **combine point of sale systems with electronic funds transfer.**

### 4.8 Smart cards

A **smart card** is **a plastic card in which is embedded a microprocessor chip**. A smart card would typically contain a **memory** and a **processing capability**. The information held on smart cards can therefore be updated (eg using a PC and a special device).

### 4.9 Voice recognition

Computer software has been developed that can **convert speech into computer sensible form**: the input device needed in this case is a microphone. Users are required to speak clearly and reasonably slowly.

## 5 OUTPUT DEVICES

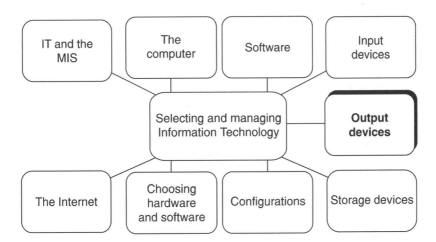

The commonest methods of computer output are printers and screen display. Other methods include output onto **microfilm** or microfiche and onto transparencies for **overhead projection**. Many computers also produce sound output through **speakers**.

### 5.1 The choice of output medium

Choosing a suitable output medium depends on a number of factors.

| Factor | Comment |
|---|---|
| **Hard copy** | Is a printed version of the output needed? If so, what quality must the output be? |
| **Volume** | The **volume** of information produced may affect the choice. For example, a VDU screen can hold a certain amount of data, but it becomes more difficult to read when information goes 'off-screen' and can only be read a 'page' at a time. |
| **Speed** | The **speed** at which output is required may critical. For example, to print a large volume of data, if a single enquiry is required it may be quicker to make notes from a VDU display. |

NOTES

| Factor | Comment |
|---|---|
| **Suitability for further use** | The **suitability** of the output medium to the purpose for which the output is needed. Output on to a magnetic disk or tape would be appropriate if the data is for further processing. Large volumes of reference data for human users to hold in a library might be held on microfilm or microfiche, and so output in these forms would be appropriate. |
| **Cost** | The 'best' output device may not be justifiable on the grounds of cost - another output medium should be chosen. |

## 5.2   Printers

A **line printer** prints a complete line in a single operation. They offer the operational speeds necessary for **bulk printing requirements**.

**Character printers** print a single character at a time. An examples is a dot matrix printers. Dot matrix printers are still reasonably widely used in accounting departments. Their main drawback is their **low-resolution.** They are also relatively **slow** and **noisy**.

**Bubblejet** and **inkjet** printers are small and reasonably cheap (under £100), making them popular where a 'private' output device is required. They work by sending a jet of ink on to the paper to produce the required characters. They are fairly **quiet and fast**, but they may produce **smudged** output if the paper is not handled carefully.

**Laser printers** print a whole page at a time, rather than line by line. Unlike daisywheel and dot matrix printers, they print on to individual **sheets of paper** (in the same way as photocopiers do) and so they do not use 'tractor fed' continuous computer stationery.

The resolution of printed characters and diagrams with laser printers is **very high** making laser printing output good enough to be used for commercial printing.

Laser printers are **more expensive** than other types - a good one will cost about £500 - but it is quite possible that several users will be able to **share** a single laser printer.

## 5.3   The VDU

Screens were described earlier, as they are used together with computer keyboards for **input**. It should also be clear that they can be used as an **output** medium, primarily where the volume of output is low, for example a single enquiry. The input/output process using a VDU is best described by looking at the features of **Graphical User Interfaces** (GUIs).

GUIs were designed to make computers more 'user-friendly'. A GUI involves the use of **W**indows, **I**cons, **M**ouse and **P**ull-down menus or 'WIMP'.

A GUI allows the screen to be divided into sections or windows. This enables two or more documents to be viewed and edited together, and sections of one to be inserted into another.

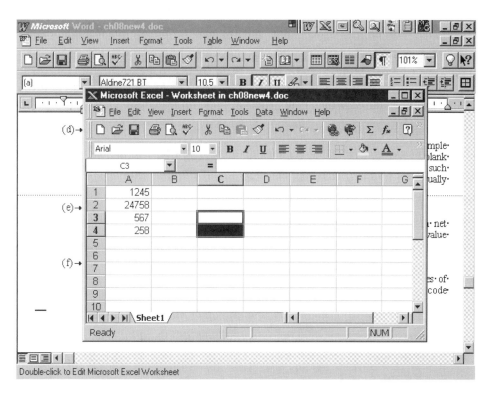

An **icon** is an image of an object used to represent an abstract idea or process. In software design, icons may be used instead of numbers, letters or words to identify and describe the various functions available for selection, or files to access. A common icon is a waste paper bin to indicate the deletion of a document.

Both icons and menus are shown in the following illustration.

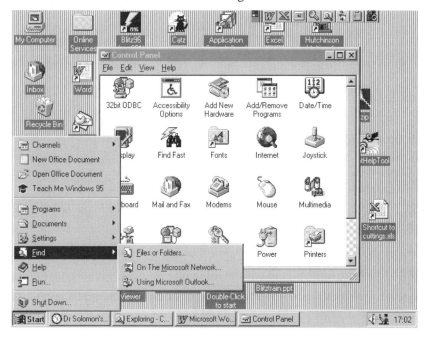

*Pull-down menu*

An initial **menu** (or 'menu-bar') will be shown across the top of the screen. Using the mouse to move the pointer to the required item in the menu, the pointer '**pulls down**' a subsidiary menu. The pointer and mouse can then be used to select (input) the required item (output) on the pulled-down menu.

*Form filling*

The main part of the screen area will be the 'page' on which you will be entering data. In a standard word processing system, there is a 'blank page' available for document creation and manipulation, accounting packages contain **pre-formatted structures** into which data can be inserted. Formatting includes several features.

- Different colours for different screen areas
- Reverse video (where colours in a selected area are the reverse of the rest of it)
- Flashing items
- Larger characters for titles
- Paging or scrolling depending on the volume of information

# 6 STORAGE DEVICES

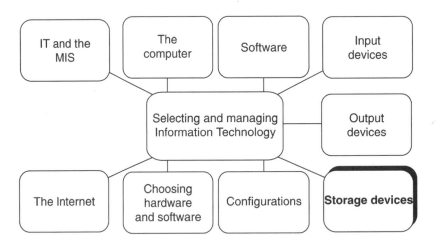

## 6.1 Hard disks

Disks offer **direct access** to data, a feature that is essential for **real-time** systems, **interactive** processing, and **database** systems. A modern business PC invariably has an **internal hard disk**. At the time of writing the average new **PC** has a hard disk size of around 5 **Gigabytes**, but 15 Gb disks are not uncommon. In larger computer systems **removable disk packs** are commonly used.

A **Zip Drive** is a **removable** hard disk for PCs, suitable for back-up, mass storage or for moving files between computers.

## 6.2 Floppy disks

The floppy disk provides a **cost-effective** means of on-line storage for **small** amounts of information. A 3$^{1}/_{2}$" disk can hold up to **1.44 Mb** of data.

## 6.3 Tape storage

Like an audio or video cassette, data has to be recorded **along the length** of a computer tape and so it is **more difficult to access** than data on disk. **Reading and writing are separate operations**, using separate heads, and so two drives are necessary for the two operations.

Tape cartridges have a **much larger capacity** than floppy disks and they are still widely used as a **backing storage** medium. Fast tapes which can be used to create a back-up file very quickly are known as **tape streamers**.

Tapes can only be **updated** by producing a completely new carried forward tape, and this provides an automatic means of **data security**. The brought forward tapes can be kept for two or three 'generations' to safeguard against the loss of data on a current file.

This **'grandfather-father-son' technique** allows for files to be reconstructed if a disaster should occur. Once the stipulated number of generations has passed, the former 'grandfather' tape can be purged and used again for other processing.

### Grandfather, Father, Son back-up rotation scheme

| Tape No. | Tape name | When written to | Overwritten |
|----------|-----------|-----------------|-------------|
| Tape 1 | Son 1 | Every Monday | **Weekly** |
| Tape 2 | Son 2 | Every Tuesday | Weekly |
| Tape 3 | Son 3 | Every Wednesday | Weekly |
| Tape 4 | Son 4 | Every Thursday | Weekly |
| Tape 5 | Father week 1 | First Friday | **Monthly** |
| Tape 6 | Father week 2 | Second Friday | Monthly |
| Tape 7 | Father week 3 | Third Friday | Monthly |
| Tape 8 | Father week 4 | Fourth Friday | Monthly |
| Tape 9 | Father week 5 (if needed) | Fifth Friday | Monthly |
| Tape 10 | Grandfather month 1 | Last business day month 1 | **Quarterly** |
| Tape 11 | Grandfather month 2 | Last business day month 2 | Quarterly |
| Tape 12 | Grandfather month 3 | Last business day month 3 | Quarterly |

## 6.4 CD-ROM

Optical disks, which use similar technology to the laser-based compact disc audio system, are being used increasingly for data storage. Optical disks have **very high capacity** compared with other media and they are **more difficult to damage**. A CD-ROM can store 650 megabytes of data.

The **speed** of a CD-ROM drive is relevant to how fast data can be retrieved: an **eight speed** drive is quicker than a **four speed** drive.

CD recorders are now available for general business use with blank CDs (CD-R) and **rewritable disks** (CD-RW) are now available.

## 6.5 DVD

The CD format has started to be superseded by DVD. DVD development was encouraged by the advent of multimedia files with video graphics and sound - requiring greater disk capacity.

**Digital Versatile Disk (DVD)** technology can store almost 5 gigabytes of data on one disk. Access speeds are improved as is sound and video quality. Many commentators believe DVD will not only replace CD-ROMs, but also VHS cassettes, audio CDs and laser discs.

---

**Activity 2**                          **(20 minutes)**

For magnetic disk, magnetic tape and CD-ROM outline at least two features of each and describe an application of each.

---

# 7 CONFIGURATIONS

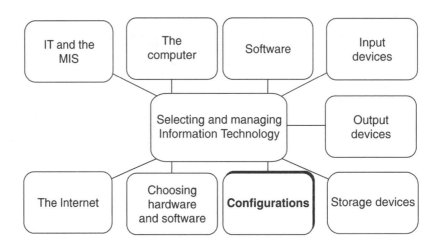

A computer **configuration** might consist of a stand-alone computer and peripheral equipment, a central computer and several terminals, or networks of computers with shared files. Mainframes can be linked to each other, but more common types of computer-to-computer links are PC to mainframe or mini, or PCs linked to one another.

---

**Activity 2**                          **(15 minutes)**

When would you expect a **stand-alone** computer to be used?

---

## 7.1 Multi-user systems

With a multi-user system one central computer is linked to **dumb terminals.** Dumb terminals are essentially a VDU and keyboard. A dumb terminal relies on the central computer for data processing power.

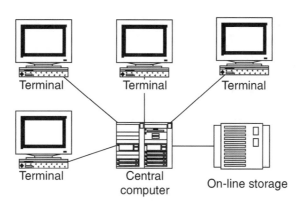

The terminals in a multi-user system might be sited in the **same room** or building as the central computer, or may be **geographically distant** from the central computer, connected by an external data link.

**Definition**

> **Remote access** describes access to a central computer installation from a terminal which is physically 'distant'.

**Benefits** of multi-user systems are:

(a) More departments or sections can have **access** to the computer, its data files and its programs. This improves the data processing capabilities of 'local' offices.

(b) By giving departments more computing power and access to centralised information files, multi-user systems also make it easier for an organisation to **decentralise authority** from head office to local managers.

(c) The **speed of processing,** for both local offices and head office, is very fast.

(d) Local offices **retain their input documents,** and do not have to send them to a remote computer centre for processing.

**7.2 Distributed processing**

Distributed processing links several computers together. A typical system might consist of a mainframe computer with PCs as **intelligent terminals,** with a range of peripheral equipment and with files either held centrally or at dispersed sites.

**Definition**

> A **distributed system** is a combines processing hardware located at a central place (eg a mainframe), with other, usually smaller, computers located at various sites within the organisation. The central and dispersed computers are linked by a communications network. (CIMA, *Computing Terminology*)

Key features of distributed processing.

(a) Computers distributed or spread over a **wide geographical area**.

(b) A computer can **access** the information files of **other computers**.

NOTES

(c)   The ability for computers within the system to **process data 'jointly'** or **'interactively'**.

(d)   **Processing** is **either** carried out centrally, or at dispersed locations.

(e)   **Files** are held **either** centrally or at local sites.

(f)   **Authority is decentralised** as processing can be performed autonomously by local computers.

(g)   **End-users** of computing facilities are given responsibility for, and control over, their own data.

One form of distributed data processing system is illustrated below.

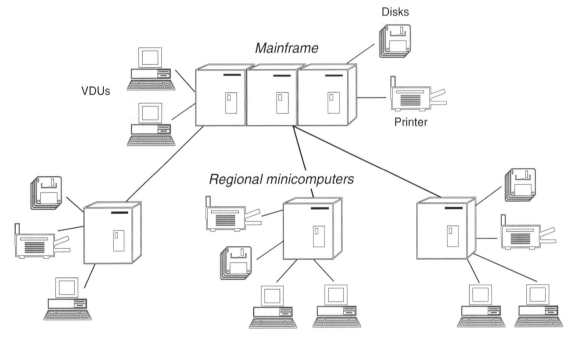

**Advantages** of distributed processing.

(a)   There is **greater flexibility** in system design. The system can cater for both the specific needs of each local user of an individual computer and also for the needs of the organisation as a whole, by providing communications between different local computers in the system.

(b)   Since data files can be held locally, **data transmission is restricted** because each computer maintains its own data files which provide most of the data it will need. This reduces the costs and security risks in data transmission.

(c)   **Speed of processing** for both local branches and also for the central (head office) branch.

(d)   There is a possibility of a **distributed database**. Data is held in a number of locations, but any user can access all of it for a global view.

(e)   The effect of **breakdowns** is **minimised**, because a fault in one computer will not affect other computers in the system. With a centralised processing system, a fault in the mainframe computer would put the entire system out of service.

(f)   The fact that it is possible to acquire powerful PCs at a 'cheap' price enables an organisation to dedicate them to particular applications. This in turn means that the computer system can be more readily **tailored** to the organisation's systems, rather than forcing the organisation to change its systems to satisfy the requirements for a mainframe computer.

(g)    Decentralisation allows for **better localised control** over the physical and procedural aspects of the system.

(h)    Decentralised processing may facilitate **greater user involvement** and increase familiarity with the use of computer technology. The end user must accept responsibility for the accuracy of locally-held files and local data processing.

**Disadvantages** of distributed processing.

(a)    There may be a **duplication of data** on the files of different computers incurring unnecessary storage costs.

(b)    A distributed network can be more **difficult to administer** and to **maintain**

(c)    The items of equipment used in the system must be **compatible** with each other.

## 7.3   Networks

**Definition**

> A **network** is an interconnected collection of **autonomous** processors. (Strictly, in a 'distributed' system, the user should be unaware that the system has more than one processor.)

The key idea of a network is that users need **equal access to resources** such as data, but they do not necessarily have to have equal computing power. There are two main types of network, a **local area network** (LAN) and a **wide area network** (WAN).

*Local area networks (LANs)*

A local area network (LAN) is a network of computers located in a single building or on a **single site**. The parts of the network are linked by **computer cable** rather than via telecommunications lines. This means that a LAN does not need modems.

Network topology means the physical arrangement of **nodes** in a network. A node is any device connected to a network: it can be a computer, or a peripheral device such as a printer.

There are several types of LAN system configuration. For example, in a **bus structure** (shown below), messages are sent out from one point along a single communication channel, and the messages are received by other connected machines.

Each device can **communicate with every other device** and communication is quick and reliable. Nodes can be **added or unplugged** very easily. Locating cable faults is also relatively simple.

*Bus system*

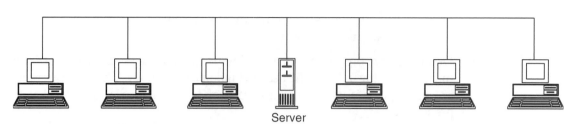

Server

Local area networks have been **successful** for a number of reasons. First of all, personal computers of sufficient **power** and related software (for example Unix) were developed, so that network applications became possible. Networks have been made available to computer users at a fairly **low price**.

*Wide area networks (WANs)*

**Wide area networks** (WANs) are networks on a number of sites, perhaps on a wide geographical scale. WANs often use minicomputers or mainframes as the 'pumps' that keep the data messages circulating, whereas shorter-distance LANs normally use PCs for this task.

A wide area network is similar to a local area network in concept, but the key differences are.

(a) The **geographical area** covered by the network is greater, not being limited to a single building or site.

(b) WANs will send data over **telecommunications links,** and so will need modems. LANs, in contrast, will use direct cables only for transmitting data.

(c) WANs will often use a **larger computer** as a file server.

(d) WANs will often be larger than LANs, with **more terminals or computers** linked to the network.

(e) A WAN can link two or more LANs, using **gateways**.

    (i) Connections may be **leased**. This is the preferred option where there is a high volume of inter-office communication.

    (ii) Connections may be made over the **public telephone network**. Standard call charges will apply, so this is beneficial where communication levels are relatively low.

### 7.4 Client-server computing

The term client-server computing is widely used. This is a way of **describing the relationship between the devices in a network**. With client-server computing, the tasks that need to be carried out are distributed among the various machines on the network.

**Definition**

> A **client** is a machine which **requests a service** from the server.
>
> A **server** is a machine which is dedicated to providing a particular function or service requested by a client. Servers include file servers (see below), print servers, e-mail servers and fax servers.

A client-server system allows **computer power** to be distributed to where it is most needed. The **client**, or user, will use a powerful personal workstation with local processing capability. The **server** provides services such as shared printers, communications links, special-purpose processing and database storage.

This approach has a number of benefits.

(a)    It reduces network **communications** costs.

(b)    It allows the central computer to be used for **administrative** tasks such as network management.

(c)    The technological flexibility of this type of system allows the use of **sophisticated applications** such as multimedia and DIP.

A server computer (or file server) may be a powerful PC or a minicomputer. As its name implies, it **serves** the rest of the network offering a generally-accessible hard disk file for all the other processors in the system and sometimes offering other resources, such as a **shared printer** for the network.

Clients on a network generally have their **own hard disk** storage capability. **Programs** or data (eg a database) for **common use** can be stored on the file server. Accounting packages written for small businesses are usually available in a multi-user version for this purpose.

The advantages of client-server computing include those shown below.

| Advantage | Comment |
|---|---|
| **Greater resilience** | Processing is spread over several computers. If one server breaks down, other locations can carry on processing. |
| **Scalability** | They are highly scalable. Instead of having to buy computing power in large quantities you can buy just the amount of power you need to do the job. |
| **Shared programs and data** | Program and data files held on a file server can be shared by all the PCs in the network. With stand-alone PCs, each computer would have its own data files, and there might be unnecessary duplication of data.<br><br>A system where everyone uses the same data will help to improve data processing and decision making. |
| **Shared work-loads** | Each PC in a network can do the same work.<br><br>If there were separate stand-alone PCs, A might do job 1, B might do job 2, C might do job 3 and so on. In a network, any PC, (A, B or C) could do any job (1, 2 or 3). This provides flexibility in sharing work-loads. |
| **Shared peripherals** | Peripheral equipment can be shared. For example, in a LAN, five PCs might share a single on-line printer, whereas if there were stand-alone PCs, each might be given its own separate printer. |
| **Communication and time management** | LANs can be linked up to the office communications network, thus adding to the processing capabilities in an office. Electronic mail can be used to send messages, memos and electronic letters from node to node. Electronic calendar and diary facilities can also be used. |

| Advantage | Comment |
|---|---|
| **Compatibility** | Client/server systems are more likely than centralised systems to have Windows interfaces, making it easier to move information between applications such as spreadsheets and accounting systems. |
| **Ad hoc enquiries** | They enable information to be moved to a separate server, allowing managers to make ad hoc enquiries without disrupting the main system. |

The **disadvantages** of client/server computing.

    (a)    **Mainframes** are better at dealing with **very large volumes** of transactions.

    (b)    It is easier to **control** and **maintain** a system centrally. In particular it is easier to keep data **secure**.

## 8    CHOOSING HARDWARE AND SOFTWARE

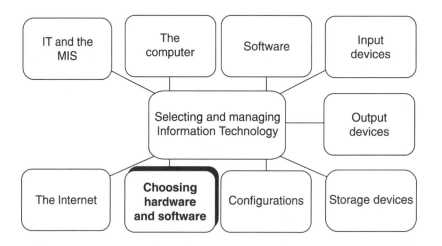

### 8.1   Hardware

In general terms, the choice of computer hardware will depend on the following factors.

| Factor | Comment |
|---|---|
| **User requirements** | The ease with which the computer configuration fits in with the user's requirements (eg direct access facilities, hard-copy output in given quantities). |
| **Power** | The power of the computer must be sufficient for current and foreseeable requirements. This is measured by:<br><br>• Processor type (Pentium, Pentium II etc)<br>• RAM in Mb<br>• Clock speed in MHz<br>• Hard disk size in Mb or Gb |
| **Reliability** | There should be a low expected 'break-down' rate. There should be back-up facilities, and in the case of a microcomputer, this might mean being able to resort temporarily back to a manual system when the computer is down. |

| Factor | Comment |
|---|---|
| **Simplicity** | Systems should be as simple as possible, whilst still capable of performing the tasks required. |
| **Ease of communication** | The system (hardware and software) should be able to communicate well with the user. Software is referred to as 'user-friendly' or 'user-unfriendly' but similar considerations apply to hardware (eg not all terminals are of standard screen size; the number and accessibility of terminals might also have a bearing on how well the user is able to put data into the computer or extract information). |
| **Flexibility** | The hardware should be able to meet new requirements as they emerge. More powerful CPUs tend to be more flexible. |
| **Security** | Keeping out 'hackers' and other unauthorised users is easier with more powerful systems, although security can be a major problem for any computer system. |
| **Cost** | The cost must be justified in terms of the benefits the hardware will provide. |
| **Changeover** | Whether the choice of hardware will help with a smooth changeover from the old to the new system. |
| **Networking** | Networking capacity, if a PC has been purchased. |
| **Software** | The hardware must be capable of running whatever software has been chosen. |

## 8.2 Software

The following table shows the factors that should be considered when choosing a software package.

| Factor | Comment |
|---|---|
| **User requirements** | The package should fit the user's particular requirements. Matters to consider include report production, anticipated volume of data, data validation routines, data security and recovery and ease of use. |
| | If using the package would mean substantial changes to the way in which the organisation operates, serious consideration must be given as to whether the changes are practical. The package should ideally be suited to the user and the user might rightly object to having to adjust his organisation to the dictates of the software. |
| **Processing times** | Are the processing times fast enough? If response times to enquiries, for example, are fairly slow, the user might consider the package unacceptable. |
| **Documentation and on-line help** | Is there full and clear documentation for the user and an on-line help facility? User manuals can be full of jargon and hard for a non-technical person to understand - they shouldn't be. |

| Factor | Comment |
|---|---|
| **User-friendliness** | Is the package easy to use? Is the software user friendly with menus and clear on-screen prompts for the keyboard operator? A user-friendly package will provide prompts and will be menu-driven, giving the operator a clear choice of what to do next. Some packages also provide 'wizards' to simplify common tasks. |
| **Controls** | What controls are included in the package (eg passwords, data validation checks, spell checks, standard accounting controls and reconciliations, an audit trail facility etc)? |
| **Maintenance / up-to-dateness** | How will the package be maintained and kept up-to-date? (eg what if a fault is discovered in the program by the software manufacturer? In an accounting package, what if the rate of VAT alters? etc). |
| **Modification** | Can the package be modified by the user - eg allowing the user to insert amendments to the format of reports or screen displays etc? Or will the software supplier agree to write a few tailor-made amendments to the software? |
| **Other users** | How many other users have bought the package, and how long has it been on the market? New packages might offer enhanced facilities, whereas well-established packages are likely to have already had any major 'bugs' corrected. |
| **Compatibility** | Will the package run on the user's computer - eg does the package need more RAM and processing power than is available? |
| | Will additional peripheral equipment have to be bought - eg, can dot-matrix and laser printers be used? |
| | Is the software able to use file formats, field lengths and so on used by other existing systems that will remain in use? |
| **Support** | What support service will the software supplier provide in the event that the user has difficulty with the package? |
| **Cost** | Off-the-shelf packages are fairly cheap on the whole, and a company should really buy what it needs for efficient operations rather than the least-cost package available. |
| | The savings in purchase price would not be worth the trouble and expense caused by trying to use a package for a business application it is not suited to. |
| | The package must not cost so much that the costs are greater than the benefits of using it. |

### 8.3 Bespoke or off-the-shelf?

A key question regarding software is whether to develop a system specially or buy what is already available.

NOTES

## Definitions

> A **bespoke package** is one designed and written for a specific situation or task. The package may be written 'in-house' or by an external software house.
>
> An **off-the shelf package** is one like Microsoft Word or Sage Line 50, that is sold to a wide range of users and intended to handle the most common user requirements.

*Bespoke software*

**Advantages** of having software specially written include the following.

(a)   The company **owns** the software and may be able to **sell it** to other potential users.

(b)   Alternatively, the company may be able to do things with its software that **competitors** cannot do with theirs. In other words it is a source of competitive advantage.

(c)   The software will be able to **do everything** that the company requires it to do, both now and (with further enhancements in the face of changing business needs) in the future.

However, only **large organisations** are likely to have sufficiently complex processing requirements to justify employing full time computer programmers. Key **disadvantages** are as follows.

(a)   The software may **not work** at all.

(b)   There may be a **long delay** before the software is ready.

(c)   The **cost** is considerable, compared with a ready-made package (the latter can be sold to lots of different users, not just one).

*Off-the shelf packages*

The **advantages** of using an off-the-shelf package as opposed to designing a system from scratch are as follows.

(a)   It is **available now** and ready for use.

(b)   It is almost certainly **cheaper** than a specially commissioned product because it is mass-produced.

(c)   It should have been written by software specialists and so should be of a **high quality**.

(d)   A successful package will be **continually updated** by the software manufacturer, and so the version that a customer buys should be up-to-date.

(e)   **Other users** will have used the package already, and a well established package should be **error-free** and well-suited to the general needs of users.

(f)   Good packages are **well-documented**, with easy to follow user manuals. Good documentation is a key feature of successful software development.

(g)   Some standard packages can be **customised** to the user's specific needs (but see below).

The **disadvantages** of ready-made packages are as follows.

(a)     The computer user gets a **standardised solution** to a data processing task. A standard solution may not be well suited to the individual user's particular needs.

(b)     The user is **dependent on the supplier** for maintenance of the package - ie updating the package, providing assistance in the event of problems for the user or even program errors cropping up. This is especially true if the general package is tailored in any way.

(c)     Competitors may well use the same package and so there is **no competitive edge** from having a system that can do something that other systems don't allow competitors to do.

### 8.4     Customised versions of standard packages

Standard packages can be **customised** so that they fit an organisation's specific requirements. This can either be done by **purchasing the source code** of the package and making modifications in-house or by paying the maker of the package to customise it.

**Advantages** of customisation are similar to those of producing a bespoke system, with the additional advantages that:

(a)     Development time should be much **quicker,** given that most of the system will be written already.

(b)     If the work is done in-house the organisation gains considerable **knowledge of how the software works** and may be able to 'tune' it so that it works more efficiently with the company's hardware.

**Disadvantages** of customising a standard package include the following.

(a)     It may prove more **costly** than expected, because **new** versions of the standard package will **also** have to be customised. For instance upgrades to Sage Sterling, the most popular off-the-shelf package for small and medium sized businesses in the UK, are released at least twice a year. Each new version would have to be customised, too.

(b)     Customisation may **delay delivery** of the software.

(c)     Customisation may introduce **bugs** that do not exist in the standard version.

(d)     If done **in-house,** the in-house team may have to **learn new skills.**

(e)     If done by the **original manufacturer** disadvantages such as those for off-the-shelf packages may arise.

### 8.5     Add-ons and programming tools

Two other ways of trying to give a computer user more flexibility with packages are:

(a)     The sale of '**add-ons**' to a basic package, which the user can buy if they suit his particular needs.

(b)     The provision of **programming tools**, such as fourth generation languages, with a package, which allows a computer user to write his own amendments to the package software (without having to be a programming expert).

## 9 THE INTERNET

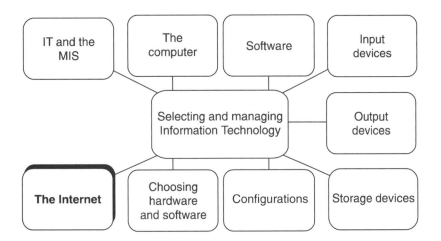

### 9.1 What is the Internet?

**Definition**

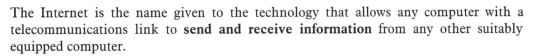

> The **Internet** is a global network connecting millions of computers.

The Internet is the name given to the technology that allows any computer with a telecommunications link to **send and receive information** from any other suitably equipped computer.

The **World Wide Web** is the multimedia element which provides facilities such as full-colour, graphics, sound and video. Web-sites are points within the network created by members who wish to provide an information point for searchers to visit and benefit by the provision of information and/or by entering into a transaction.

Most companies now have a **Website** on the Internet. A site is a collection of screens providing **information in text and graphic form,** any of which can be viewed simply by clicking the appropriate button, word or image on the screen.

Connection is made via an **Internet Service Provider (ISP)**. The number of ISPs has gown rapidly in the last few months. Many now offer free access to the Internet, meaning users pay only the local telephone charges incurred during connection. Free ISPs include Virgin Net and Freeserve. Other ISPs such as **AOL** charge a subscription and fee.

ISPs provide their own services, in addition to Internet access and e-mail capability. For instance, AOL offers a main menu with options such as Life, Travel, Entertainment, Sport, Kids. It is rather like a quality Sunday newspaper, except that the sections are updated at least daily, and it provides **much larger information resources**.

The Internet is viewed through interface programs called **browsers**. The most widely used are Microsoft Internet Explorer and Netscape Navigator. Searching the Internet is done using a **search engine** such as Yahoo!, Excite or AltaVista. The user simply types in a word or phrase to find a list of related websites.

A website address will typically be given in the format of a **U**niversal **R**esource **L**ocator (**URL**), eg '**http://www.bbc.co.uk**'.

NOTES

| URL element | Explanation |
|---|---|
| **http://** | **Hypertext Transfer Protocol**, the protocol used on the World Wide Web for the exchange of documents produced in what is known as 'hypertext mark-up language' (HTML). A common alternative to http is ftp (file transfer protocol) explained briefly later. The two forward slashes after the colon introduce a 'host name' such as www. |
| **www** | This stands for **World Wide Web.** As noted before, to put it simply the web (via its use of HTML), is what makes the Internet user-friendly |
| **bbc** | This is the **domain name** of the organisation or individual whose site is located at this URL |
| **co** | This indicates the type of organisation concerned. The Internet spans many different physical networks around the world including commercial (**com** or **co**), university (**ac** or **edu**) and other research networks (**org, net**), military (**mil**) networks, and government (**gov**) networks. |
| **uk** | Obviously, this indicates that the organisation is located in the UK |

### 9.2 Current uses of the Internet

The scope and potential of the Internet are still developing. Its uses already embrace the following:

(a) **Dissemination** of information.

(b) **Product/service development** - through almost instantaneous test marketing.

(c) **Transaction processing** - both business-to-business and business-to-consumer.

(d) **Relationship enhancement** - between various groups of stakeholders, but principally (for our purposes) between consumers and product/service suppliers.

(e) **Recruitment** and job search - involving organisations worldwide.

(f) **Entertainment** - including music, humour, art, games and some less wholesome pursuits!

The Internet provides opportunities to organise for and to automate tasks which would previously have required more costly interaction with the organisation. These have often been called low-touch or zero-touch approaches.

Tasks which a website may automate include:

(a) **Frequently-Asked Questions (FAQs)**: carefully-structured sets of answers can deal with many customer interactions.

(b) **Status checking**: major service enquiries (Where is my order? When will the engineer arrive? What is my bank balance?) can also be automated, replacing high-cost human service processes, and also providing the opportunity to proactively offer better service and new services.

(c) **Keyword search**: the ability to search provides web users with opportunities to find information in large and complex websites.

(d) Wizards (interview style interface) and intelligent algorithms: these can help diagnosis, which is one of the major elements of service support.

(e)     **E-mail and systems to route and track inbound e-mail**: the ability to route and/or to provide automatic responses will enable organisations to deal with high volumes of e-mail from actual and potential customers.

(f)     **Bulletin boards**: these enable customers to interact with each other, thus facilitating self-activated customer service and also the opportunity for product/service referral. Cisco in particular has created communities of Cisco users who help each other - thus reducing the service costs for Cisco itself.

(g)     **Call-back buttons**: these enable customers to speak to someone in order to deal with and resolve a problem; the more sophisticated systems allow the call-centre operator to know which web pages the users were consulting at the time.

## 9.3     Problems with the Internet

To a large extent the Internet has grown organically **without any formal organisation**. There are specific communication rules, but it is not **owned** by any one body and there are no clear guidelines on how it should develop.

Inevitably, also, the **quality** of much of the information on the Internet leaves much to be desired.

Speed is a major issue. Data only downloads onto the user's PC at the speed of the slowest telecommunications link - downloading data can be a painfully **slow** procedure. However, future developments will mean that speeds will improve: most crucially, telecoms links that can carry voice, video TV and the Internet need to become the norm rather than the exception.

## 9.4     Internet security issues

Establishing organisational links to the Internet brings numerous security dangers.

(a)     Corruptions such as **viruses** on a single computer can spread through the network to all of the organisation's computers. (Viruses are described at greater length later in this chapter.)

(b)     Disaffected employees have much greater potential to do **deliberate damage** to valuable corporate data or systems because the network could give them access to parts of the system that they are not really authorised to use.

(c)     If the organisation is linked to an external network, persons outside the company (**hackers**) may be able to get into the company's internal network, either to steal data or to damage the system.

    Systems can have **firewalls** (which disable part of the telecoms technology) to prevent unwelcome intrusions into company systems, but a determined hacker may well be able to bypass even these. (There is more on hackers below.)

(d)     Employees may **download inaccurate information** or imperfect or **virus-ridden software** from an external network. For example 'beta' (free trial) versions of forthcoming new editions of many major packages are often available on the Internet, but the whole point about a beta version is that it is not fully tested and may contain bugs that could disrupt an entire system.

(e)     Information transmitted from one part of an organisation to another may be **intercepted**. Data can be 'encrypted' (scrambled) in an attempt to make it unintelligible to eavesdroppers, but there is not yet any entirely satisfactory method of doing this. (See below. The problem is being worked upon by those with a vested interest, such as credit card companies, and will no doubt be resolved in time.)

(f) The **communications link itself may break down or distort data**. The worldwide telecommunications infrastructure is improving thanks to the use of new technologies, and there are communications 'protocols' governing the format of data and signals transferred (see below). At present, however, transmitted data is only as secure as the medium through which it is transmitted, no matter what controls are operated at either end.

*Encryption and other safety measures*

**Encryption** is the only secure way to prevent eavesdropping (since eavesdroppers can get round password controls, by tapping the line or by experimenting with various likely passwords).

**Definition**

> **Encryption** involves scrambling the data at one end of the line, transmitting the scrambled data, and unscrambling it at the receiver's end of the line.

**Authentication** is a technique of making sure that a message has come from an authorised sender. Authentication involves adding an extra field to a record, with the contents of this field derived from the remainder of the record by applying an algorithm that has previously been agreed between the senders and recipients of data.

**Dial-back security** operates by requiring the person wanting access to the network to dial into it and identify themselves first. The system then dials the person back on their authorised number before allowing them access.

All attempted **violations of security** should be automatically **logged** and the log checked regularly. In a multi-user system, the terminal attempting the violation may be automatically disconnected.

*Hacking*

A **hacker** is a **person who attempts to invade the privacy of a system**.

Hackers require only limited programming knowledge to cause large amounts of damage. The fact that billions of bits of information can be transmitted in bulk over the public telephone network has made it **hard to trace** individual hackers, who can therefore make repeated attempts to invade systems. Hackers, in the past, have mainly been concerned to **copy** information, but a recent trend has been their desire to **corrupt it**.

Phone numbers and passwords can be guessed by hackers using **electronic phone directories** or number generators and by software which enables **rapid guessing** using hundreds of permutations per minute.

**Default passwords** are also available on some electronic bulletin boards and sophisticated hackers could even try to 'tap' messages being transmitted along phone wires (the number actually dialled will not be scrambled).

## FOR DISCUSSION

Sending credit card details to a secure-site on the Internet is less risky than providing credit card details over the telephone, yet people seem more willing to to the latter. Discuss.

*Viruses*

## Definition

> A **virus** is a piece of software which infects programs and data and possibly damages them, and which replicates itself.

Viruses need an opportunity to spread. The programmers of viruses therefore place viruses in the kind of software which is most likely to be copied. This includes:

(a) **Free software** (for example from the Internet).

(b) **Pirated software** (cheaper than original versions).

(c) **Games software** (wide appeal).

(d) **E-mail attachments** (often with instructions to send the message on to others).

The problem has been exacerbated by the portability of computers and disks and the increased availability and use of e-mail.

It is consequently very difficult to keep control over **what disks** are inserted into an organisation's computers and similarly **what** files are received via e-mail.

The two most destructive viruses of recent times are:

- **Melissa** – which corrupts Microsoft Office documents
- **Love bug** – which attacks the operating system

Viruses can spread via floppy disk, but the most destructive viruses utilise e-mail links – **travelling as attachments to e-mail messages**. When the file attachment is opened or executed, the virus infects that system. Recent viruses have been programmed to send themselves to all addresses in the users electronic address book.

| Type of virus | Explanation/Example |
|---|---|
| **File viruses** | File viruses infect program files. When you run an infected program the virus runs first, then passes control to the original program. While it has control, the virus code copies itself to another file or to another disk, replicating itself. |
| **Boot sector viruses** | The boot sector is the part of every hard disk and diskette which is read by the computer when it starts up. If the boot sector is infected, the virus runs when boot the machine. |
| **Overwriting viruses** | An overwriting virus overwrites each file it infects with itself, so the program no longer functions. Since this is very easy to spot these viruses do not spread very well. |

| Type of virus | Explanation/Example |
| --- | --- |
| **Worms** | A worm is a program which spreads (usually) over network connections. It does not attach itself to a host program. |
| **Dropper** | A dropper is a program, not a virus itself, that installs a virus on the PC while performing another function. |
| **Macro viruses** | A macro virus is a piece of self-replicating code written in an application's 'macro' language. Many applications have macro capabilities including all the programs in **Microsoft Office**. The distinguishing factor which makes it possible to create a virus with a macro is the existence of **auto-execute events**. Auto-execute events are opening a file, closing a file, and starting an application. Once a macro is running, it can copy itself to other documents, delete files, and create general havoc! Melissa was a macro virus that infected many systems in 1999. |

### EXAMPLE: LOVE BUG VIRUS CREATES WORLDWIDE CHAOS

A computer virus which exploits office workers' yearnings for love shut down computer systems from Hong Kong to the Houses of Parliament yesterday and caused untold millions of pounds worth of delays and damage to stored files across the world.

The virus, nicknamed 'the love bug' and 'the killer from Manila' after its apparent Philippine origins, is carried in an email with the heading 'ILOVEYOU'.

The text of the message reads: 'Kindly check the attached love letter from me!' A click on the attached file launches the virus, which promptly spreads by sending itself to everyone in the recipient's email address book, overloading email systems.

Once embedded in a host computer, the virus can download more dangerous software from a remote website, rename files and redirect Internet browsers. 'It's a very effective virus. It's one of the most aggressive and nastiest I've ever seen,' said Kieran Fitzsimmons of MessageLabs, which screens millions of company emails for viruses. 'It manifests itself almost everywhere in the computer.'

One tenth of the world's mail servers were down as a result of the love bug, he said. Estimates suggested that between 10% and 30% of UK businesses were hit. Among the firms and organisations affected in the UK yesterday were Microsoft, News International - publishers of the Times and the Sun - the BBC, a number of FTSE-100 companies and parliament.

In an announcement to the Commons, Margaret Beckett, leader of the House, said that the parliamentary email system had crashed. 'I have to tell you that, sadly, this affectionate greeting contains a virus which has immobilised the house's internal communication system,' she said.

At the UK arm of Reed International, publisher of trade magazines, IT engineers alerted staff with Tannoy announcements after the bug had already crippled their computer system. 'It completely wipes out your network,' said Sarah Perkins of PC Pro magazine. 'Ours is down and we're going to lose a day's business.'

The virus spread west from Asia as offices opened and workers checked their emails. The only clue to its origins lies in the first few lines of the code which makes it work. They are headed: 'I hate go to school.' The next line identifies the author as 'spyder' and the next refers to 'Manila, Philippines'.

Daphne Ghesquiere, a Dow Jones spokesman in Hong Kong, said: 'It crashed all the computers. You get the message and the topic says ILOVEYOU, and I was among the stupid ones to open it. I got about five at one time and I was suspicious, but one was from Dow Jones Newswires, so I opened it.' Later Germany, France, Switzerland and the Low Countries were seriously affected.

IT specialists described the love bug as '**a visual basic worm**' far **more dangerous** and fast-spreading than the similar **Melissa virus, which also replicated itself by email**. Melissa infected about a million computers and caused £50m of damage.

ILOVEYOU is eight times bigger, sends itself to everyone in a recipient's address book instead of just the first 50 (and then deletes the address book), and, unlike Melissa, **tampers with operating systems**.

By yesterday afternoon MessageLabs had picked up 10,000 infected emails. The highest number in one day until now has been 700. Last night another virus tracker, TrendMicro, was reporting more than 800,000 infected files around the world, the bulk of them in the US. One expert said the love bug spread 'like wild fire' in Britain after 11.30am. 'It's taking out computers right, left and centre,' he said.

*The Guardian May 5, 2000*

---

*Jokes and hoaxes*

Some programs claim to be doing something destructive to your computer, but are actually 'harmless' jokes. For example, a message may appear suggesting that your hard disk is about to be reformatted. Unfortunately, it is **easy to over-react** to the joke and cause more damage by trying to eradicate something that is not a virus.

There are a number of common hoaxes, which are widely believed. The most common of these is **Good Times**. This hoax has been around for a couple of years, and usually takes the form of a virus warning about viruses contained in e-mail. People pass along the warning because they are trying to be helpful, but they are wasting the time of all concerned.

*We look at other aspects of computer security and privacy in Chapter 8.*

### 9.5 Electronic commerce

**Definition**

> **Electronic commerce** is the process of trading on the Internet.

Electronic commerce or e-commerce has increasingly been used to describe the use of the **Internet** and Websites in the sale of products or services.

At present, in spite of phenomenal growth the market is still fuzzy and undefined. Many e-businesses have **yet to make a profit**, the best-known example being **Amazon.co.uk** the Internet book-seller.

Unless the e-business is one started completely from scratch any new technology installed will probably **need to link up with existing business systems**, which could potentially take years of programming. Under-estimating the time and effort involved is a common obstacle.

E-commerce suffers from a lack of **trust**. The lack of a **physical presence** on the Internet discourages some people from conducting transactions. Large, reputable businesses are less affected than smaller entities.

Concerns over providing **credit and debit card** information over the Internet have been addressed to a certain extent through the development of 'secure sites' – utilising encryption technology.

## FOR DISCUSSION

How many of your group have purchased a product or service over the Internet? What was purchased? Did the purchase process run smoothly?

### Chapter roundup

- **Computers** can be classified as supercomputers, mainframes, minicomputers and PCs.

- The amount of **RAM** and the **processor speed** are key determinants of computer performance. Hard drive size is another important factor.

- The **operating system** provides the interface between hardware, software and user.

- There are a range of **input** and **output** devices available. The most efficient method will depend on the circumstances of each situation.

- Hard disks are used for internal **storage** - external storage may be on floppy disk, zip drive, CD-ROM or DVD.

- There are a range of **configurations** available to an organisation - again the 'best' configuration depends on the individual situation.

- **Bespoke** software is written for a specific situation.

- **Off-the-shelf** software is sold to a wide range of users.

- Many organisations are now utilising **the Internet** as a means of gathering and disseminating information, and conducting transactions.

### Quick quiz

1    List four types of computer. (See section 2.1)

2    What does the operating system do? (See section 3.1)

3    What factors influence the choice of output medium? (See section 5.1)

4    What is a CD-RW? (See section 6.4)

5    What are the benefits of a multi-user system? (See section 7.1)

6    List the advantages of client-server computing? (See section 7.4)

7 What factors should be considered when choosing hardware? (See section 8.1)

8 What factors should be considered when choosing software? (See section 8.2)

9 What is the Internet? (See section 9.1)

10 List five uses of the Internet. (See section 9.2)

## Answers to Activities

1 The laptop or notebook would be more expensive. The reason for this is that the smaller but equally powerful components are more expensive to produce. Some organisations and individuals are prepared to pay for the portability and space-savings a laptop/notebook provides.

2 (a) *Magnetic disks* offer fast access times (in addition to serial or sequential access), direct access to data and offer suitability for multi-user environments. Magnetic disk storage is therefore the predominant storage medium in most commercial applications currently. Direct access is essential for many commercial applications (eg databases) and in addition speed is necessary for real-time applications.

(b) *Magnetic tapes* offer cheap data storage, portability and serial or sequential access only. As other file storage media have fallen in price, and as applications requiring direct access are used frequently, magnetic tape (in reel or cassette form, for micros) is most valuable as a backup medium, on to which the contents of a disk file can be dumped at the end of every day, or period of processing.

(c) *CD-ROM* offers the capacity to store vast amounts of data and, when used with an efficient CD-ROM drive, fast access speed. They are most suitable for software installations and backup/archiving.

3 Stand-alone computers are used in the following situations.

(a) When the data processing requirements can be handled by one user with one computer. Office PCs are often stand-alone machines for use by individuals, for example for developing a personal spreadsheet model.

(b) When the data processing is centralised, for example where very large volumes of transaction data are being handled by a mainframe, or with a centralised minicomputer being used for the processing requirements of a department.

(c) When security could be compromised by the use of a multi-user system.

## Further question practice

*Now try the following practice question at the end of this text.*

Exam style question     **5**

# Chapter 6 :
# USING SOFTWARE: WORD PROCESSING AND SPREADSHEETS

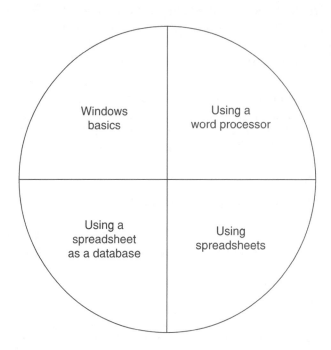

## Introduction

The chapter covers the basics of using Windows and common office software. To understand many of the issues surrounding Information Technology it is helpful to experience the strengths and weaknesses of the technology first hand. For that reason, this chapter and Chapter 7 are very practical. Use the chapter in a way that best suits your needs. If you are a regular user of the software we describe, you may prefer to skim through the chapters.

Also remember there is often more than one valid method to perform a task. If you prefer a method that differs from any we describe, use it. These chapters are not comprehensive software guides – they aim to provide an overview and a few hints.

## Your objective

After completing this chapter you should understand the practical use of word processors and spreadsheets to provide information.

## 1 WINDOWS BASICS

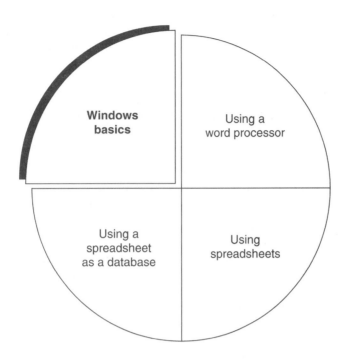

A 'window' is a frame that appears on your computer screen. Several different frames may be visible at once, or a single window may occupy the whole screen.

In Windows 95 and Windows 98 the initial screen is called the **Desktop**. The next illustration shows the desktop (in the background) with a Window that has been called up using the Start button menus.

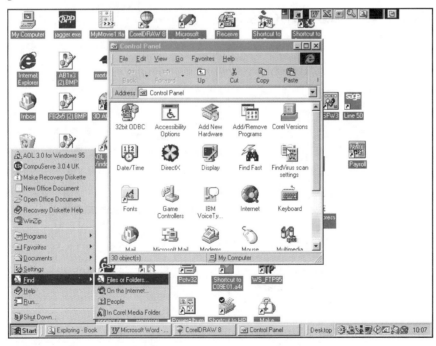

Nearly all windows have the three features explained below.

*Title bar*

A title, shown in a strip at the top the window. This is sometimes called the **title bar**.

*Top left hand corner*

Look up at the very top left-hand corner of the windows illustrated above. There is a symbol in the **top-left hand corner**. You can use this to do a variety of things, but its main use is to *close* the window. (The symbol is different depending upon which program you are using.)

*Top right-hand corner*

Now look up at the top **right hand** corner of a window. In Windows 95/98 you have three symbols in the top right-hand corner.

(a)    There is a line, which minimises the window, reducing it to a button on the 'task bar' at the bottom of the screen (where the Start button is).

(b)    There are two squares, one on top of the other. This makes the window a little bit smaller so you can see what else there is on your screen or look at two different windows at once. If your window is already in its 'smaller' state only one square is shown and this makes the window bigger again.

(c)    There is an **X.** This closes the window altogether.

## FOR DISCUSSION

What are the advantages and disadvantages for the computer user of one operating system (Windows) dominating the market?

## 2    USING A WORD PROCESSOR

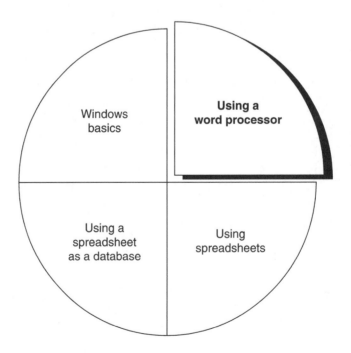

We could devote a whole book to the many facilities offered by a modern word processing package. All we are going to do here is give you an overview. Word processors are increasingly being seen as part of an integrated software package eg Microsoft Word is the word processing tool of Microsoft Office.

### 2.1 Integrated software

**Definition**

> Integrated software refers to programs, or packages of programs, that perform a variety of different processing operations, using **data which is compatible** with whatever operation is being carried out.

The term is generally used in two different situations.

(a) **Accounts packages** often consist of program **modules** that can be integrated into a larger accounting system. There will be a module for each of the sales ledger system, the purchase ledger system, the nominal ledger, and so on. Output from one 'module' in an integrated system can be used as input to another, without the need for re-entry of data.

(b) There are some PC software packages that allow the user to carry out a **variety of processing operations**, such as word processing, using spreadsheets and creating and using a database. Examples of integrated software packages that provide these varied facilities are Lotus Smartsuite and Microsoft Office.

Such packages allow **data to be freely transferred** between elements of the package, for example data from a spreadsheet can be imported into a report which is being word processed.

A potential **disadvantage** of such packages is that they may not offer the range of features which a specialist user of a stand-alone element.

### 2.2 Word processing

**Definition**

> A **word processing** program is used primarily to produce text based documents.

We are going to tell you a bit about Microsoft Word, one of the most commonly used word processors. There is little difference between the main competitors these days: manufacturers are quick to copy each others' good features, and it is in their interests that users find it easy to transfer from another system to the one that they make.

If you start up Word you will be presented with a window something like (but not exactly like) the following.

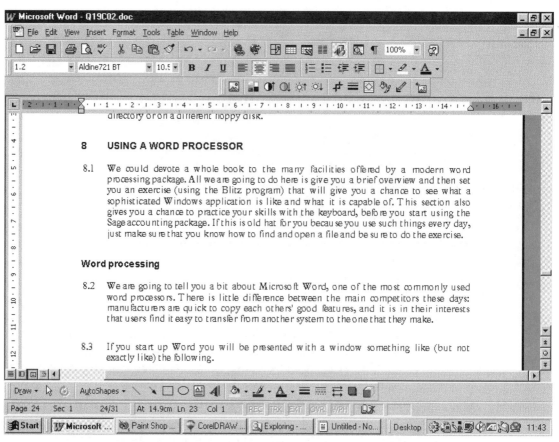

The main part of the screen is the area where you type, of course. At the top of the screen there is a bank of buttons and arrows that do useful things like **embolden** or *italicise* a word or words that you have selected, change the font style or size of selected text, or place text in the centre of the page, or set it to one side of the page. A host of other things can be done and you can create your own customised buttons to do them if you like.

In recent versions of Word, if you let the mouse pointer linger over a particular button (without clicking on it) a little label soon pops up telling you what it does. This is more fun than reading a book about it so we won't describe the buttons further.

---

**Activity 1** (15 minutes)

Open your word processor and experiment – maybe by typing in a paragraph from this book and playing with the formatting facilities.

---

The ruler below the buttons is used to set the left and right margins of the page and to indent paragraphs. You do this by dragging and dropping the triangular markers that you can see at either end of the ruler. The paragraphs on this page that you are reading now, for example, are indented by moving the lower of the two left-hand triangles in to the 1 mark.

The menu choices just below the title bar of the screen offer a huge range of further options. We are going to look at several of the most commonly used.

## File: Open

Click on the word **File** and a menu will drop down which includes the item **Open.** If you click on this, a window like the following will appear.

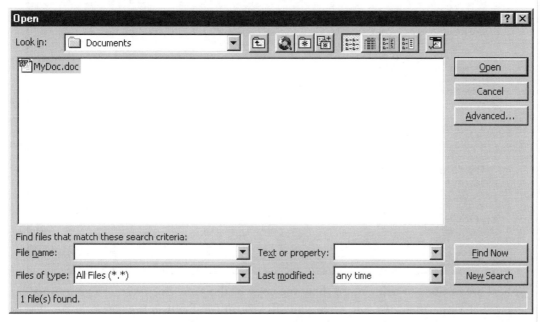

To open a particular file you would click on the **Look in** box arrow to specify the drive (if it is not the one shown already) then *double-click* in the directories box to pick the directory. A list of all the Word type files in the chosen directory will appear. Click on the file name that you want and that name will appear in the File Name box. Then you click on OK to open the file.

*Double-clicking* on a file name has the effect of both selecting it and clicking on OK to open it.

## File: Save As

This option enables you to open a file that has one name, make some changes to it, and then save it with another name. The effect is that the file you originally opened remains in its original form, but the file with the new name retains all of your changes..

## File: Close

Once you have finished with your file you should close it. Click on **File** and then on **Close** in the drop down menu. If you haven't already done so you will be asked if you want to save any changes you made.

## File: Print

If you have a document open and you wish to print it, click on the **Print** option in the **File** menu. The following box will appear.

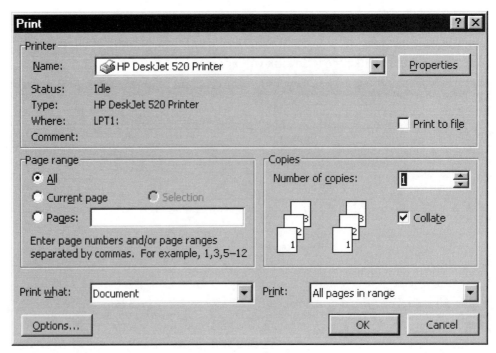

There are options to print more than one copy of the same document, to print only the page that your cursor was on when you clicked on the Print option or to print specific pages of your document. Just click in the relevant white spaces or on the arrows to make changes to any of the settings that come up when the window is first displayed.

An important point to check before you click on OK is the first line, which tells you which printer the document will be printed on.

### Edit: Cut, Copy and Paste

The cut, copy and paste facilities are so useful that there are probably toolbar buttons for them as well as menu items. They are used as follows.

(a)   Select some text. Do this by positioning the mouse pointer at the beginning of the first word, holding down the left mouse button and, keeping the button held down, moving the mouse to the end of the last word (not forgetting any punctuation marks) and then releasing the button. This portion of text will now be highlighted.

(b)   Click on **Edit** at the top of the screen. A menu drops down.

(i)   To retain the highlighted text in its current place and also to make a copy of it which is retained temporarily in the computer's memory, click on **Copy.**

(ii)   To remove the highlighted text from its current place, but also keep it temporarily in the computer's memory, click on **Cut.** The highlighted text will disappear.

(c)   Move the cursor to the point in your document where you want to move the highlighted text or place a copy of it. Do this using the direction arrow keys or by pointing and clicking with the mouse.

(d)   Click on Edit again and choose **Paste.** The text you highlighted will reappear in this new place.

Note that what you paste will be the last thing you cut or copied. If you cut out some text meaning to put it in later, but before you get there you cut or copy something else, the first thing you cut will be lost.

Note also that there are keyboard shortcuts for cutting, copying and pasting. These are listed on the **Edit** menu. In Word you can even *drag* the selected text and *drop* it in the new place. Try this with a sentence of the text you typed in at the beginning of this section.

### Edit: Find and Replace

The **Find** and **Replace** options on the **Edit** menu are very useful. Suppose you had a document that included lots of references to a certain product made by your company: the 'Widget 98', say. If your company releases a new 'Widget 2000' version of the product, it will be a slow process to scroll through the entire document and retype every instance of the product name when you see it. Fortunately you don't have to.

(a)  Click on **Edit** and then on **Replace**.

(b)  A window appears that allows you to type in one box 'Widget 98' and in another 'Widget 2000'.

(c)  You then have a choice of buttons to click.

    (i)  The **Find next** button will take you directly to each successive instance of 'Widget 98' in the document.

    (ii)  The **Replace** button will replace a particular instance of 'Widget 98' with 'Widget 2000'.

    (iii)  The **Replace All** button will automatically replace *every* instance of 'Widget 98' with 'Widget 2000'. This sounds better than option (ii), but there may be cases where you only want *some* of the examples of 'Widget 98' replaced.

You might think that it would be simpler still to find '98' and Replace All with '2000', but give this some thought: there may be other instances of the number 98 in the document, such as 'This is the new improved version of the well-loved Widget 98'.

### Format: Paragraph

This item on the **Format** menu offers you (amongst other things) a better way of spacing out paragraphs than pressing return several times to leave blank lines.

Clicking on the **Paragraph** option in the **Format** menu brings up a window with a Spacing section which allows you to specify the number of 'points' (small units of vertical space) before paragraphs and after them. For example there are '18 pts' between this paragraph and the previous one.

### Tools: Spelling

Finally we come to what is the best feature of word processors for bad spellers and clumsy typists. Click on **Tools** and then on **Spelling** in the drip down menu. Word will work right through your document seeing if the spelling matches the spelling of words in the computer's dictionary. If not it suggests alternatives from which you choose the correct one. For example, if you type 'drp', the choices you are offered include 'drip', 'drop', 'dry' and 'dip'. Do you think this paragraph has been spell-checked?

People sometimes forget that computer spell-checkers only recognise mistakes if they don't match a word in the computer's dictionary. For example, if you type 'form' instead of 'from' the computer will not realise you have made a mistake. It is also easy to make mistakes with a spell-checker if you are too eager to accept its first suggestion. The previous paragraph has a deliberate example.

# 3 USING SPREADSHEETS

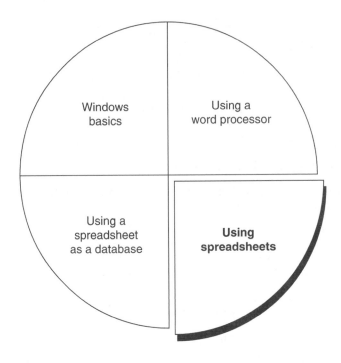

## 3.1 What is a spreadsheet?

**Definition**

> A **spreadsheet** is essentially an **electronic piece of paper** divided into **rows and columns**. It provides an automated way of performing calculations.

The main examples of spreadsheet packages are Lotus 1-2-3 and Microsoft Excel. We will be referring to Microsoft Excel, as this is the most widely-used spreadsheet.

When a 'blank' spreadsheet is loaded into a computer, the VDU monitor will show lines of empty rows and columns. **Rows** are always **horizontal** and **columns vertical**. The **rows** are **numbered** 1, 2, 3 ... etc and the **columns lettered** A, B C ... etc.

Each square is called a '**cell**'. A cell is identified by its reference according to the row or column it is in, as shown in the following illustration.

| | A | B | C | D | E | F | G | H |
|---|---|---|---|---|---|---|---|---|
| 1 | A1 | B1 | C1 | D1 | E1 | F1 | G1 | H1 |
| 2 | A2 | B2 | | | | | | |
| 3 | A3 | | C3 | | | | | |
| 4 | A4 | | | D4 | | | | |
| 5 | A5 | | | | E5 | | | |
| 6 | A6 | | | | | F6 | | |
| 7 | A7 | | | | | | G7 | |
| 8 | A8 | | | | | | | H8 |

The screen **cursor** will highlight any particular cell - in the example above, it is placed over cell C6.

The contents of any cell can be one of the following.

(a)   Text. A cell so designated contains words or numerical data (eg a date) that will not be used in computations. On newer versions of all popular spreadsheets, text can be formatted in a similar way to what is possible using a WP package. Different fonts can be selected, text can be emboldened or italicised, and the point size of the lettering can be changed.

(b)   Values. A value is a number that can be used in a calculation.

(c)   Formulae. A formula refers to other cells in the spreadsheet, and performs some sort of computation with them. For example, if cell C1 contains the formula =A1-B1 this means that the contents of cell B1 should be subtracted from the contents of cell A1 and the result displayed in cell C1. Note that a formula starts with a specific command or choice or symbols in most packages to distinguish it from text.

   (i)   In Excel, a formula always begins with an equals sign: =

   (ii)   Where a long row or column of cells (referred to as a range) is to be added together, a **'sum' function** can be used. In Excel this would be entered as =SUM(B7:B18)

### 3.2   Some hands-on skills

The instructions here refer to **Excel 97**. Later versions of Excel also work in the way described here, although they contain extra features.

Load up your spreadsheet by finding and double-clicking on the Excel **icon** or button (it will look like an X), or by choosing Excel from somewhere in the **Start** menus (maybe from within the **Microsoft Office** option).

*Moving about (F5)*

Press the function key labelled **F5** at the top of the keyboard. A **Go To** dialogue box will appear with the 'cursor' (a flashing line or lit up section) in a box. Delete anything that is in the box with the Delete key and then type C5 (or c5 – case does not matter) and press Enter. The 'cursor' will now be over cell C5. This is the **active cell** and it will have a thick black line all round it.

Press **Ctrl** + ↑ and then **Ctrl** + ←. (This means that you hold down one of the keys marked Ctrl and, keeping it held down, press the other key. )

The cursor will move back to cell A1. Try holding down Ctrl and pressing each of the direction arrow keys in turn to see where you end up. Try using the **Page Up** and **Page Down** keys and also try **Home** and **End** and Ctrl + these keys. Try **Tab** and **Shift +**

**Tab,** too. These are all useful shortcuts for moving quickly from one place to another in a large spreadsheet.

*Entering data and the active cell*

Get your cursor back to cell A1. Then type in 123. Then press the ↓ key. Note that the cell below (A2) now becomes the **active cell**.

Type 456 in cell A2 and then press the → key. The cell to the left (B2) is now the active cell.

Get back to cell A1. Above cell A1 you should be able to see a rectangle at the top left *telling* you that you are in cell A1 and, to the right of this a line containing the numbers 123. In other words this line at the top of the screen shows you the **cell reference** and the **contents** of the currently **active cell**.

*Editing data (F2)*

Assuming you have now made cell A1 the active cell, type 45. Note what happens both in the cell and in the line above. The previous entry (123) is replaced by the number 45. Press ↓. The active cell is now A2 (check in the line at the top of the screen).

Suppose you wanted to **change the entry** in cell A2 from 456 to 123456. You have four options. Option (d) is the best.

    (a)    **Type** 123456 and press **Enter.**

           To undo this and try the next option press **Ctrl + Z**: this will always undo what you have just done.

    (b)    **Double-click** in cell A2. The cell will keep its thick outline but you will now be able to see a vertical line flashing in the cell. You can move this line by using the direction arrow keys or the Home and the End keys. Move it to before the 4 and type 123. Then press Enter.

           When you have tried this press Ctrl + Z to undo it.

    (c)    Click once on the number 456 in the line that shows the active cell reference and cell contents at the top of the screen. Again you will get the vertical line and you can type in 123 before the 4. Then press Enter, then Ctrl + Z.

    (d)    Press the **function key F2**. The vertical line cursor will be flashing in cell A2 at the *end* of the figures entered there (after the 6). Press Home to get to a position before the 4 and then type in 123 and press Enter, as before.

Now make cell A3 the active cell. Type **1 2** (a 1, a space, and then a 2) in this cell and press Enter. Note that because the software finds a space it thinks you want **text** in this cell. It **aligns it to the left**, not the right. If you ever need to enter a number to be treated as text, you should enter an **apostrophe** before it. eg '1.

*Deleting*

Get to cell A3 if you have not already done so and press **Delete**. The contents of this cell will disappear.

Move the cursor up to cell A2. Now hold down the **Shift** key (the one above the Ctrl key) and keeping it held down press the ↑ arrow. Cell A2 will stay white but cell A1 will go black. What you have done here is **selected** the range A1 and A2. **Anything you do next will be done to both cells A1 and A2.**

Press Delete. The contents of cells A1 and A2 will disappear.

### 3.3 Graphs and charts

Some spreadsheet packages, such as Microsoft Excel, give the user an option to produce and print graphs or charts from numerical data.

### EXAMPLE

Carter Doyle Ltd had the following sales turnover in 20X7.

| Quarter | Sales |
|---------|-------|
|         | £000  |
| 1       | 75    |
| 2       | 100   |
| 3       | 175   |
| 4       | 150   |
| Total   | 500   |

If this data were input into a program with a graph production facility, any of the following graphs or charts could be prepared.

**Pie chart: Annual sales**

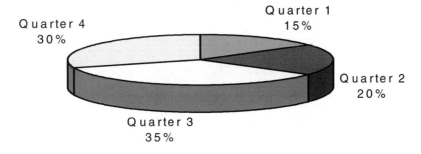

**Graph: Time series**

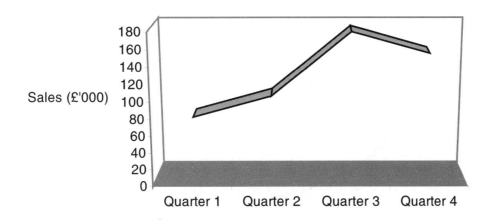

NOTES

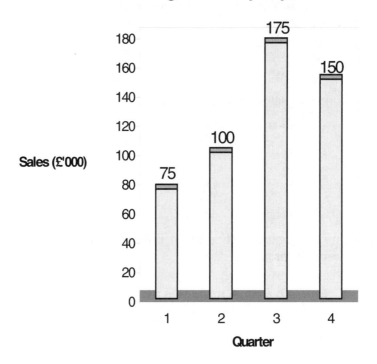

## Histogram: Sales per quarter

Sales (£'000)

175
150
100
75

180
160
140
120
100
80
60
40
20
0

1    2    3    4

Quarter

## 4 USING A SPREADSHEET AS A DATABASE

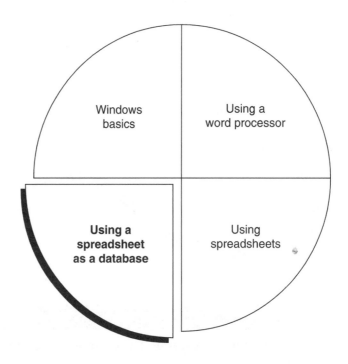

Windows basics

Using a word processor

**Using a spreadsheet as a database**

Using spreadsheets

**Definition**

A database is a collection of **structured data.** Any item of data within the database can be used as a subject of enquiry.

## 4.1 Spreadsheets and databases

Spreadsheet packages are **not true databases,** but they often have database-like facilities for manipulating tables of data, if only to a limited extent compared with a true database.

A database is a **collection of data** which is integrated and organised so as to provide a **single comprehensive system.** The data is governed by rules which define its structure and determine how it can be accessed.

The **purpose** of a database is to provide **convenient access** to common data for a **wide variety** of **users** and **user needs.** The point of storing all the data in a single place is to avoid the problems that arise when several similar versions of the same data exist, so that it is not clear which is the **definite version,** and also to avoid the need to have to input the same data more than once.

For instance, both the sales administration and the marketing departments of an organisation may need **customer name and address details.** If these two departments operated **separate** systems they will **both** need to input details of any change of address. If they **share a common database** for this information, it **only needs to be input once.**

## 4.2 Sorting facilities

In the illustration below data has been sorted by highlighting columns A to C and then clicking on **Data** and then **Sort.** It has been sorted into **ascending** product name order and **descending** order of number of parts used in that product. Then the data has been copied into columns E to G where it can be **re-sorted** according to part number and product name.

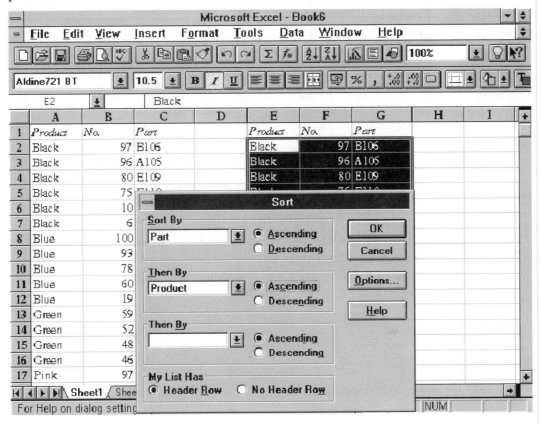

**BPP**
PUBLISHING

NOTES

## EXAMPLE: SPREADSHEETS AND DATABASES

Here is a spreadsheet used for **stock control**.

| | A | B | C | D | E | F | G | H | I |
|---|---|---|---|---|---|---|---|---|---|
| 1 | Component | Product | Quantity | In stock | Re-order level | Free stock | Reorder quantity | On order | Supplier |
| 2 | A001 | A | 1 | 371 | 160 | 211 | 400 | - | P750 |
| 3 | A002 | B | 5 | 33 | 40 | - | 100 | 100 | P036 |
| 4 | A003 | A | 5 | 206 | 60 | 146 | 150 | - | P888 |
| 5 | A004 | D | 3 | 176 | 90 | 86 | 225 | - | P036 |
| 6 | A005 | E | 9 | 172 | 120 | 52 | 300 | - | P750 |
| 7 | A006 | C | 7 | 328 | 150 | 178 | 375 | - | P684 |
| 8 | A007 | C | 2 | 13 | 10 | 3 | 25 | - | P227 |
| 9 | A008 | C | 6 | 253 | 60 | 193 | 150 | - | P036 |
| 10 | A009 | E | 9 | 284 | 90 | 194 | 225 | - | P888 |
| 11 | A010 | B | 3 | 435 | 100 | 335 | 250 | - | P720 |
| 12 | A011 | B | 2 | 295 | 110 | 185 | 275 | - | P036 |
| 13 | A012 | A | 3 | 40 | 190 | - | 475 | 475 | P036 |
| 14 | A013 | A | 7 | 23 | 120 | - | 300 | 300 | P227 |
| 15 | A014 | C | 4 | 296 | 110 | 186 | 275 | - | P750 |
| 16 | A015 | D | 7 | 432 | 40 | 392 | 100 | - | P684 |
| 17 | A016 | D | 4 | 416 | 100 | 316 | 250 | - | P141 |
| 18 | A017 | A | 3 | 463 | 150 | 313 | 375 | - | P888 |

If you scrutinise this table you may notice that there are certain common items. For instance both components A001 and A003 are used to make Product A. Both components A001 and A005 are bought from supplier P750.

Wouldn't it be handy if we could **manipulate** this data in some way, say, to get a full list of all components used to make product A, or a list of all components supplied by supplier P750? Of course, we **can** do this, almost at the click of a button.

In Excel you simply click in the **Data** menu and choose the option **Filter ... Auto filter.** A downward pointing arrow now appears beside each heading, and if you click on one of the arrows a list of each different item in the corresponding column drops down.

| | A | B | C | D | E | F | G | H | I |
|---|---|---|---|---|---|---|---|---|---|
| 1 | Component | Product | Quantity | In stock | Re-order level | Free stock | Reorder quantity | On order | Supplier |
| 2 | A001 | A | 1 | 371 | 160 | 211 | 400 | - | (All) |
| 3 | A002 | B | 5 | 33 | 40 | - | 100 | 100 | (Top 10...) |
| 4 | A003 | A | 5 | 206 | 60 | 146 | 150 | - | (Custom...) |
| 5 | A004 | D | 3 | 176 | 90 | 86 | 225 | - | P036 |
| 6 | A005 | E | 9 | 172 | 120 | 52 | 300 | - | P141 |
| 7 | A006 | C | 7 | 328 | 150 | 178 | 375 | - | P227 |
| 8 | A007 | C | 2 | 13 | 10 | 3 | 25 | - | P684 |
| 9 | A008 | C | 6 | 253 | 60 | 193 | 150 | - | P720 / P036 |
| 10 | A009 | E | 9 | 284 | 90 | 194 | 225 | - | P750 / P888 |
| 11 | A010 | B | 3 | 435 | 100 | 335 | 250 | - | P888 / P720 |
| 12 | A011 | B | 2 | 295 | 110 | 185 | 275 | - | P036 |
| 13 | A012 | A | 3 | 40 | 190 | - | 475 | 475 | P036 |
| 14 | A013 | A | 7 | 23 | 120 | - | 300 | 300 | P227 |
| 15 | A014 | C | 4 | 296 | 110 | 186 | 275 | - | P750 |
| 16 | A015 | D | 7 | 432 | 40 | 392 | 100 | - | P684 |
| 17 | A016 | D | 4 | 416 | 100 | 316 | 250 | - | P141 |
| 18 | A017 | A | 3 | 463 | 150 | 313 | 375 | - | P888 |

Sheet1 / Sheet2 / Sheet3 /

In this illustration the user has clicked on the arrow in the Supplier column and is about to select Supplier 750. This is what happens.

| | A | B | C | D | E | F | G | H | I |
|---|---|---|---|---|---|---|---|---|---|
| 1 | Component | Product | Quantity | In stock | Re-order level | Free stock | Reorder quantity | On order | Supplier |
| 2 | A001 | A | 1 | 371 | 160 | 211 | 400 | - | P750 |
| 6 | A005 | E | 9 | 172 | 120 | 52 | 300 | - | P750 |
| 15 | A014 | C | 4 | 296 | 110 | 186 | 275 | - | P750 |

Sheet1 / Sheet2 / Sheet3 /

This shows that supplier P750 supplies components A001, A005 and A014, that there is nothing on order from this supplier at present, that this supplier is important for products A, E and C only, and so on.

If the original data were restored (by clicking on the Supplier arrow and choosing All) and then we clicked on the arrow in the **Product** column we would be able to see at a glance all the components used for product A and all the suppliers for those components, whether any components were on order at present (possibly meaning delays in the availability of the next batch of Product A) and so on.

*We look at a true database application (Microsoft Access) in Chapter 7.*

### 4.3    Spreadsheets and data tables

**Definition**

> The term **data table** is used by some spreadsheet packages (for example Excel) to refer to a group of cells that show the results of changing the value of variables.

**Data tables** can be most clearly explained using a simple example.

### EXAMPLE: A ONE-INPUT DATA TABLE

Don't be put off by the terminology here. All this means is that **one** of the bits of the calculation changes and the other bits don't.

Suppose a company has production costs which it would expect to be in the region of £5m were it not for the effects of inflation. Economic forecasts for the inflation rate in the coming year range from 2% to 10%.

If this were part of a **scenario** that the company was trying to model on a spreadsheet a 'data table' could be produced showing the range of effects of these various possible levels of inflation simply by:

(a)    Entering the basic data.

(b)    Entering just one formula per item affected (production costs and profits in the example illustrated).

(c)    Using the computer's data table tool.

Here is the problem set up on Microsoft Excel.

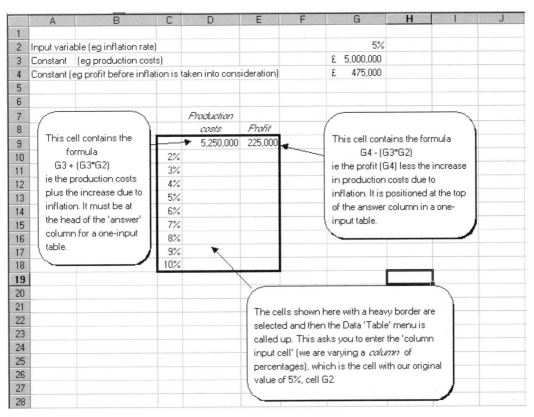

This is what happens after a single cell reference (G2) is entered, as prompted by the **data table menu**.

| | A | B | C | D | E | F | G | H | I |
|---|---|---|---|---|---|---|---|---|---|
| 1 | | | | | | | | | |
| 2 | Input variable (eg inflation rate) | | | | | | 5% | | |
| 3 | Constant (eg production costs) | | | | | | £5,000,000 | | |
| 4 | Constant (eg profit before inflation is taken into consideration) | | | | | | £ 475,000 | | |
| 5 | | | | | | | | | |
| 6 | | | | | | | | | |
| 7 | | | | Production | | | | | |
| 8 | | | | costs | Profit | | | | |
| 9 | | | | 5,250,000 | 225,000 | | | | |
| 10 | | | 2% | 5,100,000 | 375,000 | | | | |
| 11 | | | 3% | 5,150,000 | 325,000 | | | | |
| 12 | | | 4% | 5,200,000 | 275,000 | | | | |
| 13 | | | 5% | 5,250,000 | 225,000 | | | | |
| 14 | | | 6% | 5,300,000 | 175,000 | | | | |
| 15 | | | 7% | 5,350,000 | 125,000 | | | | |
| 16 | | | 8% | 5,400,000 | 75,000 | | | | |
| 17 | | | 9% | 5,450,000 | 25,000 | | | | |
| 18 | | | 10% | 5,500,000 | (25,000) | | | | |
| 19 | | | | | | | | | |
| 20 | | | | | | | | | |

The shaded cells are automatically filled by the spreadsheet package to show the impact of inflation on production costs and profits.

## 4.4 Two-input data tables

It is also possible to use this facility if **two** of the numbers in the calculation are to be changed.

## EXAMPLE: A TWO-INPUT DATA TABLE

Suppose the company is not sure that its production costs will be £5m - they could alternatively be only £4.5m or else they could be up to £5.5m. The problem is set up in a similar way on Excel. Study the diagram carefully.

| | A | B | C | D | E | F | G | H |
|---|---|---|---|---|---|---|---|---|
| 1 | | | | | | | | |
| 2 | **Column** input variable (eg inflation rate) | | | | 5% | | | |
| 3 | **Row** input variable (eg production costs) | | | | £5,000,000 | | | |
| 4 | | | | | | | | |
| 5 | | | | | | | | |
| 6 | | | | *Production* | | | | |
| 7 | | | | *costs* | | | | |
| 8 | | 5,250,000 | 4,500,000 | 5,000,000 | 5,500,000 | | | |
| 9 | | 2% | | | | | | |
| 10 | | 3% | | | | | | |
| 11 | | 4% | | | | | | |
| 12 | | 5% | | | | | | |
| 13 | | 6% | | | | | | |
| 14 | | 7% | | | | | | |
| 15 | | 8% | | | | | | |
| 16 | | 9% | | | | | | |
| 17 | | 10% | | | | | | |
| 18 | | | | | | | | |
| 19 | | | | | | | | |
| 20 | | | | | | | | |
| 21 | | | | | | | | |
| 22 | | | | | | | | |
| 23 | | | | | | | | |
| 24 | | | | | | | | |
| 25 | | | | | | | | |
| 26 | | | | | | | | |
| 27 | | | | | | | | |
| 28 | | | | | | | | |
| 29 | | | | | | | | |
| 30 | | | | | | | | |
| 31 | | | | | | | | |
| 32 | | | | | | | | |

This cell contains the formula G3 + (G3*G2), as in the last example, but it must be positioned here in the corner for a two-input table.

The cells shown here with a heavy border are selected and the Data 'Table' menu is called up again. This time cell reference G3 is entered as the 'row input variable' (the different levels of production costs shown in a row at the top of the table), as well as the column input variable (G2) - the inflation rate.

## SOLUTION

Our solution is shown over the page. It may be obtained with three or four clicks of the mouse!

| | A | B | C | D | E | F | G | H |
|---|---|---|---|---|---|---|---|---|
| 1 | | | | | | | | |
| 2 | **Column** input variable (eg inflation rate) | | | | 5% | | | |
| 3 | **Row** input variable (eg production costs) | | | | £5,000,000 | | | |
| 4 | | | | | | | | |
| 5 | | | | | | | | |
| 6 | | | | *Production* | | | | |
| 7 | | | | *costs* | | | | |
| 8 | | 5,250,000 | 4,500,000 | 5,000,000 | 5,500,000 | | | |
| 9 | | 2% | 4,590,000 | 5,100,000 | 5,610,000 | | | |
| 10 | | 3% | 4,635,000 | 5,150,000 | 5,665,000 | | | |
| 11 | | 4% | 4,680,000 | 5,200,000 | 5,720,000 | | | |
| 12 | | 5% | 4,725,000 | 5,250,000 | 5,775,000 | | | |
| 13 | | 6% | 4,770,000 | 5,300,000 | 5,830,000 | | | |
| 14 | | 7% | 4,815,000 | 5,350,000 | 5,885,000 | | | |
| 15 | | 8% | 4,860,000 | 5,400,000 | 5,940,000 | | | |
| 16 | | 9% | 4,905,000 | 5,450,000 | 5,995,000 | | | |
| 17 | | 10% | 4,950,000 | 5,500,000 | 6,050,000 | | | |
| 18 | | | | | | | | |

Once more the cells shown here with shading are filled in automatically by the spreadsheet package

## Chapter roundup

- The most widely used operating system is Windows. Certain features are common to all software produced for use in conjunction with Windows.

- The term integrated software can be used to refer to accounting packages made up of different modules or to 'office' type packages.

- A spreadsheet is an electronic piece of paper divided into rows and columns.

- A database is a collection of structured data.

- We looked at some practical uses of word processors, spreadsheets and databases in this chapter.

*We look at more aspects of spreadsheets in the next chapter.*

## Quick quiz

1 What is the purpose of the **X** symbol shown in the top right hand corner of a window? (See section 1)

2 What is the integrated software? (See section 2.1)

3 What is a spreadsheet? (See section 3.1)

4 What is the purpose of a database? (See section 4.1)

5 What is the purpose of a data table within a spreadsheet? (See section 4.3)

**BPP**
PUBLISHING

## Answers to Activities

1    Try out the buttons on the standard toolbar on sections of text and the complete paragraph.

2    Make sure you do this using the spreadsheet facilities rather than just by looking through the table!

(a)    A003, A009 and A017.
(b)    A005 and A009.
(c)    P036 and P227.

## Further question practice

*Now try the following practice question at the end of this text.*

Exam style question    **6**

# Chapter 7 :
# USING SOFTWARE: MORE SPREADSHEETS, DATABASES AND E-MAIL

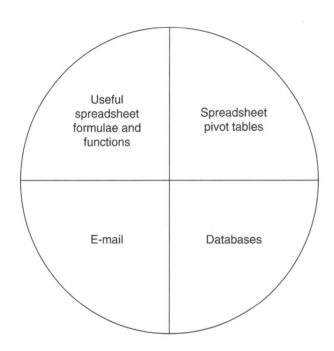

## Introduction

In this chapter we explain the workings of some useful spreadsheet formulae and functions. It is important that you explore the many other features of a modern spreadsheet package for yourself. Remember, the on-line help facility provides an excellent source of information.

Later in the chapter we look at databases and what many people believe to be the most significant development of recent years – e-mail.

## Your objective

After completing this chapter you should be aware of some common uses of spreadsheets, databases and e-mail.

Business Basics: Information Technology

# 1 USEFUL SPREADSHEET FORMULAE AND FUNCTIONS

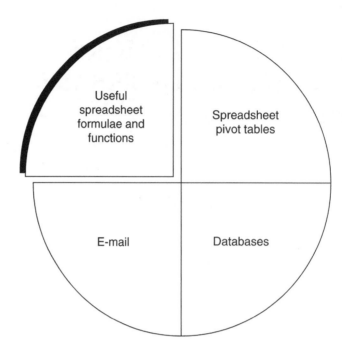

In this section we shall have a quick look at some functions that are useful when you are presented with pre-prepared data in a spreadsheet and you want to extract certain items.

## 1.1 Left, right and mid

You may need to extract only specific characters from the data entered in a cell. For instance, suppose a set of raw materials codes had been entered into a spreadsheet as follows.

| | A | B |
|---|---|---|
| 1 | 6589D | |
| 2 | 5589B | |
| 3 | 5074D | |
| 4 | 8921B | |
| 5 | 3827B | |
| 6 | 1666D | |
| 7 | 5062A | |
| 8 | 7121D | |
| 9 | 7457C | |
| 10 | 9817D | |
| 11 | 6390C | |
| 12 | 1148A | |
| 13 | 4103A | |
| 14 | 8988A | |
| 15 | 6547C | |
| 16 | 5390A | |
| 17 | 6189D | |
| 18 | 8331C | |
| 19 | 1992B | |
| 20 | 7587A | |

148

The four **digits** are, say, a number derived from the supplier's reference number, while the **letter** indicates that the material is used to make Product A, B, C or D.

If you wanted to sort this data in **alphabetical** order of **Product** you would have a problem, because it is only possible to arrange it in ascending or descending **numerical** order, using the standard Sort method.

To get round this you can extract the letter from each cell using the **RIGHT** function, as follows.

| | A | B |
|---|---|---|
| 1 | 6589D | =RIGHT(A1,1) |
| 2 | 5589B | =RIGHT(A2,1) |
| 3 | 5074D | =RIGHT(A3,1) |
| 4 | 8921B | =RIGHT(A4,1) |
| 5 | 3827B | =RIGHT(A5,1) |
| 6 | 1666D | =RIGHT(A6,1) |

The formula in cell B1 means 'Extract the last (or rightmost) one character from cell A1'. If we wanted to extract the last **two** characters the formula would be **=RIGHT(A1,2)**, and so on.

The formula can then be filled down and then the data can be sorted by column B, giving the following results.

| | A | B |
|---|---|---|
| 1 | 5062A | A |
| 2 | 1148A | A |
| 3 | 4103A | A |
| 4 | 8988A | A |
| 5 | 5390A | A |
| 6 | 7587A | A |
| 7 | 5589B | B |
| 8 | 8921B | B |
| 9 | 3827B | B |
| 10 | 1992B | B |
| 11 | 7457C | C |
| 12 | 6390C | C |
| 13 | 6547C | C |
| 14 | 8331C | C |
| 15 | 6589D | D |
| 16 | 5074D | D |
| 17 | 1666D | D |
| 18 | 7121D | D |
| 19 | 9817D | D |
| 20 | 6189D | D |

The function **LEFT** works in the same way, except that it extracts the **first** (or leftmost) character or characters.

The function **MID**, as you might expect, extracts a character or characters from the **middle** of the cell, starting at the **position** you specify, counting from left to right:

**=MID([Cell],[Position],[Number of characters]).**

In Excel the first character extracted is the one at the position specified, so if you want to extract the **third** character you specify position 3. In Lotus 1-2-3 it is the next character after the position specified, so if you want to extract the third character you specify position 2.

---

**Activity 1**                                                       **(10 minutes)**

Cell A1 contains the data: **12-D-496**

(a)      What formula would you use to extract the **D** into a different cell?

(b)      What formula would you use to extract the **12** into a different cell?

---

### 1.2 Lookup

The LOOKUP function allows you to enter data that corresponds to a value in one cell in a column and return the data in the corresponding row in a different column. A simple example will make this clearer.

|   | A | B | C | D | E | F | G |
|---|---|---|---|---|---|---|---|
| 1 | 1 | Red | | | | | |
| 2 | 2 | Green | | | | | |
| 3 | 3 | Blue | | | | | |
| 4 | 4 | Yellow | | | | | |
| 5 | | | | | | | |
| 6 | | | | | 1 | Red | |
| 7 | | | | | | | |
| 8 | | | | | | | |

Here the user enters a figure between 1 and 4 in cell E6 and the spreadsheet returns the corresponding colour from the range A1:B4. If the user had entered **3** then cell F6 would say **Blue**.

Here is the formula that is used to do this.

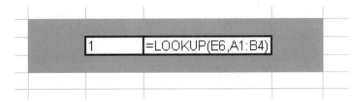

### 1.3 Merging the contents of cells

The next formula that is only available in Excel 97 and above.

Suppose data had been entered into a spreadsheet as follows.

What if you wanted the data in cells A1, B1 and C1 in a single cell: 21A64? To do this in Excel 97 you can simply join the contents of individual cells together using the **&** symbol, as follows. The formula could be filled down to give the same results for the rest of the list.

|   | A | B | C | D |
|---|---|---|---|---|
| 1 | 21 | A | 64 | =A1&B1&C1 |
| 2 | 62 | P | 14 | |
| 3 | 87 | T | 26 | |
| 4 | | | | |

### 1.4    Paste special

Sometimes you may wish to convert a formula into an absolute value, for example you may want the contents of cell D1 in the above example to be '21A64', not a formula that gives this result.

To convert a formula to an absolute value, copy the relevant cell or cells in the normal way, then highlight another cell (say, E1 in the above example) and **right click**. From the menu that appears, choose **Paste Special.** The following dialogue box will appear.

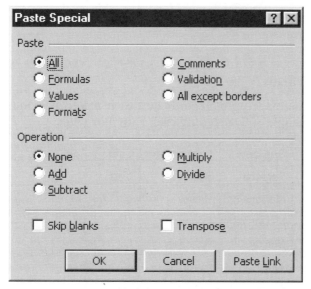

Here, if you choose **Values** then what will be pasted into cell E1 is the value '21A64', not the formula in cell D1.

## 2    SPREADSHEET PIVOT TABLES

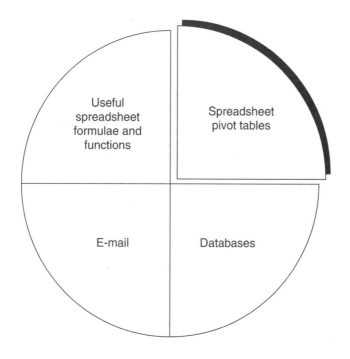

### 2.1 What is a pivot table?

### Definition

A **pivot table** is an interactive table that summarises and analyses data from lists and tables.

To understand pivot tables we first need to get a little bit more understanding of records and fields.

### 2.2 Records and fields

A typical database is made up of **records** and each record is made up of a number of **fields**. Here's an example of five records, each with four fields.

| Surname | First name | Title | Age |
|---------|-----------|-------|-----|
| Foreman | Susan | Miss | 42 |
| McDonald | David | Dr | 56 |
| McDonald | Dana | Mrs | 15 |
| Sanjay | Rachana | Ms | 24 |
| Talco | Giovanni | Mr | 32 |

(a) Each **Row** is one **Record**. (Notice that both Row and Record begin with the letter R.)

(b) Each **Column** is one **Field**. (If you can remember that Rows are Records, this shouldn't be too hard to work out!)

The example above has records for five people, and each record contains fields for the person's surname, first name, title and age.

### 2.3 Analysing and interpreting data

There are lots of ways of analysing this data.

(a) We could find the **total number** of occurrences of each surname to see which was the most and least common. Likewise first names.

(b) We could find the **total number** of each title, as an indication of the most and least common marital status of the people.

(c) We could find the **average** age of the people

(d) We could find the **maximum** and **minimum** ages.

These simple statistics - **totals, averages, and highest and lowest** - are the most common way of finding some meaning amongst a mass of figures. We are also often interested in **unusual** information (for instance an age of minus seven), because it tends to highlight areas where there could be errors in our information.

### 2.4 Pivot tables

To extract information quickly and easily from a table in Excel we can simply highlight it and click on **Data** and then **Pivot Table Report**. This starts up a Wizard which first asks you to confirm the location of the data you want to analyse and then offers you the following options.

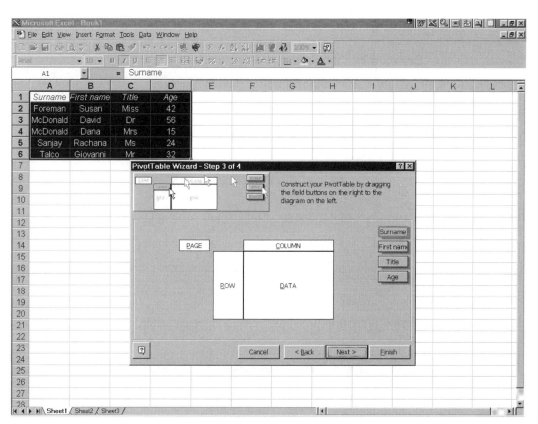

All you have to do to analyse the data is drag any of the labelled buttons on the right into the appropriate part of the white area. For instance, if we wanted to know the total number of surnames of each type we could drag the Surname label into the row area and then drag another instance of the surname label into the Data area. This is what you would see.

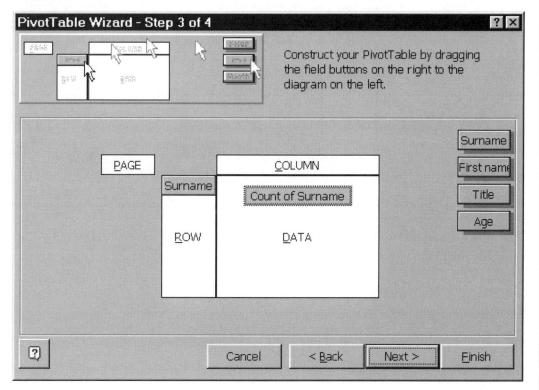

Note that in the Data area the name of the Surname label changes to Count of Surname but we do not have to accept this if it is not what we want. If we double-click on Count of Surname we are offered other options such as Sum, Average, Max, Min.

For now we will accept the Count option. Clicking on Next and Finish gives the following results.

|  | A | B |
|---|---|---|
| 1 | Count of Surname |  |
| 2 | Surname | Total |
| 3 | Foreman | 1 |
| 4 | McDonald | 2 |
| 5 | Sanjay | 1 |
| 6 | Talco | 1 |
| 7 | Grand Total | 5 |

More elaborate analyses than this can be produced. For instance, you could try setting up a pivot table like this.

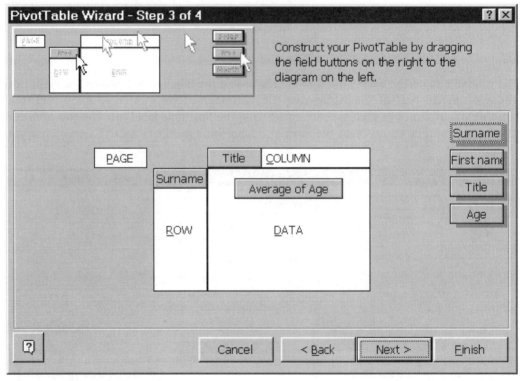

The result is as follows, showing that the average age of people called McDonald is 35.5 and the average age overall is 33.8.

|   | A | B | C | D | E | F | G |
|---|---|---|---|---|---|---|---|
| 1 | Average of Age | Title | | | | | |
| 2 | Surname | Dr | Miss | Mr | Mrs | Ms | Grand Total |
| 3 | Foreman | | 42 | | | | 42 |
| 4 | McDonald | 56 | | | 15 | | 35.5 |
| 5 | Sanjay | | | | | 24 | 24 |
| 6 | Talco | | | 32 | | | 32 |
| 7 | Grand Total | 56 | 42 | 32 | 15 | 24 | 33.8 |

This arrangement of the data also draws attention to the fact that the data includes a 'Mrs' who is only 15 years old. This is not impossible, but it is quite unusual and should be checked because it could be an inputting error.

If we don't happen to like the way Excel arranges the data it can be changed in a flash, simply by dragging the labels in the results to another part of the table. For instance if Title is dragged down until it is over cell B3 the data is automatically rearranged as follows.

|   | A | B | C |
|---|---|---|---|
| 1 | Average of Age | | |
| 2 | Surname | Title | Total |
| 3 | Foreman | Miss | 42 |
| 4 | Foreman Total | | 42 |
| 5 | McDonald | Dr | 56 |
| 6 | | Mrs | 15 |
| 7 | McDonald Total | | 35.5 |
| 8 | Sanjay | Ms | 24 |
| 9 | Sanjay Total | | 24 |
| 10 | Talco | Mr | 32 |
| 11 | Talco Total | | 32 |
| 12 | Grand Total | | 33.8 |

## FOR DISCUSSION

What other features of spreadsheets do people in your group find useful?

# 3 DATABASES

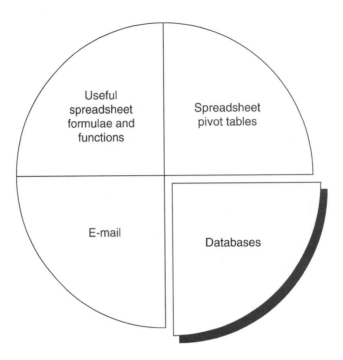

We are going to take a look at the use of a proper database package to analyse data. This is only an **introduction** to a topic that quickly becomes rather complex. We will concentrate on **Microsoft Access**. Other database packages follow the same principles.

As explained in the previous chapter, a database is an organised collection of data.

## 3.1 What distinguishes a database from a spreadsheet?

Spreadsheets do have some database capabilities such as sorting and filters. However, spreadsheets are designed more for flexibility in manipulation and presentation of information. Generally, mathematical manipulation of data is more easily achieved in a spreadsheet.

Databases are designed to store **greater volumes of data**, and they enable data required for different purposes to be stored in a single location. Databases can manipulate data using **Queries**, which are particularly useful when dealing with large data volumes. In very simple terms, a spreadsheet is the electronic equivalent of a piece of graph paper, while a database could be likened to a filing cabinet.

## 3.2 Importing data

Databases store data in **tables**. Tables can be created within the database package, and data records manually added to the table. This is time consuming, as data volumes handled by database packages are often large. The more common scenario is to **import data from a text file** (ASCII text), downloaded from an accounting software package. Or, the situation may arise where data held on a **spreadsheet** needs to be transferred into a database, perhaps to be held alongside other related data.

The **procedure for importing data** from either a text file or spreadsheet into a Microsoft Access table is outlined below.

*Step 1.* Make a note of the file name and location that contains the source data. If the data is held on a spreadsheet, also note the name of the particular sheet you want to import(eg 'Sheet 3').

*Step 2.* Save and Close the spreadsheet, or, if importing from a text file ensure the file is not being accessed by another application.

*Step 3.* Database packages are quite hungry for memory, so close all applications that you don't need.

*Step 4.* Open up Access, choose the option to create a new blank database, and give it a suitable file name. The elements of an Access database are arranged on a series of tabs as shown in the next illustration.

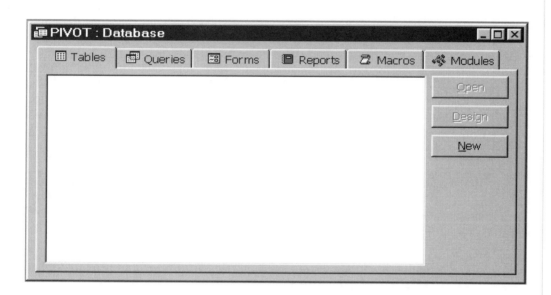

*Step 5.* Ensure the Table tab is active. Select the **File** menu, choose the **Get External Data** and then the **Import** option. Clicking on this produces a dialogue box identical to the familiar **Open file** dialogue. Change the **file type** to that required. For instance, if importing from an Excel spreadsheet change to Microsoft Excel; for a text file change to Text File. Then locate the file and click on **Import**.

*Steps 6 and 7.*

The options Access presents you with next will vary depending on the file type you selected in Step 5. In both cases, the 'Import Wizard' steps are straightforward.

| Importing from a spreadsheet | Importing from a text file |
|---|---|
| You will get a list of all the **worksheets** in the spreadsheet file you specify. Choose the sheet that you want to import (you noted this down earlier) and click on **Next.** | You will be asked to identify how the text file is formatted to identify the positioning of column breaks. **Fixed width,** means the position of the characters within each line is consistent. **Delimited** means a character, such as a comma, identifies the division between columns. (You, or the person that created the file should know what format the file is. If in doubt, opening the file in Notepad or a similar text editor enables the contents to be viewed and the delimiter identified). Click on **Next.** |
| If the first row of your spreadsheet contains column headings, check the box that says **First Row Contains Column Headings,** then click on Next. | For fixed width files you are given the opportunity to identify the position of column breaks using the mouse. For delimited files you are asked to identify the delimiter (eg comma). |

***Step 8.*** As a rule you will want to store your data in a **New Table,** so this is the next option to choose. The ability to 'Append' (add to the bottom of an existing table), exists. This is useful when importing data into the same table, but from different source files.

***Step 9.*** You are given the choice of specifying **further information** about the fields (columns) that you are importing, but there is no need to do this at this basic level, so click **Next**.

***Step 10.*** You then have the choice of defining your own 'Primary Key', which is the unique field in each line, or letting Access do it for you. It is usually acceptable to **let Access do it** for you, the default selection. Click **Next.**

***Step 11.*** Finally **choose a name** for your table if you do not like the one that Access suggests, and click on **Finish.** You will then see an entry for your new database table.

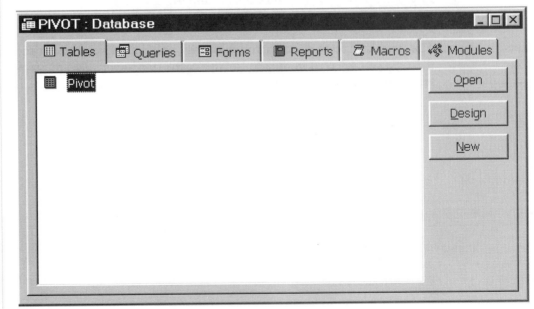

If you **select your table and click Open** you will see how data is stored within the table. This view is known as the **datasheet**.

| ID | Surname | First name | Title | Age |
|---|---|---|---|---|
| 1 | Foreman | Susan | Miss | 42 |
| 2 | McDonald | David | Dr | 56 |
| 3 | McDonald | Dana | Mrs | 15 |
| 4 | Sanjay | Rachana | Ms | 24 |
| 5 | Talco | Giovanni | Mr | 32 |
| (AutoNumber) | | | | |

Record: |◄| |►| 1 |►| |►|| |►*| of 5

Within the datasheet you can select columns, right click then **sort** the data in them in ascending or descending order. You can apply and remove **filters** simply by right clicking on a record and including or excluding the item as you wish. In the illustration below, clicking on **Filter By Selection** would show you table including only the details for people called McDonald.

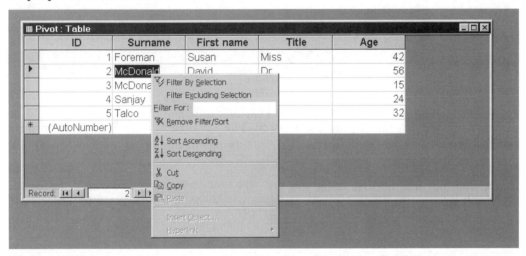

New records can be entered or existing ones edited, and there is a **Find** option in the edit menu to help locate particular items of information.

To see, or edit, the **table design** it is necessary to **open the datasheet**, then select the **Design View** icon below the File menu option. Field size and formats are then available for editing. Modifying table design should not be necessary at this level, but investigate if you wish to discover more about the workings of the database package.

### 3.3 Queries

The **real power** of a database, however, lies in its ability to **analyse and manipulate** data using practically any criteria you can dream up.

If you close your table, return to the set of index tabs, select **Queries** and click on **New** you get the following options.

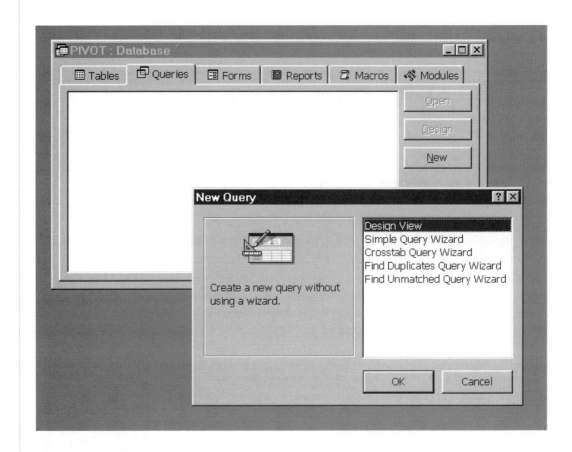

We shall not look at all of these options. The Simple Query Wizard takes you step by step through the process of building a query. The CrossTab Query Wizard performs a similar function to a Pivot Table. The functions of the other wizards speak for themselves. In this case, however, we are going to choose **Design View**.

If you click on this the first thing you are asked to do is to specify **which tables** the query will apply to. In our example we have only one table so we can simply select it and click on **Add** and then close the **Show Table** dialogue box. The screen will now look like this.

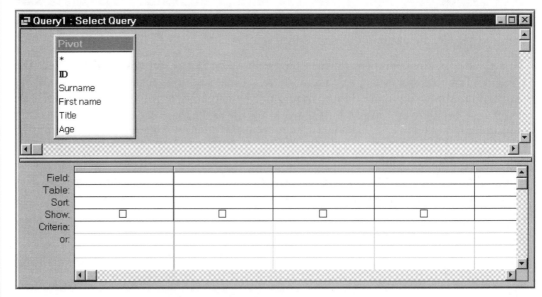

To design a query we click on the fields we wish to analyse in the list at the top to make them appear in the **design grid** below. For instance if we wish to perform an analysis of the **ages** in our table we would click on Surname (so we know which record is which) and Age to produce the following.

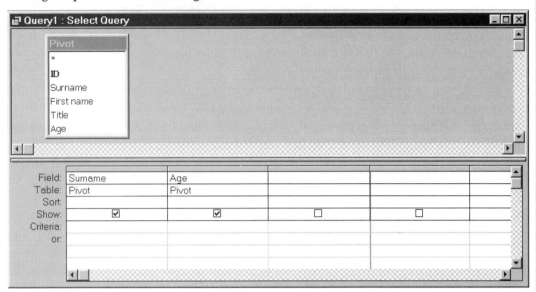

The cell entitled Criteria is the one that wants our attention. For instance, if we wanted to find the records of everyone who was over 40 or under 20 we could make the following entries for the Age field.

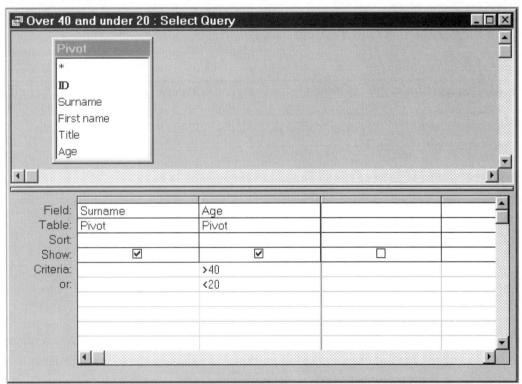

Clicking on Query and Run produces the following results.

NOTES

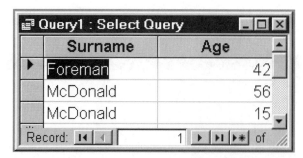

If you are satisfied that you have the information you want you can **save** the query for future use (for instance to be run again when you have entered more records). If you are not satisfied you can switch back to design view (**View ... Design**), and alter it as you wish.

### 3.4    Queries using multiple tables

A query can pull together data from more than one Table.

For example we may have a Customer table containing customer codes and names, an Items table containing stock codes and descriptions, and a Transactions table. The three tables are shown below.

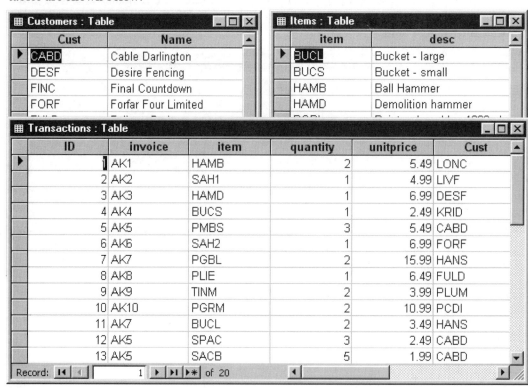

To write a query that combines data from multiple tables follow the following steps.

*Step 1.*    Before we are able to combine information from separate Tables, we need to tell Access how the information is related. To do this we form a **Relationship.** Ensure the Tables tab is active and select **Tools, Relationships.** Then select **Relationships, Show Table** and **Add** all three tables to the view. The window will now look like this.

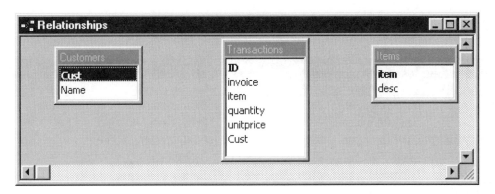

***Step 2.*** Click and hold down the mouse while dragging the **common field** over to the other table. In the example above you would click over **Cust** in Customers, hold the left mouse button down, and drag over to the **Cust** in Transactions. Release the mouse button, click on **Create** and the **link** will show. The same procedure would be followed to link Item between the Transactions and Items tables.

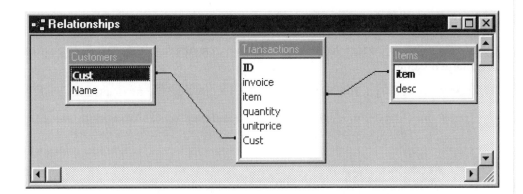

***Step 3.*** Close the Relationship window, saving your changes.

***Step 4.*** Activate the **Query tab** and click **New**. The options are as shown earlier under 5.12. If we chose the **Design View** option, the same principles explained in 5.13 to 5.15 can be applied to build this Query. Alternately, select the **Simple Query Wizard** option and click OK.

***Step 5.*** Select each of the three tables in turn under the Tables/Queries option. For each Table select which fields you wish to appear in the Query using the **>** or **>>** buttons. After you have completed this procedure for all three tables, Click Next.

***Step 6.*** Accept the default of Detail for the next option by clicking Next.

***Step 7.*** Give your Query a title that will enable you to remember its purpose, and click **Finish**.

A sample of the resulting datasheet is shown.

| Cust | Name | invoice | item | desc | quantity | unitprice |
|------|------|---------|------|------|----------|-----------|
| CABD | Cable Darlington | AK5 | PLUE | Electric plug | 6 | 1.99 |
| CABD | Cable Darlington | AK5 | SACB | Black sacks | 5 | 1.99 |
| CABD | Cable Darlington | AK5 | PMBS | Paint - matt black 200ml | 3 | 5.49 |
| DESF | Desire Fencing | AK3 | BUCL | Bucket - large | 6 | 3.49 |
| DESF | Desire Fencing | AK3 | HAMD | Demolition hammer | 1 | 6.99 |
| FORF | Forfar Four Limited | AK6 | SAH2 | Hacksaw - medium | 1 | 6.99 |
| FULD | Fulham Drainage | AK8 | PLIE | Pliers | 1 | 6.49 |
| HANS | Hansens | AK7 | SPAF | Sandpaper - fine | 4 | 2.49 |

Transactions Query : Select Query

Record: I◄ ◄ 1 ► ►I ►* of 19

### 3.5 Exporting data

The situation may arise where you wish to **extract data from a database** using a query, then export this sub-set of data into a spreadsheet, to perform further manipulations and formatting. The procedure for exporting data from Microsoft Access into a spreadsheet is explained below.

*Step 1.* Design, run and save the query following the instructions above.

*Step 2.* Select the Query tab, then click the name of the table or query you want to export. Select the **File** menu, and click **Save As/Export**.

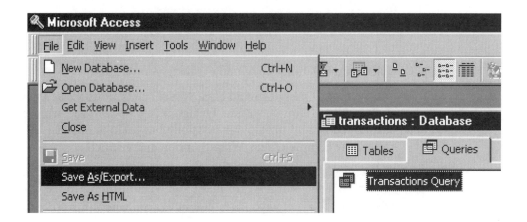

*Step 3.* In the Save As box, select **To An External File Or Database**, and then click OK.

*Step 4.* In the Save As Type box, change the **file type** to that required, for example Microsoft Excel.

*Step 5.* Within the Save In box, change the **location** to where you wish the spreadsheet to be saved. Enter the **name** you wish to give the spreadsheet in the File Name box.

*Step 6.* Click **Export**. Microsoft Access creates the spreadsheet file containing the data from your query.

*Step 7.* Close Microsoft Access (to free up memory), start your spreadsheet application and open the new file from the location you specified in Step 5.

Note that the same procedure can be followed to export the contents of a complete Table. Simply select the Table itself in step 2 rather than a query.

### 3.6    Expressions

When building queries a very wide variety of '**expressions**' can be used to define how the data in the table is displayed. Expressions are entered either in the **Criteria** cell or in the **Field** cell. Here are a couple of examples.

(a)    **Extracting parts of fields only**. For instance you can enter the expression **Left([First name],1)** in the first Field cell and set Surname as the second field to display in the normal way, as follows.

| Field: | Expr1: Left([First name],1) | Surname |
|---|---|---|
| Table: | | Pivot |
| Sort: | | |
| Show: | ☑ | ☑ |
| Criteria: | | |
| or: | | |
| | | |

(Access itself inserts the **Expr1:** part).

You will get the following results when you run the query.

| | Expr1 | Surname |
|---|---|---|
| ▶ | S | Foreman |
| | D | McDonald |
| | D | McDonald |
| | R | Sanjay |
| | G | Talco |
| * | | |

(b)    **Performing calculations**. For instance the following query would extract records of people who will have reached retirement age in 10 years time.

| Field: | Surname | Expr1: [Age]+10 | ▾ |
|---|---|---|---|
| Table: | Pivot | | |
| Sort: | | | |
| Show: | ☑ | ☑ | |
| Criteria: | | >65 | |
| or: | | | |

### 3.7    Reports

Microsoft Access includes a powerful report writer. This enables professional presentation of meaningful data drawn from the database.

Report writing in databases is not as simple as formatting a spreadsheet. For this reason, always consider the possibility of exporting the data to a spreadsheet, and using the manipulation and formatting functions available within the spreadsheet to produce your report.

The steps involved in producing a report within Access are outlined below.

***Step 1.*** **Design a query** that will extract the data you wish the report to contain. Run and save the query following the instructions given earlier.

***Step 2.*** Close your query, return to the set of index tabs, select **Reports** and click on **New.** The following options are now available.

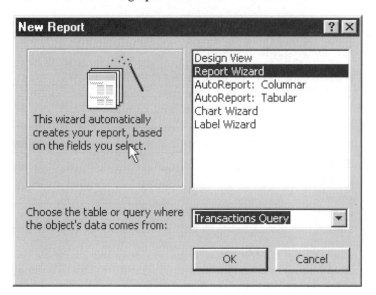

***Step 3.*** Highlight Report Wizard, and in the lower box select the Query you wrote in Step 1. Click OK.

***Step 4.*** You are now asked to select the fields you wish to report on. As we designed a query specifically for this report (in step1), we can simply ensure the name of this query is displayed in the Tables/Query box, and click on the double arrow (>>)box to select all fields. Click Next.

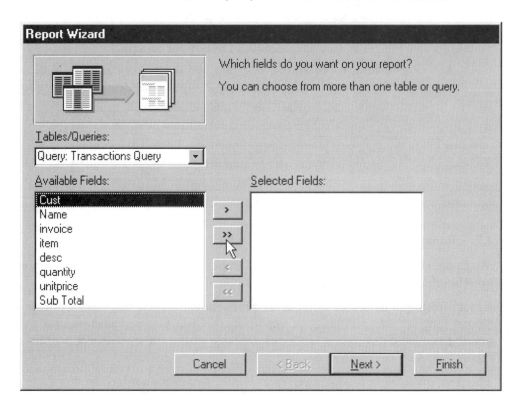

***Step 5.*** You are then asked how would you like to view your data. This relates to grouping, and the criteria selected will depend on the purpose of the Report. Highlight the item you wish the report to be grouped by, such as Customers and click Next.

***Step 6.*** Sorting criteria within these groupings is then requested. Up to four criteria can be selected by using the down arrows on the right of each box. (One criteria would often be sufficient.) Select your criteria and click Next.

***Step 7.*** The layout options will then be presented. The options presented will vary depending on the data reported on, and the answers to the previous wizard questions. Make your layout and page orientation selections, and ensure the 'Adjust field width so all fields fit on a page' box is checked, then click Next.

***Step 8.*** Select the style of the Report. Corporate is an appropriate style for business documents. Click Next.

***Step 9.*** Enter a meaningful title for your report. If data relates to a particular date or time frame, be sure to disclose that in your title. Ensure the 'Preview the report' option is checked, and click Finish.

***Step 10.*** The report will appear in Print Preview mode on screen. Print it out, and close the report window.

As a learning exercise, don't be afraid to **repeat the report producing process** a number of times, taking different options along the way. Unwanted reports can be deleted from the Reports index tab by highlighting the title to be deleted, right mouse clicking and selecting delete.

Reports can be **renamed** through right mouse clicking and selecting rename. To change the **heading** within the report highlight the report, click on the Design button, then double click in the Report Header text box. Overtype the title, select File save, and then File close.

As mentioned earlier, report writing in databases is not simple. **Experience** and **experimentation** will help ensure the correct choices are made at each Wizard stage for different types of reports.

This section has demonstrated some of the features of database packages. To fully appreciate the value of queries and the power of databases, consider these principles in the context of **vast stores of data** rather than the small number of records used here.

## FOR DISCUSSION

Does anybody from your group use Access at work? For what purpose?

## 4    E-MAIL

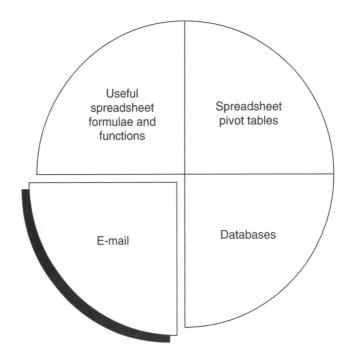

### 4.1    Electronic mail (E-mail)

**Definition**

> The term 'electronic mail', or **e-mail**, is used to describe various systems of sending data or messages electronically via a telephone or data network and a central computer.

E-mail has the following **advantages** over paper-based mail.

(a)    **Speed** (transmission, being electronic, is almost instantaneous). E-mail is far faster than post. It is a particular time-saver when communicating with people overseas.

(b)    **Economy** (no need for stamps etc). E-mail is reckoned to be 20 times cheaper than fax.

(c)    **Efficiency** (a message is prepared once but can be sent to thousands of employees at the touch of a button).

(d)    **Security** (access can be restricted by the use of passwords).

(e)    Documents can be retrieved from **word-processing** and graphics packages.

(f)    Electronic **delivery and read receipts** can be requested.

(g)    E-mail can be used to send **documents and reports** as well as short memos, for instance by **attaching** a file.

Typically information is 'posted' by the sender to a central computer which allocates disk storage as a **mailbox** for each user. The information is subsequently collected by the receiver from the mailbox.

(a)  Senders of information thus have **documentary evidence** that they have given a piece of information to the recipient and that the recipient has picked up the message.

(b)  Receivers are **not disturbed** by the information when it is sent (as they would be by face-to-face meetings or phone calls), but collect it later at their convenience.

Each user will typically have **password protected access** to his own inbox, outbox and filing system. He can prepare and edit text and other documents using a **word processing** function, and send mail using **standard headers and identifiers** to an individual or a group of people on a prepared **distribution list**.

E-mail systems may serve one department or the whole organisation. It is also possible to connect an e-mail system to outside organisations.

E-mail use is now widespread both **within organisations** and **between** them – via the Internet.

---

**Activity 2**                                                   **(15 minutes)**

There are many types of e-mail system. Perhaps the most common is Microsoft Outlook. Ensure you can send a message using the e-mail system at your work or college. Find out how to attach a file (such as a spreadsheet) to your message.

---

*We look at some of the drawbacks of e-mail in Chapter 9. In the next chapter we discuss the security and privacy implications of holding information.*

**Chapter roundup**

- In this chapter we looked at some useful spreadsheet formulae and functions including:

  ° Left, right and mid
  ° Lookup
  ° Pivot tables

- Databases generally store greater volumes of data than spreadsheets. We looked at the workings of Microsoft Access including:

  ° Importing/exporting
  ° Tables
  ° Queries
  ° Expressions
  ° Reports

- E-mail is a system of electronic messaging. Advantages over paper-based mail include speed, cost and efficiency.

**Quick quiz**

1   When would you use the left, right or mid function provided in Excel? (See section 1.1)

2   What does the lookup function do? (See section 1.2)

3   What is a pivot table? (See section 1.2)

4   A field is made up of many records – TRUE or FALSE? (See section 2.2)

5   What is the difference between a database and a spreadsheet? (See section 3.1)

6   List five advantages of e-mail over paper-based mail. (See section 4.1)

**Answers to Activities**

1   (a)   =MID(A1,4,1). The starting position is position 4 because the hyphen between the 2 and the D counts as position 3.

    (b)   =LEFT(A1,2).

**Further question practice**

*Now try the following practice question at the end of this text.*

Exam style question   **7**

# Chapter 8 :
# SECURITY AND PRIVACY

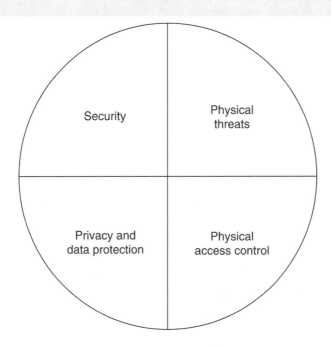

## Introduction

This chapter deals with the **security** of information systems. We also look at how information systems may **threaten** personal **privacy** rights - and at legislation to prevent this.

## Your objectives

After completing this chapter you should understand:

(a)    The threats to computer systems.

(b)    Common methods that aim to ensure the security of the MIS.

(c)    Issues of confidentiality and compliance with statutes.

*We looked at the security issues surrounding the Internet in Chapter 5.*

# 1 SECURITY

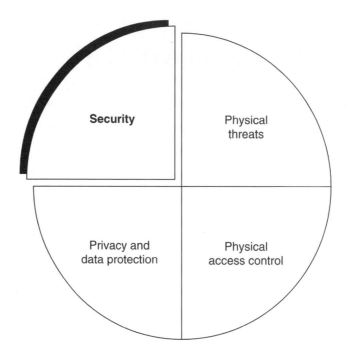

## 1.1 The responsibilities of ownership

If you own **something that you value** – you **look after it**. You keep it somewhere safe, you regularly check to see that it is in good condition and you **don't allow it to upset others.**

**Information** is a valuable possession and it deserves similar care.

**Definition**

> **Security**, in information management terms, means the protection of data from accidental or deliberate threats which might cause unauthorised modification, disclosure or destruction of data, and the protection of the information system from the degradation or non-availability of services.

Security refers to **technical** issues related to the computer system, psychological and **behavioural** factors in the organisation and its employees, and protection against the unpredictable occurrences of the **natural world**.

Security can be subdivided into a number of aspects.

(a) **Prevention**. It is in practice impossible to prevent all threats cost-effectively.

(b) **Detection**. Detection techniques are often combined with prevention techniques: a log can be maintained of unauthorised attempts to gain access to a computer system.

(c) **Deterrence**. As an example, computer misuse by personnel can be made grounds for dismissal.

(d)   **Recovery procedures**. If the threat occurs, its consequences can be contained (for example checkpoint programs).

(e)   **Correction procedures**. These ensure the vulnerability is dealt with (for example, by instituting stricter controls).

(f)   **Threat avoidance**. This might mean changing the design of the system.

## 2   PHYSICAL THREATS

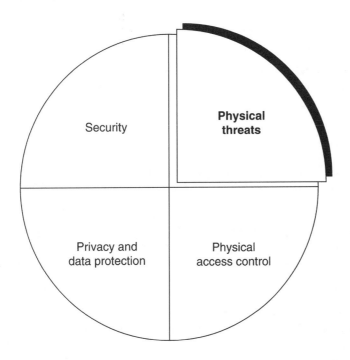

The **physical environment** quite obviously has a major effect on information system security, and so planning it properly is an important precondition of an adequate security plan.

### 2.1   Fire

Fire is the **most serious hazard** to computer systems. Destruction of data can be even more costly than the destruction of hardware.

A proper fire safety plan is an essential feature of security procedures, in order to prevent fire, detect fire and put out the fire. Fire safety includes:

(a)   **Site preparation** (for example, appropriate building **materials,** fire doors).

(b)   **Detection** (for example, **smoke detectors**).

(c)   **Extinguishing** (for example, **sprinklers**).

(d)   Training for staff in observing **fire safety procedures** (for example, **no smoking** in computer room).

### 2.2   Water

Water is a serious hazard. **Flooding** and water damage are often encountered following **firefighting** activities elsewhere in a building.

This problem can be countered by the use of **waterproof ceilings and floors** together with the provision of **adequate drainage**.

In some areas **flooding** is a natural risk, for example in parts of central London and many other towns and cities near rivers or coasts. **Basements** are therefore generally not regarded as appropriate sites for computer installation!

### 2.3 Weather

Wind, rain and storms can all cause substantial **damage to buildings**. In certain areas the risks are greater, for example the risk of typhoons in parts of the Far East. Many organisations make heavy use of **prefabricated** and portable offices, which are particularly vulnerable.

**Cutbacks in maintenance** expenditure may lead to leaking roofs or dripping pipes, which can invite problems of this type, and maintenance should be kept up if at all possible.

### 2.4 Lightning

Lightning and electrical storms can play havoc with **power supplies**, causing power **failures** coupled with power **surges** as services are restored.

One way of combating this is by the use of **uninterrupted (protected) power supplies**. This will protect equipment from fluctuations in the supply. Power failure can be protected against by the use of a **separate generator**.

### 2.5 Terrorist activity

The threat of bombs planted by **political terrorists** has beset UK organisations for many years. Other parts of the world such as the Middle East, central Europe and the US have been equally or worse afflicted. Political terrorism is the main risk, but there are also threats from individuals with **grudges.**

In some cases there is very little that an organisation can do: its buildings may just happen to **be in the wrong place** and bear the brunt of an attack aimed at another organisation or intended to cause general disruption.

There are some avoidance measures that should be taken, however.

(a)   **Physical access** to buildings should be controlled (see the next section).

(b)   Activities likely to give rise to terrorism such as **exploitation** of workers or **cruelty** to animals should be stopped.

(c)   The organisation should consult with police and fire authorities about potential risks, and **co-operate** with their efforts to avoid them.

### 2.6 Accidental damage

**People** are a physical threat to computer installations because they can be **careless and clumsy**: there can be few of us who have not at some time spilt a cup of coffee over a desk covered with papers, or tripped and fallen doing some damage to ourselves or to an item of office equipment.

Combating accidental damage is a matter of:

(a)   Sensible **attitudes** to office behaviour.
(b)   Good office **layout**.

---

**Activity 1**

Your company is in the process of installing a mainframe computer. You have been co-opted onto the project team with responsibility for systems installation. What issues should be considered in relation to the risks of fire or flooding in the discussions about site selection?

---

# 3 PHYSICAL ACCESS CONTROL

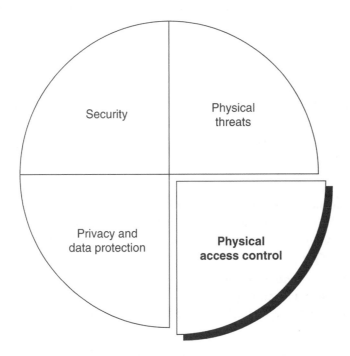

## 3.1 Controlling access

Access control aims to prevent intruders getting near the computer equipment or storage media. Methods of controlling human access range from:

(a) **Personnel** (security guards).
(b) **Mechanical devices** (eg keys, whose issue is recorded).
(c) **Electronic identification devices** (eg card-swipe systems).

Obviously, the best form of access control would be one which **recognised** individuals immediately, without the need for personnel, who can be assaulted, or cards, which can be stolen. However, machines which can identify a person's fingerprints or scan the pattern of a retina are too **expensive** for many organisations.

It may not be cost effective or convenient to have the same type of access controls around the whole building all of the time. Instead, the various **security requirements of different departments** should be estimated, and appropriate boundaries drawn. Some areas will be very restricted, whereas others will be relatively open.

Guidelines for security against physical threats which should be applied **within the office** include:

(a) **Fireproof cabinets** should be used to store files, or **lockable metal boxes** for floppy disks. If files contain confidential data, they should be kept in a safe.

(b) Computers with **lockable keyboards** are sometimes used. Computer terminals should be **sited carefully**, to minimise the risk of unauthorised use.

(c) If computer printout is likely to include confidential data, it should be **shredded** before it is eventually thrown away after use.

(d) **Disks** should not be left lying around an office. They can get lost or stolen. More likely still, they can get damaged, by spilling **tea or coffee** over them, or allowing the disks to gather **dust**, which can make them unreadable.

(e) The computer's **environment** (humidity, temperature, dust) should be properly controlled. This is not so important with PC systems as for mainframes. Even so, the computer's environment, and the environment of the files, should **not be excessively hot**.

*PINs*

In some systems, the user might have an individual **personal identification number**, or PIN, which identifies him or her to the system. Based on the security privileges allocated, the user will be **allowed** access and editing rights to certain parts of the system, but **forbidden** access or editing rights to other parts.

*Door locks*

Conventional door locks are of value in certain circumstances, particularly where users are only required to pass through the door a **couple of times a day**. If the number of people using the door increases and the frequency of use is high, it will be difficult to persuade staff to lock a door every time they pass through it.

If this approach is adopted, a 'good' lock must be accompanied by a **strong door**, otherwise an intruder may simply bypass the lock. Similarly, other points of entry into the room/complex must be as well protected, otherwise the intruder will simply use a **window** to gain access.

One difficulty with conventional locks is the matter of **key control**. Inevitably, each person authorised to use the door will have a key and there will also be a master key maintained by security. Cleaners and other contractors might be issued with keys. Practices such as lending out keys or taking duplicate keys may be difficult to prevent.

One approach to this is the installation of **combination locks**, where a numbered keypad is located outside the door and access allowed only after the correct 'code', or sequence of digits has been entered. This will only be fully effective if users ensure the combination is kept confidential, and the combination is **changed** frequently.

*Card entry systems*

There is a range of card entry systems available. This is a more sophisticated means of control than the use of locks, as **cards can be programmed** to allow access to certain parts of a building only, between certain times.

These allow a high degree of monitoring of staff movements; they can for example be used instead of clock cards to record details of time spent on site. Such cards can be incorporated into **identity cards**, which also carry the photograph and signature of the user and which must be 'displayed' at all times.

*Computer theft*

A problem which is related to the problem of physical access control is that of equipment theft. As computer equipment becomes **smaller** and **more portable,** it can be 'smuggled' out of buildings with greater ease. Indeed much equipment is specifically **designed for use off-site** (for example laptops, notebooks, handhelds, bubblejet printers) and so control is not simply a question of ensuring that all equipment stays on site.

A **log of all equipment** should be maintained. This may already exist in basic form as a part of the fixed asset register. The log should include the **make, model** and **serial number** of each item, together with some other organisation-generated code which identifies the **department** which owns the item, the **individual** responsible for the item and its **location.** Anyone taking any equipment off-site should book it out and book it back in.

Computer theft may be carried out by persons who have official access to equipment. It may equally be carried out by those who do not. **Burglar alarms** should be installed.

**Smaller items** of equipment, such as laptop computers and floppy disks, should always be **locked securely away.** Larger items cannot be moved with ease and one approach adopted is the use of **bolts** to secure them to desks. This discourages 'opportunity' thieves. Larger organisations may also employ site security guards and install closed circuit camera systems.

---

**Activity 2**

Your department, located in an open-plan office, has five networked desktop PCs, a laser printer and a dot matrix printer.

You have just read an article suggesting that the best form of security is to lock hardware away in fireproof cabinets, but you feel that this is impracticable. Make a note of any alternative security measures which you could adopt to protect the hardware.

---

**FOR DISCUSSION**

What methods are used to control access to the premises of your place of work?

---

## 4    PRIVACY AND DATA PROTECTION

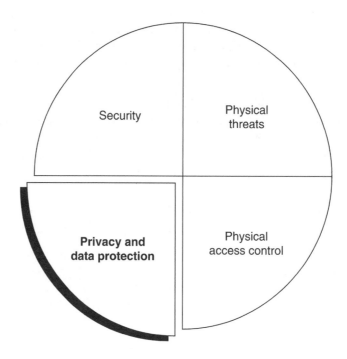

### Definition

> **Privacy** is the right of the individual to control the user of information about him or her, including information on financial status, health and lifestyle (ie prevent unauthorised disclosure).

### 4.1    Why is privacy an important issue?

In recent years, there has been a growing popular fear that **information** about individuals which was stored on computer files and processed by computer could be **misused**.

In particular, it was felt that an individual could easily be harmed by the existence of computerised data about him or her which was inaccurate or misleading and which could be **transferred to unauthorised third parties** at high speed and little cost.

In the UK the current legislation is the **Data Protection Act 1998**. This Act replaced the Data Protection Act 1984.

In July 1995 the European Parliament adopted a new **Directive on Data Protection**, with two main purposes.

(a)    To protect **individual privacy**. Previous UK law only applied to **computer-based** information. The directive applies to **all personal data, in any form.**

(b)    To **harmonise data protection legislation** so that, in the interests of improving the operation of the single European market, there can be a **free flow of personal data** between the member states of the EU.

This directive **led to the introduction of the new Data Protection Act in 1998.**

## 4.2    The Data Protection Act 1998

The Data Protection Act 1998 is an attempt to protect the **individual**.

*Definitions of terms used in the Act*

In order to understand the Act it is necessary to know some of the technical terms used in it.

## Definitions

> **Personal data** is information about a living individual, including expressions of opinion about him or her. Data about other organisations (eg supplier or customer companies) is not personal data, unless it contains data about individuals who belong to those other organisations.
>
> **Data users** are organisations or individuals who control the contents of files of personal data and the use of personal data which is processed (or intended to be processed) automatically - ie who use personal data which is covered by the terms of the Act.
>
> A **data subject** is an individual who is the subject of personal data.

*The data protection principles*

There are certain Data Protection Principles which registered data users must comply with.

### DATA PROTECTION PRINCIPLES

Schedule 1 of the 1998 Act contains the revised data protection principles.

1    Personal data shall be processed fairly and lawfully and, in particular, shall not be processed unless:

    (a)    At least one of the conditions in Schedule 2 is met (see paragraph 4.11 (c) in this section).

    (b)    In the case of sensitive personal data, at least one of the conditions in Schedule 3 is also met (see 4.11 (d)).

2    Personal data shall be obtained only for one or more specified and lawful purposes, and shall not be further processed in any manner incompatible with that purpose or those purposes.

3    Personal data shall be adequate, relevant and not excessive in relation to the purpose or purposes for which they are processed.

4    Personal data shall be accurate and, where necessary, kept up to date.

5    Personal data processed for any purpose or purposes shall not be kept for longer than is necessary for that purpose or those purposes.

6    Personal data shall be processed in accordance with the rights of data subjects under this Act.

7    Appropriate technical and organisational measures shall be taken against unauthorised or unlawful processing of personal data and against accidental loss or destruction of, or damage to, personal data.

8    Personal data shall not be transferred to a country or territory outside the European Economic Area unless that country or territory ensures an adequate level of protection for the rights and freedoms of data subjects in relation to the processing of personal data.

*The coverage of the Act*

Key points of the Act can be summarised as follows.

(a) With certain exceptions, all **data users** have had to **register** under the Act with the **Data Protection Registrar**.

(b) **Individuals** (data subjects) are awarded certain **legal rights**.

(c) Data holders must adhere to the data protection principles.

*Registration under the Act*

The Data Protection Registrar keeps a Register of all data users. Each entry in the Register relates to a data user. Unless a data user has an entry in the Register he may not hold personal data. Even if the data user is registered, he must only hold data and use data for the **purposes** which are registered. A data user must apply to be registered.

*The rights of data subjects*

The Act establishes the following rights for data subjects.

(a) A data subject may seek **compensation** through the courts for damage and any associated distress caused by the **loss, destruction** or **unauthorised disclosure** of data about himself or herself or by **inaccurate data** about himself or herself.

(b) A data subject may apply to the courts for **inaccurate data** to be **put right** or even **wiped off** the data user's files altogether. Such applications may also be made to the Registrar.

(c) A data subject may obtain **access** to personal data of which he is the subject. (This is known as the 'subject access' provision.) In other words, a data subject can ask to see his or her personal data that the data user is holding.

(d) A data subject can **sue** a data user (or bureau) for any **damage or distress** caused to him by personal data about him which is **incorrect** or **misleading** as to matter of **fact** (rather than opinion).

Features of the 1998 legislation are:

(a) Everyone has the right to go to court to seek redress for **any breach** of data protection law.

(b) Filing systems that are structured so as to facilitate access to information about a particular person now fall within the legislation. This includes systems that are **paper-based** or on **microfilm** or **microfiche**. Personnel records meet this classification.

(c) Processing of personal data is **forbidden** except in the following circumstances.

(i) With the **consent** of the subject. Consent cannot be implied: it must be by freely given, specific and informed agreement.

(ii) As a result of a **contractual arrangement.**

(iii) Because of a **legal obligation.**

(iv) To **protect the vital interests** of the subject.

(v) Where processing is in the **public interest.**

(vi) Where processing is required to exercise **official authority.**

(d) The processing of '**sensitive data**' is forbidden, unless express consent has been obtained or there are conflicting obligations under employment law.

Sensitive data includes data relating to **racial origin, political opinions, religious beliefs,** physical or mental **health, sexual proclivities** and **trade union** membership.

(e) If data about a data subject is **obtained from a third party** the data subject must be given.

   (i) The identity of the **controller** of the data.

   (ii) The **purposes** for which the data are being processed.

   (iii) **What data** will be disclosed and **to whom.**

   (iv) The existence of a right of subject **access** to the data.

(f) Data subjects have a right not only to have a **copy of data** held about them but also the right to know **why** the data are being processed and **what is the logic** behind the processing.

The 1998 Act provided for a transitional period for data controllers to bring existing systems into line with the new law. The Act finally came into force on March 1 2000, and all data controllers will have to comply fully with the Act by October 2001.

---

**Activity 3**

Your MD has asked you to recommend measures that your company, which is based in the UK, could take to ensure compliance with data protection legislation. Suggest what measures should be taken.

### 4.3 The Computer Misuse Act

The Computer Misuse Act 1990 was enacted to respond to the growing threat of hacking to computer systems and data. Hacking means obtaining unauthorised access, usually through telecommunications links (see Chapter 5). The Act can not prevent hacking, but by setting out offences and punishments it may deter some potential hackers.

| Crime | Explanation |
|---|---|
| Unauthorised access | This means that a hacker, who, knowing he or she is unauthorised, tries to gain access to another computer system. It is the **attempt** which is the crime: the hacker's success or failure is irrelevant. |
| Unauthorised access with the **intention** of committing another offence | This results in **stricter penalties** than unauthorised access alone. However, it might be a suitable charge if a hacker had been caught in the early stages of a fraud. |
| Unauthorised **modification** of data or programs | In effect this makes the deliberate introduction of computer **viruses** into a system a criminal offence. However, this does not apply to the simple addition of data, just its corruption or destruction. Guilt is based on the **intention to impair** the operation of a computer or program, or prevent or **hinder access** to data. |

NOTES

*Hackers were identified as one of the security issues associated with the Internet in Chapter 5.*

## Chapter roundup

- **Security** is the protection of data from accidental or deliberate threats and the protection of an information system from such threats.

- **Physical threats** to security may be natural or man made. They include fire,

- flooding, weather, lightning, terrorist activity and accidental damage.

- **Physical access control** attempts to stop **intruders** or other unauthorised persons getting near to computer equipment or storage media.

- Important aspects of physical access of control are **door locks** and **card entry systems**. Computer theft is becoming more prevalent as equipment becomes smaller and more portable. All computer equipment should be tagged and registered, and portable items should be logged in and out.

- **Privacy** is the right of the individual not to have information about him or her disclosed in an unauthorised manner.

- The **Data Protection Act 1998** is a piece of UK legislation which protects individuals about whom data is held. Both manual and computerised information must comply with the Act.

    ○ Data users must register with the Data Protection Registrar and announce the uses to which the data will be put.

    ○ The Act contains eight data protection principles, to which all data users must adhere.

- The **Computer Misuse Act 1990** was enacted in the UK to respond to the growing threat to computer systems and data from hacking. While it cannot *prevent* hacking, it recognises a number of offences and provides certain punishments.

## Quick quiz

1   List six aspects of security. (See section 1.1)

2   How can fire be guarded against? (See section 2.1)

3   Should a mainframe computer be based in the basement? (See section 2.2)

4   How can problems caused by lightning be combated? (See section 2.4)

5   How can the risk of accidental damage be minimised? (See section 2.6)

6   List three methods of controlling access. (See section 3.1)

7   Define privacy. (See section 4)

8   What is a data user? (See section 4.2)

9   Summarise the eight data protection principles? (See section 4.2)

## Answers to Activities

1    (a)    **Fire**. Fire security measures can usefully be categorised as preventative, detective and corrective. Preventative measures include siting of the computer in a building constructed of suitable materials and the use of a site which is not affected by the storage of inflammable materials (eg chemicals). Detective measures involve the use of smoke detectors. Corrective measures may include installation of a sprinkler system, training of fire officers and good siting of exit signs and fire extinguishers.

       (b)    **Flooding**. Water damage may result from flooding or from fire recovery procedures. The main rule is to avoid siting the computer in a basement.

2    (a)    'Postcode' all pieces of hardware. Invisible ink postcoding is popular, but visible marking is a better deterrent. Soldering irons are ideal for writing on plastic casing.

       (b)    Mark the equipment in other ways. Some organisations spray their hardware with permanent paint, perhaps in a particular colour (bright red is popular) or using stencilled shapes.

       (c)    Hardware can be bolted to desks. If bolts are passed through the desk and through the bottom of the hardware casing, the equipment can be rendered immobile.

       (d)    Ensure that the organisation's standard security procedures (magnetic passes, keypad access to offices, signing in of visitors etc) are followed.

3    Measures could include the following.

- Obtain consent from individuals to hold any sensitive personal data you need.

- Supply individuals with a copy of any manual files you have about them if so requested.

- Consider if you may need to obtain consent to process personal data, on computer, paper or microfiche.

- Consider how you will be able to meet the notification requirements of the Directive in situations where you obtain personal data about individuals from third parties.

### Further question practice

*Now try the following practice question at the end of this text.*

Exam style question    **8**

# Chapter 9 :
# THE IMPACT OF THE IT REVOLUTION

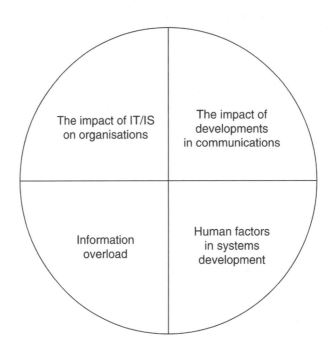

### Introduction

The impact of technology on organisations and society in general over the last ten years has been dramatic.

This chapter explores some of the wider issues arising from this rapid change.

### Your objectives

After completing this chapter you should be able to:

    (a)    Identify and evaluate the impact of developments in telecommunications.

    (b)    Recommend strategies for managing change in an IT context.

# 1 THE IMPACT OF INFORMATION TECHNOLOGY/ INFORMATION SYSTEMS ON ORGANISATIONS

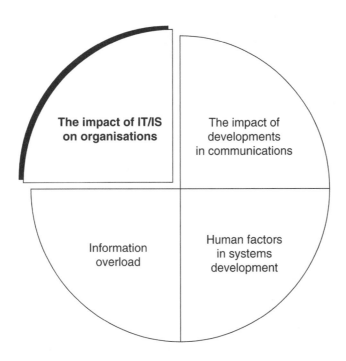

## 1.1 The organisational implications of office automation

Office automation in a variety of ways. Many of these are discussed at greater length elsewhere in this book; further points are outlined below.

*Routine processing*

The processing of routine data can be done in **bigger volumes**, at **greater speed** and with **greater accuracy** than with non-automated, manual systems.

*The paperless office*

There might be less paper in the office (but not necessarily so) with more data-processing done by keyboard. Data transmission is likely to shift from moving paper to moving data electronically. Files are more likely to be magnetic files or microform files rather than paper files.

*Staff issues*

Office staff will be affected by computerisation. The behavioural or 'human' aspects of installing a computer system are potentially fairly complex, but broadly speaking the following should be considered.

(a) Office staff must show a **greater computer awareness**, especially in areas of the office where computerisation is most likely to occur first - typically the accounts department.

(b) Staff must **learn new habits**, such as the care of floppy disks and VDUs, how to use keyboards, and remembering to make back-up copies of files for data security purposes.

(c) Managers may have to **learn to work at a workstation**, otherwise they will be less skilled than their staff.

*Management information*

The **nature and quality of management information** changes.

(a) Managers have access to **more information** - for example from a database. Information is also likely to be more accurate, reliable and up-to-date. The range of management reports is likely to be wider and their content more comprehensive.

(b) **Planning activities should be more thorough**, with the use of models (eg spreadsheets for budgeting) and sensitivity analysis.

(c) Information for **control** should be more readily available. For example, a computerised sales ledger system should provide prompt reminder letters for late payers, and might incorporate other credit control routines.

(d) Decision making by managers can be helped by **decision support systems**.

*Organisation structure*

The organisation structure might change. PCs give local office managers a means of setting up a **good local management information system**, and localised data processing. Multi-user systems and distributed data processing systems also put more data processing and information processing 'power' into the local office, giving local managers access to centrally-held databases and programs. Office automation can therefore encourage a **tendency towards decentralisation** of authority within an organisation.

On the other hand, multi-user systems and distributed data processing systems help **head office to keep in touch** with what is going on in local offices. Head office can therefore readily **monitor and control** the activities of individual departments, and retain a co-ordinating influence. It can therefore be possible for a head office to retain a co-ordinating (centralising) role, and to manage an expanding organisation with reasonable efficiency. Arguably, mega-mergers between large companies are only possible with the computerisation of management information systems.

*Technological change*

Office automation commits an organisation to **continual change**. The pace of technological change is rapid, and computer systems - both hardware and software - are likely to be superseded after a few years by something even better. Computer maintenance engineers are anyway often unwilling to enter into maintenance contracts for hardware which is more than a few years old, and so organisations are forced to consider a policy of regular replacement of hardware systems.

*Customer service*

Office automation, in some organisations, results in **better customer service**. When an organisation receives large numbers of telephone enquiries from customers, the staff who take the calls should be able to provide a prompt and helpful service if they have on-line access to the organisation's data files.

*Open systems*

Organisations develop computerised systems over a period of time, perhaps focusing on different functions at different times, and a number of consequences are likely to become apparent.

(a) They may have networks or other equipment supplied by a **range of manufacturers**.

(b) **Data is duplicated** in different areas of the business.

(c) Software may have become **inefficient** and **out of date.**

**Open systems** aim to ensure compatibility between different makes of equipment, enabling users to choose on the basis of price and performance. An open systems approach has a number of characteristics. The first is **vendor independence**. Applications can be 'ported' from one system to another. An open systems infrastructure supports **organisation-wide functions** and allows interoperability of networks and systems. Authorised users would be able to access applications and data from any part of the system.

# 2 THE IMPACT OF DEVELOPMENTS IN TELECOMMUNICATIONS

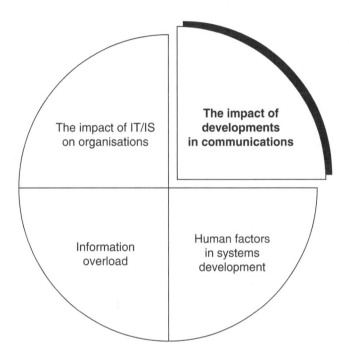

**Communications technology** is probably having a greater impact on organisational life than computers are at present. E-mail, videoconferencing and so on offer considerable benefits, but also have drawbacks.

*We talked about the practical use and advantages of e-mail in Chapter 7. We will now explore some of the wider issues associated with the widespread use of e-mail.*

## 2.1 The impact and possible drawbacks of e-mail

In spite of its advantages e-mail may not always be the best medium for communications. Possible shortcomings are as follows.

(a)   The nature of the **medium**. E-mail allows communication in the form of written words, numbers or graphics. Communication however entails more than just symbols of this type: it is estimated that perhaps 50% of the meaning that people are able to impart to each other in face-to-face conversation is non-verbal. Meaning is conveyed by body language and tone of voice to a much larger extent than is generally realised.

(b)   The nature of the **message**. People may wish to discuss detailed operational problems, whereas e-mail is best suited to short messages. Immediate two-

 **PUBLISHING**

way exchange of information is possible, but it will be hampered by the need to type in messages on a keyboard, especially if the users are not particularly competent typists.

(c)   E-mail is a relatively **permanent** means of communication. It is likely that all exchanges are recorded and can be read by others. This may be undesirable from the point of view of users since some of their exchanges may be 'off the record', for example short-cuts that get round organisational bureaucracy, but solve operational difficulties.

(d)   Senior managers may **value meetings** because they take place outside the main place of work, meaning that they are free of the usual daily pressures and better able to take an overview of the operations they manage.

(e)   Large amounts of e-mail are likely to be received each day. Staff may quickly find themselves suffering from **information overload**. They will either spend excessive amounts of time dealing with e-mail or they will skip over much of the mail they receive and possibly miss important points.

(f)   It is **uncomfortable to read** much more than a screen-full of information. Longer messages will either not be read properly or they will be printed out, in which case they may just as well have been circulated in hard copy form in the first place.

(g)   **No distinction is made between different types of communication**. A short chatty message that might in the past have been scribbled on a Post-it note, is delivered in the same format and through the same medium as an important two page report.

(h)   Depending on the system in use, the **facilities for data presentation** in an e-mail message may not be as sophisticated as they are in a spreadsheet or word processing application.

## 2.2   Voice mail

Voice mail (or v-mail) systems enable the **caller's message to be recorded at the recipient's voice mail box** similar to a mail box in an e-mail system. The main advantage of the system is that it only requires a telephone to be used. No typing or keying in is necessary. A voice mail message is basically a spoken memo: for the person sending the message it is much more convenient than typing it or having it typed and then faxing it.

Some companies allow their clients to use their voice mail network to leave messages for company representatives. The advantage of voice mail messages, compared to cellular radio or mobile communications, is that it is relatively cheap. However, it is **not suitable for conversations**. Voice mail can be used for different situations.

(a)   To contact sales representatives 'in the field'.

(b)   To leave messages in departments in **different time zones**.

(c)   In organisations where employees might be **working away at a client's premises**.

## 2.3   Voice messaging

This is a kind of **switchboard answerphone** that takes the place of a human receptionist, or at least relieves the receptionist of the burden of dealing with common, straightforward calls. Typically, when a call is answered a recorded message tells the caller to dial the extension they want if they know it, or to hold if they want to speak to the operator. Sometimes other options are offered, such as 'press 2 if you want to know about X service and 3 if you want to know about Y'.

Such systems **work well if callers frequently have similar needs** and these can be accurately anticipated. They can be **frustrating** for callers with non-standard enquiries, however, and many people find the **impersonality** of responding to an answerphone unappealing. Badly set up systems can result in the caller being bounced about from one recorded message to another and never getting through to the person they want to deal with.

## FOR DISCUSSION

Most people have experienced the frustration of being stuck in what seems like an endless 'phone-loop'. What features should a well-designed automated call-managing system have?

## EXAMPLE: INTERACTIVE VOICE RESPONSE (IVR)

Several pharmaceutical companies have installed sophisticated interactive voice response systems to deal with enquiries from doctors, chemists or patients. For example some allow the caller to press a number on their handset and have details of possible side effects sent back to them by fax.

## 2.4    Computer Telephony Integration (CTI)

**Definition**

> **Computer Telephony Integration (CTI)** systems gather information about callers such as their telephone number and customer account number or demographic information (age, income, interests etc).

The information is stored on a customer database and can be **called up and sent to the screen of the person dealing with the call**, perhaps before the call has even been put through.

Thus sales staff dealing with hundreds of calls every day might **appear to remember individual callers personally** and know in advance what they are likely to order. Order forms with key details entered already can be displayed on screen automatically, saving time for both the sales staff and the caller.

Alternatively a busy manager might note that an **unwelcome call** is coming in on the 'screen pop' that appears on her PC and choose to direct it to her voice mail box rather than dealing with it at once.

As another example, a bank might use CTI to prompt sales people with changes in share prices and with the details of the investors they should call to offer dealing advice.

Business Basics: Information Technology

## 2.5 Facsimile

Facsimile transmission (or fax) has been in widespread use since the mid 1980s. Fax involves the transmission by data link of documents. The original is fed into the fax machine, which 'reads' it and converts it into electronic form so it can be transmitted over the telephone. The latest fax machines can also be used as scanners, as printers for PC output and as photocopiers.

Alternatively a PC can be fitted with a fax modem, allowing data to be transmitted directly from the PC . However, PCs are unable to receive fax messages when turned off. Standard fax machines tend to be left on 24 hours.

Facsimile helped encourage the trend towards **speed** in business. People no longer had to wait for documents to be posted. This thirst for **instant service** has continued.

## 2.6 Data transmission

We will now explain the workings of some developments in communications technology that have contributed to the impact of IT.

A data transmission link might connect:

(a) A central computer and a remote terminal. A computer may have a number of remote terminals linked to it by data transmission equipment.

(b) Two computers located some distance from each other (for example a mainframe and a PC, which would use the link to exchange data) .

(c) Several processors in a network, with each computer in the network able to transmit data to any other.

Who provides the telecommunications link?

In the UK, British Telecom, Mercury and a range of newer suppliers (eg. NTL) provide services for the transmission of data. Public or private lines may be used.

Public lines use the ordinary telephone network. The cost is dependent upon the service used and the time the telephone link is maintained (as for any ordinary telephone call).

Private lines also use the telephone network but a special line is provided at a fixed charge per annum.

Data transmission media include:

(a) Copper wire. The simplest type of communications channel in use is a telephone line made of copper wire. This is in fact a 'twisted pair' of cables. It has low transmission rates and a relatively high error rate because there is only minimal anti-interference screening.

(b) Coaxial cable. Coaxial cable, similar to domestic television aerial cable, gives significantly better performance than twisted pair cable, as there is less risk of distortion of data at higher rates of transmission. Heavier grades of cable allow broadband transmission, increasing the number of signals which can be carried simultaneously.

(c) Fibre-optic cable. Fibre-optic cable is virtually interference-free and has extremely high data transmission rates (up to 1 billion bits per second). It is popular in WANs, but less widely used in LANs because it is a relatively high cost option.

The principle of fibre optics is that data is transmitted through very fine glass fibres. Transducers covert electrical pulses to light and back again at each end of the cable. The advantages of fibre-optic cable are as follows.

- High bandwidth supports high transmission rates
- Low cross-talk (interference between adjacent cables)
- No interference from external electrical sources
- High reliability
- No danger from electricity, heat or sparks

*Microwave*

Microwaves are ultra high frequency UHF radio signals. Microwaves can be transmitted between radio transmitters and receivers which are in sight of each other. Each of these relay stations is known as a repeater. Repeaters are sited to create a network along which signals can be sent. The ultra high frequency nature of microwaves minimises distortion.

*Satellite*

Microwave is limited by the requirement for base stations to be sited in line-of-sight of each other. Inland, strategic positioning on hills and other high ground can overcome problems, but transmission over the ocean is not possible. This problem is overcome by the use of satellites. Each satellite maintains a constant position in relation to the earth's surface; this is referred to as a geosynchronous orbit. Radio transmissions are received by the satellite, which includes a repeater and an amplifier, to boost the signal, and send it onwards to receivers on another continent.

*Bandwidth*

The amount of data that can be sent down a telecommunications line is in part determined by the bandwidth. Bandwidth is the range of frequencies that the channel can carry. Frequencies are measured in cycles per second, or in Hertz. There are three ranges.

- Narrow band (up to 300 Hertz)
- Voice band (300-3,000 Hertz)
- Broad band (over 3,000 Hertz)

The wider the bandwidth, the greater the number of messages that a channel can carry at any particular time. Broad bandwidth enables messages to be transmitted simultaneously.

*Data switching*

When communication between a number of computers (and terminals) which will transmit data to each other in an irregular and unpredictable way is required, a data switching arrangement is used.

A switch is a device for opening, closing or directing an electric circuit. A telecommunications link is a circuit like any other: when you are speaking to someone over the telephone a circuit exists between the two devices. In the telephone network, switches connect one set of lines to another.

**Circuit switching** occurs when the connection is maintained until broken at one end. If data is sent simply by circuit switching, the line between the sender and the recipient must be open for the duration of the message. As much data transmission is irregular, this is a wasteful use of the telephone line. Gaps in transmission of your message, when the line is idle, could be used by somebody else. Similarly, you may wish to transmit your data at a time when there is nobody on the other end of the line to receive it.

**Message switching** requires no direct physical connection between sender and receiver before communication can take place, as the message is stored on a central computer or switching station before being forwarded to another switching station and ultimately to its destination. A message can be sent even though the destination is not able at that time to receive it. (It is also known as the store-and-forward technique).

Data can also be sent over a packet switching system. The PSN (UK Public Packet Switched Network) is run by British Telecom. A data message is divided up into packets of data of a fixed length, usually 128 bytes, and transmitted through the network in separate packets. Each packet contains control data, which identifies the sender of the message and the address of the recipient. Each processor receives packets of data from another processor in the network, and redirects them to the next processor along the chain.At the 'local' end of the PSN link (ie. the end near the recipient of the message) the packets of data are reassembled into their full message.

*Protocols*

One of the big problems in transmitting data down a public or private telephone wire is the possibility of distortion or loss of the message. There needs to be some way for a computer to:

(a) Detect whether there are errors in data transmission (eg loss of data, or data arriving out of sequence) .

(b) Take steps to recover the lost data, even if this is simply to notify the operator to re-transmit. More 'sophisticated' systems can identify the corrupted or lost data more specifically, and request re-transmission of only the lost or distorted parts.

The mechanism used to detect and usually then to correct errors is known as a communications protocol. Protocol is defined as 'an agreed set of operational procedures governing the format of data being transferred, and the signals initiating, controlling and terminating the transfer.'

Factors covered by a protocol include the mode and speed of transmission, the format of the data and error detection and correction procedures

New technologies require **transmission systems** capable of delivering substantial quantities of data at great speed. For data transmission through the existing 'analogue' telephone network to be possible, there has to be a device at each end of the telephone line that can convert (MOdulate) the data from digital form to analogue form, and (DEModulate) from analogue form to digital form. This conversion of data is done by devices called **modems**. There must be a modem at each end of the telephone line.

**Definition**

> **Digital** means 'of digits or numbers'. Digital data is information in a coded (binary) form. Data in **analogue** form uses continuously variable signals.

An ongoing development is the introduction of **Integrated Systems Digital Networks** *(ISDN)*, which in effect will eventually make the entire telephone network **digital**. It will therefore be possible to send **voice, data, video and fax** communications from a single desktop computer system over the telecommunication link, without using a modem. The speed of data transfer with ISDN is significantly faster than with standard lines.

**ADSL** (Asymmetric Digital Subscriber Line), now in trial in a number of countries including the UK, offers data transfer rates of up to **8 Mbps**, considerably faster than ISDN. ADSL allows information to be sent out over ordinary copper wires and simultaneous use of the normal telephone service is possible.

## 2.7 Mobile communications

**Networks** for portable telephone communications, also known as '**cellular phones**', started up in the late 1980s and have boomed ever since. Digital networks have been developed and are now operating alongside earlier transmission systems. These are better able to support data transmission then the older analogue networks, with higher transmission speeds and less likelihood of data corruption.

This means that a salesperson out on the road, say, can send or receive a fax or e-mail simply by plugging a lap-top PC into a mobile handset. A combined palmtop computer and cellular phone is already on the market, as are Web capable mobile phones utilising Wireless Application Protocol (WAP) technology.

The mobile services available are increasing all the time. Here are some examples.

(a) **Messaging services** such as: voice mail; short message service (SMS) which allows text messages of up to 160 characters to be transmitted over a standard digital phone; and paging services

(b) **Call handling services** such as: call barring, conference calls and call divert

(c) **Corporate services** such as: integrated numbering, so that people have a single contact number for both the phone on their desk and for their mobile; and virtual private networks that incorporate mobile phones as well as conventional desktop phones, so that users can dial internal extension numbers directly.

(d) **Internet access.** The speed of transmission when downloading information is relatively slow at present, but improving. **Wireless Application Protocal (WAP)** technology will make parts of the Internet accessible using a mobile phone.

(e) Satellite technology enables some mobile phones to 'roam' (ie be used) in many countries around the world - rather than only in the 'country of issue'.

## 2.8 Computer conferencing and bulletin boards

A computer conferencing system is similar to e-mail in that there is a huge central mailbox on the system where all persons connected to the system can **deposit messages** for everyone to see, and, in turn, **read what other people have left** in the system.

Computer conferencing can be appropriate for a team of individuals at different locations to compare notes. It becomes a way of keeping track of progress on a **project** between routine team meetings.

Computer conferencing systems can become **organisation-wide bulletin boards**. A bulletin board system can be a way of re-establishing some of the **social ties** of office life which are alleged to have suffered from computerisation.

## 2.9 Video conferencing

Videoconferencing is the use of computer and communications technology to **conduct meetings** in which several participants, perhaps in different parts of the world, are linked up via **computer and a video system**. (Conference calls on a **telephone system**, where several people can converse at the same time, are a precursor of teleconferencing.)

Videoconferencing has become increasingly common as the ready availability of chips capable of processing video images has brought the service to desktop PCs at reasonable cost. More expensive systems feature a **separate room with several video screens**, which show the images of those participating in a meeting.

Even if the technology used is expensive, it is far **cheaper** when compared to the cost in management time and air fares of business **travel**.

### 2.10 Electronic data interchange (EDI)

Electronic data interchange (EDI) is a form of computer-to-computer **data** interchange. Instead of sending each other reams of paper in the form of invoices, statements and so on, details of inter-company transactions are sent via telecoms links, **avoiding the need for output** and paper at the sending end, and **for re-keying of data** at the receiving end.

The general concept of having one computer talk directly to another might seem straightforward enough in principle, but in practice there are two major **difficulties**.

(a) Each business wants to produce documents (and hold records on file) to its own **individual requirements** and structure. Thus a computer of X Ltd could not transmit data to a computer of Y Ltd because the records/data transmitted **would not be in a format or structure** to suit Y Ltd.

(b) Businesses may work to differing **time schedules,** especially when they are engaged in international trade. If a London company's computer wants to send a message to a computer in San Francisco, the San Francisco computer might not be switched on or otherwise able to receive the message.

Until recently different makes of computer could not easily 'talk' to each other. The problem of **compatibility** between different makes of computer was a serious one, and some form of interface between the computers had to be devised to enable data interchange to take place. This is less and less of a problem as businesses adopt common standards and set up sites on the **Internet.**

EDI encourages **closer links** between business partners.

## 3  HUMAN FACTORS IN SYSTEMS DEVELOPMENT

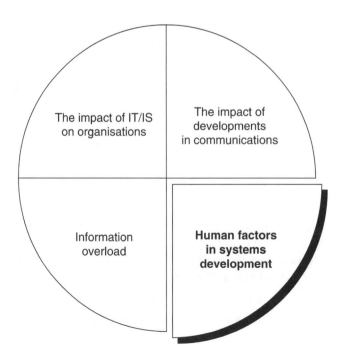

IT is by nature an area that changes constantly. This means that once automated (a big change in itself), a process will then undergo frequent changes as technology develops.

Whatever the scale of **systems development** – whether a manager who is not computer literate acquires a PC for departmental planning and ends up using it just to type memos, or whether a complex production planning and control system in a large manufacturing concern is computerised - there will inevitably be **challenges**, not only for the individuals using computers, but for other staff whose jobs interact with theirs.

## 3.1 Job security and status

Employees might think that a new system will **put them out of a job**, because the computer will perform routines that are currently done manually, and so reduce the need for human intervention. An office staff of, say, 10 people might be reduced to 8, and the threat of being out of work would unsettle the entire office staff. Even when there is no threat of losing a job, a new system might make some staff, experienced in the existing system, **feel that all their experience will be worthless** when the new system goes live, and so they will **lose 'status'** within the office.

In some cases, the resistance to a new system might stem from a fear that it will result in a loss of status for the **department** concerned. For example, the management of the department concerned might believe that a computer system will give 'control' over information gathering and dissemination to another group in the organisation. **Dysfunctional behaviour** might therefore find expression in:

(a) Interdepartmental disputes about access to information.
(b) A tendency to disregard the new sources of information.

## 3.2 Career prospects

In some instances, managers and staff might think that a new system will damage their career prospects by **reducing the opportunities for promotion**. When the effect of a system is to reduce the requirement for staff in **middle management and supervisory grades,** this could well be true. On the other hand, today's successful manager should be able to adapt to information technology, and to develop a career means having to be flexible, accepting change rather than resisting it.

## 3.3 Social change in the office

New systems might **disrupt the established 'social system'** or 'team spirit' in the office. Individuals who are used to working together might be separated into different groups, and individuals used to working on their own might be expected to join a group. Office staff used to moving around and mixing with other people in the course of their work might be faced with the prospect of having to work much **more in isolation** at a keyboard, unable to move around the office as much.

Where possible, therefore new systems should be designed so as to leave the 'social fabric' of the workplace undamaged. Group attitudes to change should then be positive rather than negative.

## 3.4 Bewilderment

It is easy for individuals to be confused and bewildered by change. The systems analyst must **explain the new system fully,** inviting and answering questions from an early stage.

### 3.5 Fear of depersonalisation

Staff may be afraid that the computer will 'take over' and they will be **reduced to being operators** chained to the machine.

Dysfunctional behaviour might manifest itself in the **antagonism of operating staff towards** those employed to introduce the new system. It might take the form of:

(a) An **unwillingness to explain the details of the current system**, any such antagonism would impair the new system design.

(b) A **reluctance to be taught** the new system.

(c) A **reluctance to help** with introducing the new system.

Another fear is that the investigation will **show how poor and inefficient** previous methods of information gathering and information use had been. If individuals feel that they are put under pressure by the revelation of any such deficiencies, they **might try to find fault with the new system** too. When fault-finding is not constructive - ie not aimed at improving the system - it will be dysfunctional in its consequences.

### 3.6 Overcoming the human problems

Hostility to IT is as much an issue in management culture as it is in industrial relations. To overcome the human problems with systems design and implementation, management and systems analysts must recognise them, and do what they can to resolve them. The following checklist is suggested as a starting point.

(a) **Keeping staff informed.**

Employees should be kept fully informed about plans to install the new system, how events are progressing and how the new system will affect what people do.

(b) **Explanations.**

It should be explained to staff why 'change is for the better'.

(c) **Participation.**

User department employees should be encouraged to participate fully in the design of the system, when the system is a tailor-made one. Participation should be genuine.

(i) Their suggestions about problems with the existing system should be fully discussed.

(ii) The systems analyst's ideas for a new system should be discussed with them.

(ii) Their suggestions for features in the new system should be welcomed.

(d) **Nature of the work.**

Staff should be informed that they will be spared boring, mundane work because of the possibility of automating such work and so will be able to take on more interesting, demanding and challenging work.

(e) **Skills.**

Employees should be told that they will be able to learn new skills which will make them more attractive candidates either for internal promotion or on the external labour market. For example, experience with using databases or spreadsheet models could greatly enhance an office worker's experience.

(f) **Training.**

A training programme for staff should be planned in advance of the new systems being introduced. If there are to be job losses, or a redeployment of staff, these should be arranged in full consultation with the people concerned.

(g) **Work patterns.**

Careful attention should be given to:

(i) The design of work organisation.

(ii) The developments or preservation of 'social work groups'.

(iii) The inter-relationship between jobs and responsibilities in the new system.

(h) **Planning.**

Change should be planned and managed. Reductions in jobs should be foreseen, and redundancies can be avoided if plans are made well in advance (eg staff can be moved to other job vacancies in the organisation). Training (and retraining) of staff should be organised.

(i) **Office expert.**

A member of the staff should be appointed as the office expert or 'guru' in the system, to whom other members of staff can go to ask for help or advice. When the software is bought as an off-the-shelf package, this office expert should be made the person who contacts the software supplier about any problems with the system.

(j) **The analyst.**

When systems are designed in-house, the systems analyst should:

(i) Produce changes gradually, giving time for personnel to accept the changes.

(ii) Build up a good personal relationship with the people he or she has to work with.

(iii) Persuade management to give sound guarantees for the future.

(iv) Work towards getting employees to accept change as a matter of course.

(v) Be willing to listen to and act on criticisms of the system under design.

(k) **Familiarisation.**

The system should not be introduced in a rush. Users of the system should be given time to become familiar with it. Implementation by means of 'parallel running' might be advisable.

(l) **Confidence.**

Confidence between the systems analyst and operational staff should be built up over time.

(m) **Management support.**

The systems analyst should have the full and clearly expressed support of senior management. There should be no danger that his authority could be undermined.

Business Basics: Information Technology

## 4 INFORMATION OVERLOAD

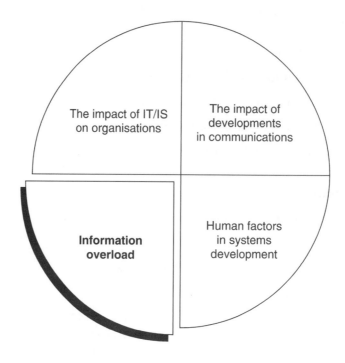

### 4.1 Too much information?

The volume of information a human being is required to process has increased dramatically over the last twenty years. Computing and communications developments have led to the capture and transmission of ever increasing amounts of information. However, only relevant information is useful. An excess of irrelevant information is harmful - a person is more likely to miss or miss-interpret vital information after being swamped with irrelevant material.

Technological developments such as e-mail adds to the problem. Now that everyone uses it, it often seems not much easier to get a reply to an e-mail message than to a phone message. In-boxes get stuffed with junk e-mails and are frequently ignored by their owners.

As a reaction to information overload new forms of software which carry out the extraction, organisation and selection of information for the **needs of the individual user** have been developed. A principal aim of the research and development going on in this area is to develop personalised information and message services, so that people receive the material which they require and nothing else.

There are two main approaches to avoiding information overload. Firstly, the **characteristics of the information passed to a human information processor** need to be considered. Secondly the **number of information sources** feeding an individual can be managed.

*The qualities of information*

***The qualities of information were covered in Chapter 1. Refer to Chapter 1, Section 2.3.***

## 4.2 Limiting the number of information sources

The approach taken to limiting the sources of information will depend on the situation. In some instances it may be sufficient to implement temporary measures to **delay** non-urgent information reaching a person at a particularly busy time. Other situations may require a **permanent change** to information flows. Some examples are shown in the following table.

| Limiting tool | Comment |
| --- | --- |
| **Delegate to colleagues** | Communications regarding certain issues may be dealt with by others within the organisation. For example, routine client contact could be delegated to junior staff, and only strategic issues referred 'up the chain'. |
| **Review reports received for duplication** | Regular reviews of information received should be made. If information is duplicated one source should be deleted. The review should also consider what information would best be received together to aid interpretation. |
| **Re-route incoming telephone calls** | A secretary could be allocated to take telephone messages, putting through only calls of significance that require immediate attention. To be effective, the instructions concerning calls that should be put through, and how messages should be relayed must be specific. |
| **Voice-mail** | While voice-mail can be frustrating when trying to reach someone, it may be useful to temporarily divert calls to voice-mail when work pressures require no interruptions - and no other staff are available to divert calls to. |
| **Filter incoming e-mail** | E-mail programs have the ability to review and re-direct messages based on the message content, priority, sender and/or intended recipients. Non-selected messages may be copied to a selected person, or redirected to a non-urgent inbox to be dealt with later. |
| **Use an Internet news-clipping service** | A person may face a constant stream of industry related journals. These should be reviewed for relevant information - a time-consuming process. However, a news-clipping service could review relevant journals and newspapers on the Internet, and forward via e-mail copies of articles that meet user-defined criteria. |
| **Use intelligent agents** | These are programs that the user can set-up to perform tasks such as retrieving and delivering relevant information and automating repetitive tasks. |

### Activity

Think about the information you receive and the information you produce in your work or study. Could the volume of information or the number of information sources be reduced without reducing the quality of information?

**Chapter roundup**

- The world has changed rapidly over the past thirty years. The **communications age** has arrived, and is still developing at a rapid rate.

- The Internet has the potential to bring about significant **changes in society** as a whole.

- Technology has also had a significant impact **on the way organisations are structured**, and on the roles of staff.

- Communications developments are making **geographically dispersed structures** increasingly viable.

- The almost **constant change** prevalent in organisations and society as a whole is placing greater **demands on people**.

- People are now exposed to greater volumes and sources of information than ever before. If information flows aren't managed efficiently, **information overload** may occur.

**Quick quiz**

1   Why are automated systems more efficient in the processing of routine data? (See section 1.1)

2   What staff issues need to be considered in an office being computerised? (See section 1.1)

3   List five possible disadvantages of e-mail. (See section 2.1)

4   Distinguish between voice mail and voice messaging. (See sections 2.2-2.3)

5   What does CTI stand for? (See section 2.4)

6   Outline the concerns staff may have when a new system is proposed. (See section 3.1-3.5)

7   How may those fears be overcome? (See section 3.6)

8   Can too much information hinder understanding? (See section 4.1)

9   List five methods that could reduce the number of information flows reaching an individual. (See section 4.2)

**Answers to Activities**

1   You may be able to use some of the techniques explained in section 4.2 to combat information overload. Be careful not to 'cut' information that is needed immediately and is not provided from another source.

**Further question practice**

*Now try the following practice question at the end of this text.*
Exam style question            **9**

**Multiple choice questions**

Ensure you work through the multiple choice questions, covering the whole Text, at the back of the book.

# Glossary

202

**Acceptance testing**: testing of a system by the user department, after the system has passed its systems test.

**Adaptive maintenance**: taking account of anticipated changes in the processing environment.

**Bandwidth**: the range of frequencies that a telecommunications line can carry.

**Bespoke package**: a software package designed and written for a specific situation or task. May be written 'in-house' or by an external software house.

**Business system:** collection of people, machines and methods organised to accomplish a set of specific functions.

**Client:** machine which requests a service from the server.

**Closed system:** system which is isolated from its environment and independent of it.

**Computer supported co-operative**: term which combines the understanding of the way people work in groups with the enabling technologies of computer networking and associated hardware, software, services and techniques.

**Computer Telephony Integration (CTI)**: a system which gathers information about callers such as their telephone number and customer account number of demographic information (age, income, interests etc).

**Corrective maintenance**: is carried out in reaction to a system failure, for example in processing or in an implementation procedure, its objective is to ensure that systems remain operational.

**Critical success factors**: the key areas of the job where things must go right for the organisation to flourish.

**Data**: the raw material for data processing.

**Data dictionary**: an index of data held in a database, used to assist in maintenance and any other access to the data.

**Data redundancy**: duplication of data items.

**Data subject**: an individual who is the subject of personal data.

**Data table**: used by some spreadsheet packages (for example Excel) to refer to a group of cells that show the results of changing the value of variables.

**Data users**: organisations or individuals who control the contents of files of personal data and the use of personal data which is processed automatically.

**Database**: a collection of structured data which may be manipulated to select or sort some or all of the data held.

**Digital**: digital data is coded in binary form. Only two states are present in digital data.

**Distributed system**: combines processing hardware located at a central place (eg a mainframe) with other, usually smaller computers located at various sites.

**Documentation**: a wide range of technical and non-technical books, manuals, descriptions and diagrams relating to the use and operation of a computer system.

**Electronic commerce**: the process of trading on the Internet.

**Electronic mail (E-mail):** various systems of sending data or messages electronically via a telephone or data network and a central computer.

**Encryption**: involves scrambling the data at one end of the line, transmitting the scrambled data, and unscrambling it at the receiver's end of the line.

**Environmental scanning**: is used to describe the process of gathering external information.

**Extranet**: an intranet that is accessible to authorised outsiders.

**Feasibility**: a formal study to decide what type of system can be developed which meets the needs of the organisation.

**Feedback**: modification or control of a process or system by its results or effects, by measuring differences between desired and actual results.

**File conversion**: converting existing files into a format suitable for the new system.

**Filtering**: removing 'impurities' such as excessive detail from data as it is passed up the organisation hierarchy.

**Fourth generation language (4GL)**: loosely denotes software which enables systems designers to 'write' a program with little programming knowledge.

**Groupware**: is a term used to describe a collection of IT tools designed for the use of co-operative or collaborative work groups.

**Information**: data that has been processed in such a way as to be meaningful to the person who receives it.

**Information technology**: the coming together of computer technology with data transmission technology, to revolutionise information systems.

**Integrated software**: programs, or packages of programs that perform a variety of different processing operations.

**Internet**: a global network allowing millions of computers around the world to communicate.

**Intranet**: an internal network used to share information. Intranets often utilise Internet 'styles' and protocols.

**Knowledge**: is information within people's minds.

**Knowledge management**: describes the process of collecting, storing and using the knowledge held within an organisation.

**Management information system (MIS)**: converts data from internal and external sources into information, and communicates that information in an appropriate form to managers at all levels.

**Methodology**: procedures, techniques, tools and documentation aids which help systems developers in their efforts to implement a new information system.

**Modem**: a device attached to a telephone line to enable digital data to be transmitted over analogue lines.

**Network**: an interconnected collection of autonomous processors.

**Off-line testing**: describes the testing of a software program carried out on machines not controlled by the central processor.

**Off-the-shelf package**: a software program (or group of programs) that is sold to a wide range of users and intended to handle the most common user requirements.

**On-line testing**: testing carried out under the control of the principal central processor.

**Open system**: a system connected to an interacting with its environment.

**Perfective maintenance**: is carried out in order to perfect the software, or to improve software so that the processing inefficiencies are eliminated and performance is enhanced.

**Personal data**: information about a living individual.

**Pivot table**: an interactive table that summaries and analyses data from lists and tables.

**Privacy**: the right of the individual to control the use of information about him or her.

**Protocol**: an agreed set of operating procedures governing the format of data being tranferred.

**Prototype**: a model of all or part of a system, built to show users early in the design process how it will appear.

**Remote access**: describes access to a central computer installation from a terminal which is physically 'distant'.

**Security**: means the protection of data from accidental or deliberate threats.

**Server**: a machine which is dedicated to providing a particular function or service requested by a client.

**Spreadsheet**: a computer file in the form of an 'electronic piece of paper' divided into rows and columns. It provides an automated way of performing calculations.

**Structured data**: a collection of data, any item of which can be used as a subject of enquiry.

**System**: a set of interacting components that operate together to accomplish a purpose.

**Virus**: a piece of software which infects programs and data and possibly damages them and which replicates itself.

**Word processing**: a program used primarily to produce text based documents.

**Workflow**: a term used to describe the defined series of tasks within an organisation to produce a final outcome.

# Multiple Choice Questions

**These multiple choice questions cover the whole of this Text. They are ordered randomly – as this is how they would usually appear in an examination.**

1    A system is often subject to control. Control depends on information, and one type of information provided is *feedback*. Feedback, in systems terminology, is

    A    Information derived from sources external to the system, indicating whether the system is achieving its goals

    B    Comments and ideas for improving a system obtained from users of the system

    C    Output information generated by the system itself, and returned to the system as input

    D    External information relating to the system used as input for control purposes

2    Feedback is described as being either positive or negative. When you receive positive feedback

    A    You know that everything is going according to plan
    B    You are encouraged to carry on deviation from the plan
    C    You realise you must bring yourself back in line with the plan
    D    You know that no alterations are needed to the plan

3    A payroll system is an example of

    A    A transaction processing system
    B    A decision support system
    C    A database management system
    D    An expert system

4    Which of the following is most appropriately described as control information?

    A    A report comparing actual monthly sales figures with budget
    B    A report prepared by the marketing department detailing long-term social trends
    C    A print-out detailing the day's cash receipts and payments
    D    A price list

5    Which of the following would be the most suitable field to identify as a key field?

    A    Lastname
    B    Company
    C    NI No
    D    Post code

6       A database administrator is

A       A civil servant, employed under the Data Protection Act, to ensure that public databases do not abuse confidential information about members of the public

B       A person in an organisation delegated with the task of controlling, maintaining and enhancing the database for user benefit

C       Another term for database management system

D       An item of software residing in the database management system, which provides the links between database files

7       Which of the following is *not* hardware?

A       Printer
B       CPU
C       Word for Windows
D       Keyboard

8       Which of the following is an input device?

A       Screen
B       Keyboard
C       Printer
D       CPU

9       Input, output and storage devices are often referred to as peripherals. Which of the following is *not* a peripheral?

A       Modem
B       Mouse
C       Scanner
D       Windows 98

10      Computers can be described by type. What type of computer would you usually find on a desk in an office?

A       Mainframe
B       PC
C       Supercomputer
D       Palmtop

11      A PC has three major components. Which of the following is *not* a PC component?

A       Input devices
B       CPU
C       VDU
D       Printer

12    The processor is dividend into three areas. Which of the following is *not* part of the processor?

    A      Operating system
    B      Control Unit
    C      ALU
    D      Memory

13    Memory is measured in bytes. How many bytes is 16 MB?

    A      1,024
    B      8,388,608
    C      16,777,216
    D      17,179,184

14    Computer data is frequently stored on disk. Which of the following would you expect to have the greatest storage capacity?

    A      CD ROM
    B      Floppy disk
    C      Hard disk
    D      DVD ROM

15    Floppy disks have a variety of uses. Which of these uses is *not* recommended?

    A      Storage
    B      Backup small file(s)
    C      Coaster
    D      Transportation between PCs

16    Data can be stored on a variety of mediums. Which of the following is *not* a storage medium?

    A      Mouse
    B      CD-ROM
    C      Magnetic tape
    D      Zip disk

17    A record can contain a number of fields. Which of the following is not a suitable field name for a customer record?

    A      Title
    B      020 7342 5768
    C      Lastname
    D      Postcode

18    Fields are usually identified as being of particular types. Which of the following would be a numeric field?

    A      Date of birth
    B      Price
    C      Phone No
    D      Catalogue number

19    Fast tapes used to create back-up files quickly are known as

    A    Tape writers
    B    Tape spoolers
    C    Tape streamers
    D    Tape copiers

20    Which of the following is *not* an advantage of magnetic disk over magnetic tape?

    A    Direct access
    B    Quicker access
    C    Suitable for internal and external storage
    D    Less chance of data corruption

21    User-friendly systems can include a number of features. Which of the following is *not* user-friendly.

    A    GUI
    B    WIMP
    C    Icons
    D    DOS

22    Documentation reading methods enable the computer to read data direct. Which of the following is *not* a document reading method?

    A    OCR
    B    OMR
    C    WISIWYG
    D    MICR

23    Which of the following is *not* true? A laser printer

    A    Can print graphics
    B    Can print in a variety of different fonts
    C    Can use continuous stationery
    D    Contains a microprocessor

24    Protocol is

    A    The way in which data is translated into a form compatible to a different computer system from the one which processed it originally

    B    A means by which access by networked microcomputers to commonly held files is governed

    C    An agreed set of operational procedures governing the format of data being transferred and the signals initiating, controlling and terminating the transfer

    D    The process by which the interface between two computer systems is efficiently managed

25    A multi-user system is

A    A system linking together several computers with their own processors

B    A system, based around one processor, that serves more than one user with apparent simultaneity

C    A data processing system of uniform stand-alone microcomputers, using standard software

D    An organisation that does data processing work for other organisations

26    Which of the following statements is *incorrect?* A Local Area Network (LAN)

A    Relies on telephone lines to link it together

B    Consists of a number of independent computers which require network software to function as a network

C    Is incapable of extensive geographical dispersion

D    Is likely to contain a central server computer

27    Which of the following is *not* a typical function of an operating system?

A    Booting

B    Translating a program from one language to another

C    Managing multi-tasking

D    File management

BPP
PUBLISHING

NOTES

PUBLISHING

**Data for questions 28-30**

You have acquired a spreadsheet package, Excel. You want to use it to devise a monthly schedule of your firm's income and expenditure over the past three months, in a format as shown below. The schedule is to be updated every month. (At the end of July, for example, the months shown will be July, June and May.) You decide that columns should represent months, with one to contain 'year-to-date' totals and each row should represent an item of income or expenditure, with a final profit figure at the bottom of each column, as in the illustration below. You also want to list the amount owing to your firm by its clients at the end of each month.

| | A | B | C | D | E |
|---|---|---|---|---|---|
| 1 | *Item* | *Total 3* | *June* | *May* | *April* |
| 2 | | *months* | | | |
| 3 | | £ | £ | £ | £ |
| 4 | Fees | | 21500 | 22000 | 22500 |
| 5 | | | | | |
| 6 | | | | | |
| 7 | Salaries | | 13500 | 12500 | 12500 |
| 8 | Postage | | 200 | 200 | 200 |
| 9 | Telephone | | 200 | 200 | 200 |
| 10 | Stationery | | 200 | 200 | 200 |
| 11 | Rent | | 1500 | 1500 | 1500 |
| 12 | Accountancy | | 300 | 200 | |
| 13 | Bank charges | | - | 400 | |
| 14 | Rates | | 600 | 600 | 600 |
| 15 | Other | | 1000 | 1200 | |
| 16 | | | | | |
| 17 | Net | | 4000 | 5000 | 6000 |
| 18 | | | | | |
| 19 | Owed by clients | | 7170 | 10995 | 9000 |
| 20 | | | | | |
| 21 | | | | | |
| 22 | | | | | |
| 23 | | | | | |

28    What should you enter in cell B4 when you construct the model, to make *best* use of the spreadsheet's facilities?

    A     66000
    B     =21500 + 22000 + 22500
    C     =SUM(C4:E4)
    D     (C:E)★4

29    Which of the following would *not* be entered in the total column, on the row entitled 'Net profit'?

    A     =B4-SUM(B7:B15)
    B     =SUM(C17:E17)
    C     B4-B7-B8-B9-B10-B11-B12-B13-B14-B15
    D     =SUM(B7:B15)+B4

30    You now wish to make your model more sophisticated, to include various items of a statistical nature. (1) The percentage change in revenue month by month is required. (2) The outstanding debt at the end of each month to be expressed as a proportion of the average daily revenue per month (assume each month has 30 days). Which of the alternatives below best expresses how you would input these requirements to your spreadsheet?

    A      (1): =(C4-D4)/D4 formatted as a percentage
           (2): =C19/(C4/30)
    B      (1): =C4-D4/D4 formatted as a percentage
           (2): =C19/C4/30
    C      (1): =C4-D4/D4 formatted as a percentage
           (2): =C19/C4/30
    D      (1): =C4-D4/D4 formatted as a percentage
           (2): =C19/(C4/30)

31    In any feasibility study the costs of a system must be estimated. Some system costs recur regularly. Others are one-off costs. One-off costs can be divided into 'capital' items and 'non-capital' items. The difference is that non-capital costs are charged in full against profit in the year the costs are incurred, whereas the 'capital' costs are spread over a number of years of the project.

Which of the following is treated as a 'capital' item?

    A      Hardware maintenance
    B      Rewiring and other installation costs
    C      Staff training
    D      Staff recruitment fees

32    An organisation with severe branches changes over the computer system in one branch first to see if the system works well. This type of systems changeover is know as

    A      Staged implementation
    B      Direct changeover
    C      Phased implementation
    D      Pilot operation

33    A situation where data is run on both old and new systems for a specified time is an example of

    A      Indirect changeover
    B      Parallel running
    C      Restricted data running
    D      Pilot operation

34    Which would be the fastest way to transmit a document from London to New York?

    A      Post
    B      Fax
    C      E-mail
    D      Telex

35    A form of electronic filing is called

    A     PABX
    B     Telex
    C     DIP
    D     EDI

36    What will *not* be reduced by telecommuting?

    A     Office rent
    B     Phone bills
    C     Travel time
    D     Conference time

37    Which of the following is *not* likely to be in the terms of reference of a feasibility study?

    A     Problem definition
    B     Establishment of key performance factors for any new system
    C     Cost benefit analysis of proposed new system (or alternative systems)
    D     Data flow analysis

38    Which of the following is a financial evaluation that is used to assess whether a systems project should be chosen, and which takes the time value of money into account as well as the full expected costs and benefits of the project?

    A     Payback
    B     Accounting return on capital employed
    C     CVP analysis
    D     DCF analysis

39    A feasibility study involves the identification of *system requirements*. Which of the following would *not* be part of this process?

    A     Deciding what processing speeds are needed
    B     Deciding what standard of output is expected
    C     Deciding the numbers and qualifications of staff who will be required by the new system
    D     Discerning the information needs of senior management

40    Which of the following will *not* be included in a feasibility report?

    A     Alternative systems considered
    B     Clear recommendation of preferred system option
    C     Implementation timescale
    D     Detailed design of proposed system

41    A disadvantage of purchasing off-the-shelf software, rather than having software custom-built from scratch, is

    A     System testing and implementation take longer
    B     Software errors will be more frequent
    C     Input errors will be more common
    D     The software may not satisfy all user needs

42  A mail-order organisation which was having difficulties recruiting clerical staff has recently computerised many of its systems using OCR as an input medium. Additionally, the sales order and stock systems have been integrated. Which of the following would be classified as an *intangible* benefit of computerisation?

    A     Savings in staff costs

    B     Better decision-making, due to more and/or better information

    C     Processing of orders more quickly resulting in fewer items being kept in a central warehouse

    D     Reduction in staff time spent correcting input errors

43  The list below shows some of the activities necessary for software development and operation in a computer system project.

*Activity*

1    Requirements analysis
2    System design
3    Program testing
4    Implementation
5    Detailed specification
6    Maintenance
7    Program writing
8    System testing

Which is the normal sequence in which these activities are carried out?

    A     1, 2, 5, 7, 3, 8, 4, 6
    B     1, 5, 2, 7, 3, 8, 4, 6
    C     1, 5, 2, 8, 7, 3, 4, 6
    D     1, 2, 5, 8, 7, 3, 4, 6

44  File conversion

    A     Is a technical issue relating to how data is transferred from one magnetic medium to another

    B     Is the process by which logical file designs are implemented physically

    C     Only occurs when the system goes live

    D     Is the process by which data from old files are transferred to files used by the new system

45    System maintenance is a stage in the system development life cycle. To which of the following items does maintenance refer?

*Item*

1    Correction of software errors

2    Alteration of programs to meet changes in user requirements

3    Alteration of programs to meet changes in external factors, such as changes in legislation and regulations

4    Changes in programs caused by user decisions to alter hardware and operating system configurations

A    Item 1 only
B    Items 1 and 2 only
C    Items 1, 2 and 3 only
D    Items 1, 2, 3, 4

46    Acceptance testing is when

A    The new system is checked on delivery
B    The systems design is agreed
C    The system is tested by the user department
D    The bill is paid

47    Parallel running is when

A    All the data in the new system flows smoothly
B    Old and new systems are run in parallel for a time
C    The new system is up and running
D    The old system is replaced by the new one in one move

48    Two terms which relate to the use of codes to ensure controls over data transmission are encryption and authentication. Which of the following statements is correct?

A    Authentication ensures that the message goes to an authorised recipient by use of a commonly determined algorithm and encryption ensures that the message has come from an authorised source

B    Authentication is carried out to ensure that a message has been encrypted successfully

C    Authentication is the reassembly and decoding of an encrypted message

D    Encryption involves scrambling in cipher a message to prevent eavesdropping by third parties, and an authentication code is a check appended to a message to ensure that the message has not been tampered with

---

**Data for questions 49-50**

Data valuation is an important software control over data. Five types of validation check are listed below.

*Type*

1    Check digit check

2    Range or limit check

3    Compatibility check

4    Format check

5    Code validity check

Data validation checks are to be incorporated into a new computerised stock control, order processing and invoicing system.

---

49    Which type of check would be most appropriate to check for errors where an input record specifies that a product is to be despatched from a warehouse which does not stock the item?

    A    Type 1
    B    Type 2
    C    Type 3
    D    Type 4

50    Which type of check would be most appropriate for checking transcription errors resulting in the input of an incorrect stock code?

    A    Type 1
    B    Type 2
    C    Type 3
    D    Type 5

51    Which of the following statements is true? The Data Protection Act 1998 covers

    A    Data about individuals
    B    Manual and computer records relating to individuals
    C    Only manually processed data relating to individuals
    D    Only data relating to individuals processed by computer

52    A *data protection officer* is

    A    One of the Data Protection Registrar's deputies

    B    Appointed by an organisation to ensure that it complies with the Data Protection Act 1998

    C    An official whose job it is to ensure that the organisation's networks are safe from unauthorised access

    D    An official in charge of an organisation's data archive

53    Which of the following is responsible for the implementation of the Data Protection Act?

    A    Comptroller & Auditor General
    B    Audit Commission
    C    Data Protection Registrar
    D    Department of Trade & Industry

54    All the following statements EXCEPT ONE are examples of the advantages that a computer-based accounting system has over a manual system.

Which statement is the exception?

    A    A computer-based accounting system is easier to update as new information becomes available

    B    A computer-based accounting system will always reject inaccurate financial information input to the system's database

    C    Financial calculations can be performed more quickly and accurately

    D    The management accountant can more readily present financial information to other business departments in a variety of forms

55    Which of the following statements, relating to information technology standards, are correct?

(i)     Properly designed standards reduce but do not eliminate the possibility of mistakes in the development and operation of computer systems.

(ii)    An example of a hardware standard is a requirement that all a business's computers must be loaded with a particular word processing application.

(iii)   An example of a systems development standard is a scheme of rules for operating a business's network of computers.

(iv)    An example of a security standards is a requirement that all employees operate a virus detecting application when starting up their computers.

    A    (i), (ii) and (iv) only
    B    (ii) and (iii) only
    C    (i) and (iv) only
    D    (i), (iii) and (iv) only

56    Exception reporting within business is

    A    The reporting of exceptional events, outside the normal course of events

    B    The analysis of those items where performance differs significantly from standard or budget

    C    Where reports on routine matters are prepared on an 'ad hoc' basis

    D    The scrutiny of all data as a matter of course, save in exceptional circumstances

57    Which *one* of the following statements, all of which relate to the use of commonly-used input, output and storage devices in a business's computer system, is correct?

    A    In recent years dot matrix printers have largely replaced laser printers because they give businesses better value for money

    B    Many businesses now use DVD-ROM for storing the large quantities of data processed by their computers

    C    Modems form part of a wide area network (WAN) communication system

    D    On shut down, a computer's random access memory (RAM) stores the document currently being worked on

58    Which *of the* following statements is incorrect?

    A    A help function is often a feature of a user-friendly program

    B    A mouse-driven program can use both keyboard and mouse as input devices

    C    Function keys on a keyboard enable the user to enter instructions quickly to the computer, in order to carry out defined operations with an application program

    D    Pulldown menus are normally used with programs that do not need a mouse for input

59    A small company's computer system comprises five desktop personal computers located in separate offices linked together in a local area network within the same building. The computers are not connected to any external network and employees are not allowed to take floppy disks into or out of the building. Confidential information is stored on one of the computers.

    Which ONE of the following statements can be concluded from this information?

    The company's computer system does NOT

    A    Need a back-up system
    B    Need a password access system
    C    Receive e-mail from customers or suppliers
    D    Include virus detection software

60    Which of the following statements, referring to the information technology communication system known as the Internet, are correct?

    (i)    The Internet is owned by the United States government which controls standards on the system.

    (ii)   The Internet is viewed through a browser.

    (iii)  The Internet provides a completely secure system for all business communications.

    (iv)   The Internet enables businesses to use electronic mail (e-mail) to communicate with suppliers and customers.

    A    (i), (ii) and (iv) only
    B    (ii) and (iii) only
    C    (ii) and (iv) only
    D    (i), (iii) and (iv) only

61    A spreadsheet software application may perform all the following business tasks *except one*. Which one of the following is the exception?

    A    The presentation of numerical data in the form of graphs and charts
    B    The application of logical tests to data
    C    The application of 'What If' scenarios
    D    Automatic correction of all data entered by the operator into the spreadsheet

62    Which one of the following would be essential equipment for a homeworker equipped with a PC connected to his or her office systems?

    A    A fax machine
    B    Electronic mail
    C    Appropriate software manuals
    D    A modem

63    The following statements relate to the electronic point of sale (EPOS) computer technology adopted in recent years by many retail businesses such as supermarkets.

    (i)    EPOS technology makes it possible for shops to calculate customers' bills quickly and accurately.

    (ii)    Shops which use EPOS technology never make mistakes when calculating customers' bills.

    (iii)    EPOS technology enables store groups to hold lower levels of stocks of goods for sale at their retail outlets.

    (iv)    EPOS technology enables a store group to collect data providing information on the shopping patterns of the business's customers.

    Which of the above are correct?

    A    (i) and (ii) only
    B    (ii) and (iii) only
    C    (iii) and (iv) only
    D    (i), (iii) and (iv) only

64    Information systems can be either open or closed. Which *one* of the following describes a closed information system?

    A    The information system is isolated from the surrounding environment
    B    The information system is open to controlled inputs but closed to uncontrolled inputs
    C    The information system automatically shuts down when not in active use
    D    Information stored within the system can be accessed only through the use of an appropriate password

65    All the following statements relate to computer communications systems.

(i)     Software applications known as 'search engines' have been developed to enable a computer user to locate information on the Internet.

(ii)    Computers can now communicate with each other by making use of satellite and fibre optic technology.

(iii)   Improvements in communications systems have facilitated the growth of teleworking and the emergence of the virtual organisation.

(iv)    External or built-in modems are always needed to enable networked computers to communicate with each other.

Which of the above statements are *correct*?

A    (i), (ii) and (iv) only
B    (ii) and (iii) only
C    (i), (ii) and (iii) only
D    (ii), (iii) and (iv) only

66    Spreadsheets are a well-known type of software application. All the following statements about spreadsheets are true expect one. Which *one* of the statements is *untrue*?

A    Spreadsheets can import information from documents created in other applications such as a database

B    Under certain circumstances it might be sensible for a small business to invest in an integrated software application such as *Microsoft Works* rather than in a dedicated spreadsheet application

C    A numerical value and a label cannot be entered as a combination in a particular spreadsheet cell

D    Most dedicated spreadsheet applications automatically check all numerical data keyed into the spreadsheet and alert the user if the data is incorrect

67    In recent years, desk-top or personal computers have been replacing mainframe computers in many businesses. This has encouraged the development of all the following except one.

Which one is the exception?

A    More business tasks being performed in employees' homes
B    Changes in the division of labour within the business organisation
C    More frequent updating of computer hardware
D    Firms setting up specialist departments to perform all computer-related business tasks

68    An information processing system in which all the hardware peripherals in use are connected to the central processing unit (CPU) of the computer is known as

A    A batch processing system
B    An on-line processing system
C    Groupware
D    A transaction processing system

69    All the following statements about a desk-top computer's Read Only Memory (ROM) are true except one.

Which is the exception?

    A    ROM is fixed in the computer's hardware
    B    ROM cannot be altered in the normal course of processing
    C    The application currently being processed is stored in the ROM
    D    Information stored in the ROM is used to start up the computer

70    There are various ways in which a business can communicate information electronically. A facility whereby a duplicate copy of a document can be sent electronically is known as:

    A    Electronic mail or e-mail
    B    Internet
    C    Telex
    D    Facsimile or fax

71    All the following statements *except one* describe the relationship between data and information. Which *one* is the exception?

    A    Information is data which has been processed
    B    The relationship between data and information is one of inputs and outputs
    C    Information from one process can be used as data in a second process
    D    Data is always in numerical form whereas information is always in text form

72    Computerisation is often described as being the way towards the 'paperless office'. Which of the following technologies is least likely to support this?

    A    Electronic data interchange
    B    Document image processing
    C    Computerised accounting systems
    D    Electronic mail

73    All of the following statements about a personal computer's Random Access Memory (RAM) are true except one.

Which one is the exception?

    A    RAM is volatile
    B    The more RAM there is available, the more processing can be performed without further recourse to the hard disk
    C    Any address in RAM can be accessed at the same speed as any other address
    D    The amount of RAM cannot be changed after installation

74    Which *one* of the following statements about the system of business communication known as electronic data interchange (EDI) is *untrue*?

A    For two businesses to communicate through EDI, their computer systems must be identical

B    EDI can enable a business to access information directly from a supplier's computer system

C    The use of EDI facilitates 'just-in-time' methods of production

D    EDI communication may not be completely secure

75    Which one of the following distinguishes a LAN from a WAN?

A    The number of users on the system
B    The power of the computers in the network
C    The nature of the links between computers
D    The operating system installed on users' computers

76    The following statements are about word-processing software.

(i)    Standard word-processing applications can be used to check spelling and undertake a word count in a document.

(ii)   Standard word-processing applications automatically correct grammatical mistakes made by the user.

(iii)  Modern word-processing applications can import information produced on other applications such as databases and spreadsheets.

(iv)   A document produced on a word-processing application such as *Word* can be saved as a document in the format of another word-processing application such as *WordPerfect*.

Which of the above are correct?

A    (i) and (iii) only
B    (i) and (ii) only
C    (i) (iii) and (iv) only
D    (ii), (iii) and (iv) only

77    Feedback in information systems terminology is

A    Output information generated by the system which is returned to the system as input

B    Information fed into the system from a backup peripheral device

C    Information on backup disks stored in a secure place for future emergency use

D    Information provided by a server computer to a client computer via a local area network

78    All the following statements, which refer to the communications system known as the Internet, are true *except one*.

Which *one* of the statements is *untrue*?

    A    Some commentators believe businesses that use the Internet may eventually decide to replace some of their personal computers with a new type of computer, known as a network computer or a 'thin client'

    B    All business communication via the Internet is secured by the standards developed by Electronic Data Interchange (EDI) communications systems

    C    Many businesses make use of specialist service providers such as CompuServe to access the Internet

    D    Many businesses now include a World Wide Web site on the Internet as an element in their marketing mix

79    All the following statements refer to electronic point of sale (EPOS) technology which is now used by many retailing businesses.

    (i)    EPOS technology enables a business to assess which items of stock are selling quickly.

    (ii)   EPOS technology can be used only by businesses selling durable goods as it is less suited to perishable products.

    (iii)  EPOS technology can facilitate electronic data interchange links between a retail business and its suppliers.

    (iv)   EPOS technology can facilitate the just-in-time (JIT) organisation of production.

Which of the above are correct?

    A    (i), (ii) and (iv) only
    B    (i) and (iv) only
    C    (i), (iii) and (iv) only
    D    (ii) and (iii) only

80    Which ONE of the following statements about a desktop computer's random access memory (RAM) is TRUE?

    A    Information stored in the RAM is used to start up the computer

    B    The total amount of RAM built into the computer cannot be increased

    C    The application currently being used is stored temporarily in the RAM

    D    In the event of a computer crash, information stored in the RAM cannot be lost

81    Which ONE of the following statements about communication between computers is CORRECT?

    A    Computers can communicate with each other via satellite and mobile telephone technology, as well as through the use of land lines

    B    Two computers can communicate with each other via the Internet, but only if the operating system software is the same

    C    Modems are always used when two computers communicate through a local area network

    D    The way in which data is translated into a form compatible to a different computer system from the one which processed it is known as protocol

82    Which ONE of the following statements about a desk-top computer's read-only memory (ROM) is TRUE?

    A    The application currently being used is stored temporarily in the ROM

    B    In the case of a computer with a CD-ROM drive, all the computer's ROM is externally stored on compact discs

    C    In the event of a computer crash, information stored in the ROM is usually lost

    D    Information stored in the ROM is used to start up the computer

83    Which ONE of the following statements about the system of business communication known as electronic data interchange (EDI) is CORRECT?

    A    EDI communication is attractive for businesses because it is always completely secure

    B    For two businesses to communicate through EDI, their computer systems must be identical

    C    A business may use EDI to transfer information directly into a client's computer system

    D    'Just-in-time' production systems require businesses to use EDI to communicate with suppliers

84    Which ONE of the following standards is intended to reduce misunderstandings between systems analysts and programmers when a new system is being designed?

    A    Performance standards
    B    Documentation standards
    C    Operating standards
    D    Programming standards

85    Which ONE of the following is NOT applications software?

    A    Database software

    B    Word-processing software

    C    Software which gives priority to different programs during processing

    D    Software designed in-house to perform a particular task for a particular user

NOTES

86 Which ONE of the following statements regarding imperfect information is correct?

A Imperfect information is prepared for a specific user, but may be able to be used by others

B Imperfect information is correct, but is out of date

C Imperfect information concerns the future and therefore 100% accuracy can not be guaranteed. Most information is imperfect but may still be useful

D Imperfect information is of no use and should be ignored

87 An Expert System is:

A A program that uses a knowledge base of experience to make logical assumptions

B A system designed by a top programmer

C A system that requires users to be proficient in computing

D A program used to train users

88 Which ONE of the following best describes Information Technology?

A Computers

B A collection of tools designed to encourage working in groups

C The Internet and the World Wide Web

D The coming together of computing technology and communications technology, particularly in relation to information systems

89 Wireless Application Protocol (WAP) is expected to enable which ONE of the following developments?

A Quicker software development

B Internet access through televisions equipped wit a set-top box

C More reliable mobile phone connections

D The accessing of websites using a mobile phones

90 In the past new computerised systems have often failed to meet expectations. The most common reason for this is:

A Not enough money was available

B Users have false expectations – they want the computer to do their thinking

C Manual systems are easier to use

D Developers did not take enough time to understand exactly what users require the new system to do

91    Which of the following statements is incorrect? Mainframes differ from PCs because:

A    Mainframes have larger storage capacity

B    Data held on a mainframe can be backed-up to tape. Data held on a PC can only be backed up to disks

C    Mainframes are physically larger

D    Many mainframes use Unix operating systems whereas with PCs the Windows operating system dominates

92    Which of the following is not present on a typical PC keyboard?

A    Function keys
B    Escape
C    Total
D    Enter

93    A smart card is:

A    A plastic card with machine-sensible data recorded on a magnetic stripe
B    A plastic card with machine-sensible data recorded on a microchip
C    A credit card with a security hologram
D    A hand-held device used to scan text

94    The system operated at many businesses whereby a customer's bank account is debited with the price of goods purchased at the time of the sale is known as:

A    EFTPOS
B    POS
C    EPOS
D    EFT

95    Which of the following statements describes a benchmark test? A benchmark test involves:

A    Testing a system to see if it works

B    Subjecting a system to increasing workloads to establish the load at which performance becomes unacceptable

C    Establishing the speed of the CPU

D    Subjecting a system to a known workload, and comparing performance against other systems subjected to the same workload

96    In the context of software development, what does RAD stand for?

A    Random Application Development
B    Rapid Access Development
C    Rapid Application Development
D    Rapid Application Disk

97  What name is given to an intranet that is accessible to authorised outsiders?

    A   Extranet
    B   Internet
    C   Protocol
    D   Wide Area Network (WAN)

98  Which one of the following is not an Internet search engine?

    A   Yahoo
    B   Microsoft Internet Explorer
    C   Lycos
    D   AskJeeves

99  Which one of the following is not a disadvantage of homeworking?

    A   Space and facilities may be inadequate
    B   Workers may be exposed to a greater number of distractions
    C   Team spirit may suffer
    D   The organisation may relocate to smaller premises

100 'Modem' is derived from two words. They are:

    A   Modern demographics
    B   Modulate demodulate
    C   Modular demonstration
    D   Model manager

101 Modifying a payroll program to allow for new income tax rates is an example of what kind of system maintenance?

    A   Corrective
    B   Perfective
    C   Adaptive
    D   Open

102 The process of collecting, storing and using information held within an organisation, particularly the information held by the people within an organisation is known as:

    A   The grapevine
    B   Groupware
    C   Intranet management
    D   Knowledge management

103 What is the name of the group of software products that includes Word, Excel, Outlook, PowerPoint and Access?

    A   Lotus Symphony
    B   Microsoft Works
    C   Microsoft Windows
    D   Microsoft Office

104  Which ONE of the following techniques should not be used to manage information overload?

    A    Delegate routine issues to colleagues

    B    The occasional screening of incoming telephone calls

    C    Ignore all incoming information until the task in hand is complete

    D    Take action to ensure the information received is concise and targeted

# Exam Style
# Questions

BPP
PUBLISHING

## Chapter 1                                                                    *40 mins*

1    A small company has one accountant. One of her responsibilities is to decide
     whether to offer credit to a customer, and if so, to determine an appropriate credit
     limit. This credit decision depends upon such factors as bank references, order
     value and customer location. This example demonstrates how information must
     be relevant to the decision-making process. Relevance is an important quality of
     information.

     Define five further qualities of information and describe their application to
     assessing the credit-worthiness and credit limit of a customer.

## Chapter 2                                                                    *30 mins*

2    CC plc is a company employing 500 staff in 10 different offices within one
     country. The company offers a wide range of specialist consultancy advice to the
     building and construction industry. This includes advice on materials to be used,
     relevant legislation (including planning applications) and appropriate sources of
     finance.

     The information to meet client requirements is held within each office of the
     company. Although most clients are serviced by a single office, a lot of the
     information used is duplicated between the different offices.

     In the past there has been no attempt to share data because of the cost of
     transferring information and the lack of trust on the part of staff in other offices.
     Some senior managers tend to keep part of client data confidential to themselves.

     The Marketing Director has suggested that an Intranet should be established in
     the company so that common information can be shared rather than each office
     maintaining its own data. This suggestion is meeting with come resistance from
     all grades of staff.

     Explain the objectives of an intranet and show how the provision of an intranet
     within CC plc should result in better provision of information.

## Chapter 3                                                                    *30 mins*

3    Many organisations undertake a feasibility study before taking the decision to
     commit to a full-scale systems development. A feasibility study will often
     commence with the terms of reference.

     (a)   Describe the main objectives of the study.

     (b)   Explain the different types of feasibility it will consider.

     (c)   Briefly explain (with examples) three elements that are usually defined
           within the terms of reference.

## Chapter 4                                                                    *30 mins*

4    A new sales and accounting system is to be implemented in a large, multi-site
     organisation using VDU terminals on-line to a central mainframe computer. This
     system will be the first experience of computing for the majority of the staff
     involved and it has been decided to base the implementation on a popular off-the-
     shelf package.

     (a)   Describe the issues to be considered under staff training.

     (b)   What are the advantages and disadvantages of formal training?

## Chapter 5                                                          *45 mins*

5   (a)   Briefly explain the meaning of the term management information system, suggest what qualities a MIS should possess, and identify the advantages of using a computerised MIS.

    (b)   Describe and briefly explain the purpose of the main types of software which might be installed in a computer system located in the offices of a small business dealing with a number of customers and suppliers.

## Chapter 6                                                          *30 mins*

6   (a)   Identify and explain three ways in which the following spreadsheet could be improved. (The comment about the formula is for your information – it is not part of the spreadsheet.)

|   | A | B | C | D |
|---|---|---|---|---|
| 1 | 6614 | 9790 | 8221.25 | |
| 2 | 5665 | 4966 | 4753 | |
| 3 | 7899 | 4462.5 | 4163 | |
| 4 | 7717 | 5212 | 9736 | |
| 5 | 12461 | 24430.5 | 26873.25 | |
| 6 | | | | |
| 7 | | | | |
| 8 | | | | |
| 9 | | | | |
| 10 | | | | |
| 11 | | | | |
| 12 | | | | |
| 13 | | | | |

The formula in this cell is =A1+A2+A3-A4

    (b)   Explain the steps in the construction and use of a spreadsheet model.

## Guidance

You may want to use this checklist and answer plan to help construct your answer.

    (a)   Comment on the **presentation**

         Is it clear (from headings and labels) what the figures mean?

         Are the numbers easy to read (eg comma format, font, percentages shown as percentages etc)

         Are decimal places consistent

         Are the numbers properly aligned?

         Are totals clearly distinguished?

    Comment on the **structure** and **logic**

         Could the data have been laid out in a different way?

         Are there rounding errors?

         Could safer, more efficient formulae have been used?

         Have the formulae been entered correctly?

(b)    **Building a model**

    Variables in input area

    Formulae in calculation area

    Results in output area (not always necessary)

    Explain why this approach is preferred (eg 'what if?' analysis)

## Chapter 7                                             *30 mins*

7    Explain how electronic mail works and what advantages it has over paper-based internal and external postal services.

## Chapter 8                                             *40 mins*

8    An Institute of Systems Analysts is currently computerising its membership details. The membership system will store personal details about each member. The Institute intends to offer an employment service to companies, providing career details of members who may be suitable for job vacancies.

    The system will have to comply with the principles of the Data Protection Act 1998. Three important principles of this Act are given below:

    •    Personal data shall be accurate and kept up-to-date

    •    Personal data held for any purpose shall not be kept longer than is necessary for that purpose

    •    Appropriate security measures shall be taken against unauthorised access to, alteration, destruction or disclosure of personal data

    (a)    Explain why each of the three principles are important in the context of the membership system and describe how each principle might be enforced.

    (b)    The Institute is also worried about computer viruses. What is a computer virus? Briefly explain what measures might be taken to prevent a computer virus entering the membership computer system.

## Chapter 9                                             *40 mins*

9    (a)    Explain how the use of information technology can bring about improvements in productivity within a business organisation.

    (b)    Explain how the use of information technology may sometimes harm a business's performance.

# Answers to Multiple Choice Questions

BPP

PUBLISHING

1    C    The term feedback is widely used in everyday speech (as in answer B). This question was testing your understanding of it in systems terminology. Additionally, answers A and D were descriptions of open loop systems where control is exercised irrespective of the system's output.

2    B    Feedback expressions are used in every day speech. Positive feedback, in system terminology, has the specific meaning given in answer B. For example, if you are driving along an empty motorway breaking the speed limit, and your passenger encourages you to go even faster, you are being given positive feedback.

3    A

4    A

5    C    A key field needs to be a unique identifier.

6    B    A database administrator is a person with responsibility for the database.

7    C    Word for Windows is wordprocessing software.

8    B    The keyboard is an input device. The screen and the printer are output devices, while the CPU performs the processing function.

9    D    Windows 98 is software – an operating system.

10   B    PCs are now widespread throughout organisations.

11   D    A printer need not be connected to the PC – it would still work, displaying its output on the screen. Input devices, such as a keyboard, are necessary, as is the screen. The CPU enables the PC to process the input information.

12   A    The CPU is divided into 3 areas, the control unit which receives program instructions, the ALU (arithmetic and logic unit) which performs the calculations allowing the instructions to be carried out, and the memory which holds the instructions in memory while the computer is operating.

13   C    16 KB is 16 × 1,024. Answer A (1,024) represents 1 Kilobyte, Answer B (8,388,608) is 8 × 1,024 or 8 Kb. Answer D (17,179,869,184) is 16 × 1,024 × 1,024 × 1,024 or 16 Gb.

14   C    Hard disks vary in size, but a typical PC hard disk offers 5 Gb – 10 Gb of storage capacity. A DVD-ROM can hold approximately 5 Gb, a CD-ROM 650 Mb and a floppy disk 1.44 Mb.

15   C    It is not recommended to use a floppy disk as a coaster for a coffee mug – the disk and the data stored on it are likely to be damaged.

16   A    The mouse is an input device and displays data. Data can be stored on CD-ROM disks, on magnetic tapes, and on ZIP disks.

17   B    A phone number is data, which would be entered in the field area on a record – in a field possibly called PhoneNo. Title, Lastname and Postcode are all suitable filed names.

18   B    Price should be classified as a numeric field, which would allow calculations to be performed, such as adding and multiplying. Date of birth should be classified as a date field. Phone No and Catalogue Nos will not be used for calculations, so should be alphanumeric.

19   C

20   D    On a magnetic disk, records can be accessed directly. If data is stored on tape, the tape has to be run from the beginning until the required record is

reached. Whether data becomes corrupt is not significantly affected by the storage medium.

21    D    DOS is an unfriendly text based operating system. DOS was widely used before the advent of Windows.

22    C    WYSIWIG (what you see is what you get) describes the fact that what you see on the screen is an accurate representation of what will be printed. OCR (optical character recognition), OMR (mark sensing and optical mark reading) and MICR (magnetic ink character recognition) are all computer readable methods of conveying data.

23    C    Laser printers print on to individual sheets of paper, much like photocopies, and do not use continuous stationery.

24    C    Protocol is not so much concerned with the transfer of data between different systems, as ensuring the integrity of data transfer itself.

25    B

26    A    A LAN is linked by direct cables not by the telecommunications network. A WAN is linked by the telecommunications network.

27    B    The operating system controls the operation of the computer. Its tasks include 'booting up' the computer when it is switched on, and responding to commands from users to carry out such tasks as deleting files or formatting floppy disks. Translating programs is not one of its jobs.

28    C    There is no point in devising a spreadsheet if you are not prepared to let it work for you, so answers A and B, are not appropriate.

29    C    Answer B adds across the monthly net profit figures. Answer A subtracts the costs listed from fee income in the year-to-date column. Answer D is effectively the same calculation as answer A. Answer C is wrong: Excel requires an '=' sign to show that it is a formula.

30    A    Both formulae in answer A are correct. Both formulae in answer B are incorrect. Formula (1) in answer B, =C4 – D4/D4 can be translated as £21,500 – £22,000/£22,000 which equals £21,500 – 1. Operations in brackets are performed first, so that, in answer A the result of £21,500 – £22,000 is divided by £22,000. As for formula 2, answer B will generate an *error* message as no priority has been given to one of the calculations: either cell C19 divided by cell C4 is first performed, or cell C4 divided by 30 days.

31    B    Equipment is normally categorised as a 'fixed asset'. Hardware maintenance and staff training are likely to be regular costs. The cost of recruiting staff is a 'one-off' non-capital cost.

32    D    Answers A and C are the same and refer to a situation where some of the data is run in *parallel* on the old and new systems but not all of it.

33    B    When data is run on both old and new systems this is an example of parallel running.

34    C    E-mail is virtually instantaneous – so long as all systems involved are operational.

35    C    In document image processing a document is scanned into a computer. PABX is a telephone system and EDI stands for electronic data interchange.

36    B    Although much data can be conveyed electronically, there will always be the need for personal communications.

| | | |
|---|---|---|
| 37 | D | Detailed analysis takes place at a later stage. |
| 38 | D | Discounted cash flow using either NPV or IRR is a technique which takes into account the time value of money. |
| 39 | C | As above, this level of detail would be examined at a later stage. |
| 40 | D | As above. |
| 41 | A | Custom-built software would fit the user's exact requirements. |
| 42 | B | Better decision making is a benefit, but is difficult to quantify. |
| 43 | A | |
| 44 | D | |
| 45 | D | |
| 46 | C | |
| 47 | B | |
| 48 | C | Encryption involves the replacement of the correct text by cipher. The transformation from a cipher text to the original is called decryption. An authentication code is a coded check, derived from an algorithm, which can reveal whether a message has been tampered with in some way. |
| 49 | C | A check can be made to ensure that the product code in a record is compatible with the warehouse code. |
| 50 | A | Check digit checks should pick up any transposition errors or other transcription errors in a stock code. |
| 51 | B | |
| 52 | B | |
| 53 | C | |
| 54 | B | Garbage in, garbage out! |
| 55 | C | In (ii) a word processing application is a piece of software, so this cannot be a hardware standard. In (iii) rules for operating a network are an example of an operating standard not a development standard. |
| 56 | B | Exception reporting focuses attention on those items where performance differs significantly from standard or budget. |
| 57 | C | DVD-ROMs can be used to store large quantities of data but the data cannot be changed once it is written onto the disk. DVD-ROMs are therefore not flexible enough for day-to-day storage methods, though they are being used increasingly for archiving purposes. Re-writeable DVDs (DVD-RW) are being developed. |
| 58 | D | Answer D is an incorrect statement. Some programs have several menus from which the user can select options. These menus are each identified by a single word, displayed in a horizontal bar across the screen. The mouse moves the pointer to the appropriate word. The menu is selected by clicking a button on the mouse, and then moving the mouse so as to pull down a secondary menu from the top of the screen. |
| 59 | C | All systems should include back-up storage and virus detection software. Passwords are needs if information is to be kept confidential. |
| 60 | C | The Internet is not owned by any one body, but by all of the bodies and individuals that use it. |

| 61 | D | Garbage in, garbage out! |
|---|---|---|
| 62 | D | A fax machine is not essential. Other possible means of communication include telephone and electronic mail; alternatively a fax card could be inserted into the PC to enable faxes to be sent directly from screen. Electronic mail, although likely, is not essential. The homeworkers might just be linked directly to the relevant system(s). Software manuals are not necessary: most applications nowadays include comprehensive on-line help facilities. A modem is necessary to link the PC, via the telephone network, to the office system. |
| 63 | D | Shop assistants quite commonly key in/scan something twice, so (ii) is clearly wrong. Statement (iii) is correct in the sense that EPOS allows better forecasting of demand and stock movements, and so less safety stock. |
| 64 | A | The other statements are irrelevant. |
| 65 | C | The first three statements are correct. Modems are not used in LANs, therefore (iv) is incorrect. |
| 66 | D | It is impossible for an application to check the precise accuracy of numerical data keyed in. |
| 67 | D | Specialist departments are more likely to be closed down. |
| 68 | B | On-line describes a device in direct communication with the processor. |
| 69 | C | Programs and data in current use are stored in RAM memory. |
| 70 | D | Fax uses photocopier type technology: 'duplicate' is the keyword here. |
| 71 | D | Data is any kind of unprocessed information. |
| 72 | C | DIP means that only a single paper copy of each document needs to be retained: duplicates can be manipulated electronically. EDI and email can be entirely screen based, although a 'file copy' may be required. Accounting systems do not eliminate the need for legal and audit records to be maintained; in addition multiple copies of many documents (invoices, delivery notes etc) are produced and various transaction listings and exception reports are produced in hard copy too for control and checking purposes. |
| 73 | D | RAM is supplied on chips which can be plugged in and unplugged fairly easily. A 32 Mb PC can, for example, be upgraded to 64 Mb to improve its performance. |
| 74 | A | Translation software enables businesses using different systems to communicate through EDI. |
| 75 | C | A LAN uses computer cabling. A WAN requires telecommunications links between sites. |
| 76 | C | Some packages (eg Word) can assess the user's grammar, but they do not correct it automatically. |
| 77 | A | B to D may or may not have been generated by the system and may or may not be fed back into it. |
| 78 | B | The Internet can be used for ED1 but it is not governed by ED1 standards. ED1 was originally developed in the 1980s as a means of transferring standard format data from the mainframe computer to another. |
| 79 | C | Statement (ii) is nonsense. |

| 80 | C | The application currently being used is stored temporarily in the RAM to enable quick and easy access to the program. The other statements are false. |
|---|---|---|
| 81 | A | It is now reasonably common for a notebook computer to be used in conjunction with a mobile phone to communicate with other computers. The other statements are nonsense. |
| 82 | D | When 'booting-up' a PC uses information stored in the ROM. The other statements are false. |
| 83 | C | EDI is used to transfer information between businesses removing the need for manual data entry. The other statements are false. |
| 84 | D | The other standards are more relevant to stages of the SDLC other than the design stage. |
| 85 | C | This is the job of the operating system. |
| 86 | C | All future orientated information is imperfect. |
| 87 | A | |
| 88 | D | |
| 89 | D | Some observers believe WAP and other similar technologies will revolutionise the way the Internet is used. |
| 90 | D | Before a system that meets user need s can be built those needs must be established in detail. |
| 91 | B | PCs can be backed up to tape if a suitable tape unit or tape drive is attached. |
| 92 | C | |
| 93 | B | |
| 94 | A | |
| 95 | D | The essence of benchmarking is allowing a realistic comparison to be made. |
| 96 | C | |
| 97 | A | |
| 98 | B | Microsoft Internet Explorer is a browser. |
| 99 | D | Smaller premises should mean lower rent – an advantage not a disadvantage. |
| 100 | B | |
| 101 | C | This is a change in the processing environment. |
| 102 | D | Knowledge management is concerned with ensuring that knowledge does not remain locked away inside peoples heads. For the organisation to benefit from this information it must be accessible. |
| 103 | D | |
| 104 | C | It is dangerous to ignore all incoming communication. At the very least a system should be in place that facilitates the receipt of truly urgent important material. |

# *Answers to Exam Style Questions*

## Chapter 1

Besides relevance, information should possess (five of) the following characteristics.

It should:

- Be complete
- Be sufficiently accurate
- Be clear
- Inspire the user's confidence
- Be communicated to the appropriate person
- Be of a manageable volume
- Be available at the right time
- Be sent through the right channel of communication
- Cost no more than it is worth

Credit control information might display these characteristics in (five of) the following ways.

Incomplete information might omit the fact that although the customer pays, they pay late, or that, the reason the customer requires an increased limit is to purchase goods to fulfil a large order.

Information that is inaccurate may result in credit being granted to a customer that appeared creditworthy but who is not. This may result in bad debts. Information that is too accurate - for example that the customer should be allowed credit up to a value of £738.29 - is not more useful than less precise information, such as 'good for up to £750'. The precise level of accuracy will depend on the level of materiality that applies to the business.

Vague information (for instance, 'the customer may be able to pay but he may not') will not be helpful in making the decision as to whether to grant credit. Information may be overlooked if it does not clearly identify the factors that are used to assess creditworthiness (for example, if trading record figures are hidden in a mass of other information).

Information about the customer's creditworthiness from an unreliable source (for instance someone who had been known to be wrong in the past, or who was closely connected with the customer) would not inspire confidence.

The customer's assurances (however valid) might be communicated informally to a sales representative rather than formally to the person who actually makes the credit decision.

The information might give a voluminous list of how many days the customer had taken to pay all previous invoices, but not provide a summary to give an overall impression of how good or bad a debtor they were likely to be.

A vital piece of information (for instance a bad reference from a bank) might not be received early enough to be taken account of when making a decision to grant credit.

Information supplied verbally or over the telephone leaves no written record, and may make what was a sound credit decision appear to have no sound basis when it is reviewed, because the wrong channel was used.

Credit checks involve telephone and postage costs, perhaps a fee to a credit agency, and the cost of processing time spent by the credit controller. For small orders the cost may well exceed the value of the sale.

The cost of extra-thorough checks might be justified in other circumstances, for instance if the potential loss through granting an over-generous limit is high, or if setting limits too low (to avoid the dangers of not checking thoroughly) causes customers to go to competing suppliers.

## Chapter 2

An intranet uses software and other technology originally developed for the Internet on internal company networks. An intranet comprises an organisation-wide web of internal documents that is familiar, easy to use and comparatively inexpensive. Each employee has a browser enabling him or her to view information held on a server computer and may offer access to the Internet.

The main objective of an intranet is to provide easy access to information that helps people perform their jobs more efficiently. Many roles require increased access to knowledge and information. An intranet is a way of making this knowledge readily available.

Other objectives are outlined below.

To encourage the use of reference documents. Documents on-line are more likely to be used than those stored on shelves, especially if the document is bulky (for instance procedure manuals).

To create a sense of organisational unity. An intranet 'pulls together' in a co-ordinated fashion information from disparate parts of an organisation. It may be the only visible way some parts of a large organisation are linked.

The provision of an Intranet within CC plc should result in better provision of information by:

- Ensuring consistency in information held and provided to clients. The intranet will enable one set of data to be held and accessed by all 10 offices.

- Providing easy access to a larger pool of data. Information that managers previously 'kept to themselves' will be available to others.

- The intranet-Internet link will ensure the most up-to-date planning information is available. It would be useful to develop an intranet page complied from appropriate websites. (This must be kept up to date.)

## Chapter 3

(a)  Objectives

A feasibility study is a formal study to decide what type of system can be developed which meets the needs of the organisation. The main objective of a feasibility study is to ensure that a project can be carried out, literally is the project *feasible*? This will be considered in terms of whether the technical and operational performance required can be achieved using existing technology for an acceptable cost. Subsidiary objectives will be defined in each of these areas, as explained in part (b).

(b)  Types of feasibility

(i)  Technical feasibility

The requirements of a project must be technically achievable. Any solution must be able to be implemented using existing or proposed hardware, software and any other equipment. Some of the criteria that the equipment may have to meet include:

- Processing a given volume of transactions
- Meeting a requirement to store files of a given size
- Guaranteeing response times
- Supporting of a given number of users

The project will be checked to ensure that the exact criteria can be met.

(ii)   Operational feasibility

The proposed solution or system must fit into the existing operational structure of the organisation. If the solution conflicts with the way that organisation operates, for example if it changes management responsibilities or reporting structures, or it involves unacceptably high costs or redundancies, the solution may not be acceptable. A project must fit into the existing operations of an organisation to gain acceptance. A project that does not meet this aim is likely to fail due to lack of management support or lack of understanding of how the new system works in the overall context of the organisation.

(iii)  Economic feasibility

Even though a project may meet the feasibility criteria above, it must still prove to be economically feasible. This means that it should be the 'best' computerised solution that is affordable from those under consideration.

Costs that will be considered include capital costs (hardware and software) and revenue costs (support, maintenance), and one-off costs such as training. Benefits are generally less tangible, but may include speed of processing, savings in staff costs, and a higher quality, more competitive product or service.

Also, the project should be judged in terms of opportunity cost, or what else the organisation can do with the money to be invested in the project. Just because the project passes the other feasibility criteria and will make a positive return does not mean that it should go ahead. Precedence may still be given to other projects (eg a new fleet of delivery vans) if this is more important to the company at the time a decision needs to be made on the project.

(c)   Terms of reference

The terms of reference for a feasibility study are normally set out by the steering committee. The terms explain the objectives of the feasibility study and will normally include the following.

(i)   Objectives

The objectives of the feasibility study including the deliverables – that is what the feasibility study should produce when it has been completed.

Many feasibility studies conclude with a series of alternatives, for example, recommendations on whether to continue with the project, and if so, what further actions are required to continue.

(ii)  Definition of system and system requirements

The requirements of any revised system will be stated in the terms of reference, and the system itself needs to be clearly identified (eg the sales order processing system might include sales order processing only, or it might be inextricably linked to stock and production systems).

This information is needed to help identify what information is already produced by existing systems. The amount of work required to implement a revised system will be tailored to take into account what is already available in an organisation.

(iii) System recommendation

The study will investigate a small number of possible solutions and recommend the most appropriate to the organisation being studied.

The study will need to take into account the specific standards and operations that already exist in an organisation. Different solutions will therefore be required in different situations. Care will have to be taken to ensure that any solution really does match the specific situation of the organisation.

(iv) Costs and resources

The terms of reference will need to set out the funds and resources available to undertake the study. For instance a team of ten systems analysts can clearly conduct a more extensive study than one analyst working alone, but will cost considerable more. and will need more equipment (PCs, analysis tools).

(v) Reporting deadline

This is the date when the feasibility report is due from the steering committee.

The reporting deadline is necessary so that the Board can set a date to make a decision regarding the recommendations from feasibility study. The format of the report will also be defined so that it can read and assimilated quickly when it is finally produced.

## Chapter 4

(a) As for the majority of staff this will be their first experience of computing, there will be little point in detailed training in the new system until it has been installed and is ready for testing. This is because what staff learn is likely to be quickly forgotten unless they can reinforce their learning with continual practice. Training can be provided by:

(i) Reading the user manuals or on-line help (which in relation to the software should be readily available, since an application package is to be purchased).

(ii) Training by computer, using tutorials provided by the software house (again this may well be available within a standard package).

(iii) Attending courses that the hardware/software supplier has agreed to provide. Since a large system is to be installed, this should be available for selected members of staff, who could then help to train others if training were not available for all.

(iv) Attending courses provided by a third party training establishment (which should be available if it is a leading software package which is to be acquired).

With a comprehensive new system being proposed, extensive training of a significant number of staff will probably be necessary, and so additional training measures might include:

(i) Presentations on general or specific aspects of the new sales system - possibly making use of visual aids such as training films, pre-prepared slides, etc.

(ii) Meetings that allow staff the opportunity to ask questions and sort out problems.

(iii) Use of the company's newsletter or circulars (or Intranet and e-mail facilities) to explain the new system in outline.

(iv) Issue of handbooks, probably obtained from the hardware/software suppliers, detailing in precise terms the documentation and procedures for the new sales system.

(v) Using trials/tests on the new system to give staff direct experience before the system 'goes live'.

(vi) Involving staff in the conversion procedures (see below) when the files for the new system are first established.

The persons responsible for communication and training must take care over the preparation of internal courses and the material used. It is essential that interest is aroused and maintained, and so both courses and material must be well written, well presented and make an impact on the staff members.

(b) Formal training can be provided in a number of different ways. Courses can be designed within the organisation and run internally. If there is sufficient expertise this can be a cost- effective and focused means of providing training. Manufacturers and suppliers of software may offer courses; typically these will be available for new purchasers of software or in conjunction with the release of new versions of software. If software is widely used (eg Microsoft Excel) then independent training establishments may run courses which are aimed to appeal to a broad base of users.

Advantages of formal training in IT applications

(i) Best practice. Formal training ensures that users follow good working practices. This is particularly important in the area of general policy and procedure eg computer security, back-up routines etc.

(ii) Software capabilities. Since the organisation is likely to have spent considerable amounts on software, it is worth making users aware of the software's capabilities on more than some kind of assumed 'need to know' basis. This will encourage users to make best use of systems and operate them in the most efficient and effective way.

(iii) Confidence. Users will be given confidence in their ability to use the system - without formal training they may be reduced to flicking through manuals and given a feeling of uncertainty as to what they are doing.

(iv) Assistance. Formal training is important if only to point out the user friendly features of a system and the existence of 'help' screens. The user will be given some indication of where to turn for assistance.

(v) Feedback. It is easier to monitor the success of formal training than informal training. Follow-up procedures will identify the aptitude of trained staff for the tasks they do, and changes can then be made where necessary.

(vi) Surroundings. Users can be given an awareness of how their job fits into the whole system entity. An understanding of how tasks are related may lead to suggestions for improvement.

Disadvantages of formal training in IT applications

(i) Cost. When an organisation buys a tailor-made system, the cost will be likely to include a certain number of days of 'free' user training. Any training beyond this may be expensive.

(ii)    Necessity. Off-the-shelf packages may include training routines. Most general purpose packages, eg spreadsheets and WP, include tutorial disks for the user to teach himself. Formal training may not therefore be necessary.

(iii)   Relevance. Externally run training courses catering for a number of users with different applications for the software may not be relevant or meet the particular requirements of the organisation.

(iv)    Adequacy. There is no guarantee that formal training courses will be well designed or run. They may turn out to be a waste of time and money.

## Chapter 5

(a)     Management Information System.

A management information system is a system for providing information which will enable managers and administrators to perform their roles properly. In any individual company such a system may be good or bad.

Qualities

A system should be effective in providing good quality information at an acceptable cost. Good management information is relevant, accurate and timely, allowing management to base decisions upon the information given.

Advantages

The nature and quality of management information will change where an MIS is computerised.

(i)     Managers are likely to have access to more information, for example from a database. Information is also likely to be more accurate, reliable and up-to-date. The range of management reports is likely to be wider and their content more comprehensive and better presented.

(ii)    Planning activities should be more thorough, with the use of models (such as spreadsheets for budgeting) and sensitivity analysis.

(iii)   Information for control should be more readily available. For example, a computerised sales ledger system should provide prompt reminder letters for late payers, and might incorporate other credit control routines. Stock systems, especially for companies with stocks distributed around several different warehouses, should provide better stock control.

(iv)    Decision making by managers can be helped by decision support systems.

(b)     Software components

The main types of software required by a small business with a number of customers and supplier will fall into one of two categories. These are operating software and applications software.

(i)     The operating software for individual PCs (probably Windows as it is the most user friendly and is loaded on most computers in business use) and for the network (probably Windows NT or Novell Netware) will be needed to make the computer hardware work. It provides a bridge between the applications software and the hardware. The operating software handles basic tasks such as file management, calling up of program files and data files from disk storage into memory, handling of interruptions (for example program abnormalities or machine failure), and managing multitasking (switching between different programs).

(ii)     Applications software is written for a particular processing function or handles data for a particular purpose. They include the following.

    (1)     General purpose packages such as Word for word processing (letters to customers and suppliers etc), Excel (a spreadsheet for number manipulation, such as an aged debtor analysis) and Access (a database package for more efficient and sophisticated data storage, interrogation and manipulation such as compiling customer mailing lists and stock control). These packages often come in an integrated format, such as Microsoft Office, so that they can communicate with each other and data can be transferred between applications.

    (2)     Accounting software, such as Sage Line 50 (given that it is only a small business). Besides basic financial ledgers, this may include a payroll processing module and a stock control module.

    (3)     Telecommunications software to control PC faxes to customers and suppliers, and Internet connections, including software of a service provider such as Demon. Communications may also include e-mail, both internal and external.

    (4)     Internet browser software such as Netscape Navigator or Microsoft Explorer. This handles the way in which information downloaded from the Internet is displayed (including animations and sound), and allows information to be saved, printed out, copied and so on.

## Chapter 6

(a)     There are many ways in which the spreadsheet could be improved, including *(three of)* the following.

    (i)      Headings should be added to the columns and labels to the rows. An overall title would also be useful, if it is not clear from the title of the file itself or of this worksheet.

    (ii)     A consistent size and type of font should be used, For instance the figures in cells A2 and C1 to C5 are in a different font size and type to the other figures.

    (iii)    The figures should be given to a consistent number of decimal places. Some are stated to nil decimal places, others to one decimal place and others to two. If one figure has to be stated to two decimal places, then all of them should be.

    (iv)     It may be easier to read the figures if they are presented in comma format.

    (v)      The totals in cells A5 to C5 should be given top and bottom borders to make it clear that they are totals.

    (vi)     The formula in cell A1 is badly constructed. A better approach would be to enter the figure in cell A4 as a negative number and use the formula =SUM(A1:A4) in cell A5. This avoids the need to type in all the cell references individually and minimises the risk of entering the wrong sign(s) in the formula.

    (vii)    The totals in cells B5 and C5 are simply the sum of the four figures above them. In other words, unlike in column A, the figures in row 4 are not treated as negative. This may be what was intended, but there is some doubt because the approach is not consistent.

(b) A spreadsheet model should be built as follows.

(i) All the variables in the problem should be identified and entered in separate cells in one part of the spreadsheet with clear labels. This is the input area.

(ii) In a different part of the spreadsheet the formulae that act upon the variables should be entered. This is the calculation area. It may also be necessary to use functions such as 'IF' functions.

(iii) The results of the calculations may be displayed in a third output section of the spreadsheet. In less complicated cases this may be combined with the calculation area.

Once built in this way the model could be used to carry out 'what if' analysis. The values of the input variables could be altered as appropriate and the impact of such changes could be instantly evaluated.

## Chapter 7

The term electronic mail or email is used to describe various systems of sending data or messages electronically over networks.

Network users who are registered as e-mail users will be given a user identity and allocated a password allowing them to enter the e-mail system. On selecting the relevant menu option, a user will be presented with a series of basic facilities such as:

- Create a new message
- Edit an existing message
- Read a new message
- Send a message
- File a message
- Move or refile a message
- Retrieve a message
- Delete a message

If the user wishes to send a memo to a user in another office they choose the New Message option. He or she will be presented with a screen that resembles a word processor. Using this a message can be created. Basic word processing functions (edit, wraparound, manipulation of blocks etc) are standard. Once the message is prepared it can be saved. If the user wishes to send it immediately, the recipients e-mail address must be entered in the correct field. Here, details of addressee and other people to whom copies should be sent are entered. There may be options for requesting a delivery receipt and/or a read receipt. The message can then be sent and at the same time given a name and filed.

The filing system consists of a number of folders; each can be used for messages relating to a different customer or subject.

Once a message has been sent, it is received by a central computer which allocates disk storage as a 'mailbox' for each user and signals the arrival of messages to recipients. Clearly the successful working of the system depends on regular checking of 'in-trays' by all users. Systems may offer a two-tier mailbox for each user, one private and one public, accessible by all users or by users in a particular grade/department.

Housekeeping controls may exist, for example, to ensure that any letter 'binned' can be retrieved for a certain period before being irretrievably lost, and that any letters not filed in a folder are binned after a certain period. The network administrator will monitor users who fail to use the system or to clear their in-trays, so that they can be 'retrained' or taken off the system. If mail is to be sent or copied to non-users, hard copy can be printed at a network printer.

Advantages

Electronic mail has the following advantages over paper-based postal services.

(a)   Speed. A message reaches its recipient within fifteen minutes of being sent.

(b)   Reliability. Receipts can be generated to confirm delivery and that the addressee has read the message.

(c)   Economy. There is an IT cost to email, but stationery, photocopying postage and courier costs and time can be saved.

(d)   Security. Each user's filing system, inbox and outbox is password protected.

(e)   Flexibility. Existing documents can be 'attached' to memos and transmitted with them (eg spreadsheets, reports etc).

## Chapter 8

(a)   *Personal data shall be accurate and, where necessary, kept up-to-date.*

This principle means that data on the membership system must be correct at all times; the implication is therefore that as members details change, so the data on the membership system must be amended to reflect those changes. If the data is not correct, then the Institute could provide prospective employers with incorrect information, which may prejudice a member's chances of obtaining a job. This action would reflect badly on the Institute and could result in legal action by the member in some situations.

The Institute can try ensure that the membership information is correct, firstly by recording where the original information came from. If members provide inaccurate information concerning their qualifications or salary then the Institute can hardly be found liable for any inaccuracies in this information. To check the accuracy of the current information on the system, a printout of the record for each member can be made and that member asked to confirm that the details are correct. Again, if the member signs the form then it is good evidence that membership information is accurate.

*Personal data shall not be kept longer than is necessary for its purpose.*

Personal data can only be collected and stored for specific purposes. When the reason for collecting that information has been expired, then there is no longer any need to maintain that information. If the data is maintained on the membership system then there is a danger that the data will be disclosed accidentally with other valid information. To avoid this situation occurring, data that is no longer required should be deleted from the membership system.

In this situation, it is likely that salary information will only be required where members are applying for jobs via the Institutes job vacancy service. When a member has found a suitable job, then the salary information is no longer required and should be deleted from the membership system.

The other situation where data should be deleted is where a person ceases to be a member of the Institute, possibly due to non-payment of subscription or resignation. If either of these situations occurs, then the details of that member should be removed. This action may be under manual control or by the computer system itself. After a specified amount of time, such as three months, if the subscription has not been paid, then the member's information can be automatically deleted from the system.

*Appropriate security measures shall be taken against unauthorised access to, or alternation, or disclosure of, personal data and against accidental loss or destruction of personal data.*

This principle means that the personal data must be kept secure, and that the data can only be accessed and disclosed in accordance with the reasons for which it is being held. To ensure that this principle is maintained, then adequate security must be placed around the membership system. The security system must be sufficient to stop not only removal of the data, but also access and amendment of that data on the company's system.

The following controls will be needed to meet these requirements.

Security over access to the membership system including door locks and security passes to enter buildings.

Access controls on computer systems such as passwords.

Appropriate backup of the data to guard against accidental or even deliberate destruction of the data at the Institute.

(b)    A computer virus is a computer program that has been written to cause deliberate damage to a computer's software, hardware or both. Various measures can be taken to stop a virus entering the computer system.

Runnig appropriate anti-virus software. The anti-virus software will automatically scan any programs and data files being transferred onto the computer and provide an alert to the user if a virus is detected. Steps can then be taken to disinfect the file before any damage is done to the computer receiving that file.

Ensuring that staff are aware of the need to ensure viruses are not transferred onto the computer. This can be carried out by having all staff signing conditions of employment which include the clause that only authorised software may be used on company computers. This will help to eliminate the spread of viruses via e-mail attachments or other unauthorised programmes.

Ensuring that the computer maintaining the membership system is not attached to a network. This control will be effective where only a limited number of people are required to access the system, and they are located in one office. Providing network or intranet access increases the risk of viruses being spread because they can easily be transferred from other computers on the network.

## Chapter 9

(a)    Many organisations invest in IT in the expectation that it will bring substantial benefits, perhaps by cutting costs or by giving the organisation competitive advantage. This is not necessarily always going to be the case: any new system should be justified by reference to its technical, operational and economic feasibility before a decision to invest is made. Many of the benefits of introducing a new system are intangible and may not be clearly identified in advance. One benefit which may be expected, but which is hard to quantify, is improved productivity.

Productivity may be defined as rate of output per person. Increased productivity could take a number of different forms. It could simply consist of faster work, but might also be seen in work which is performed with fewer errors.

The benefits of IT are sometimes identified as follows.

(i)    Computers are generally accurate, whereas humans are not.

(ii) Computers can handle large volumes of transactions more easily than humans can.

(iii) Computers can perform calculations and sorting exercises faster than humans can.

(iv) Information is more easily distributed to users throughout an organisation.

The accuracy claimed for computers must be qualified by the mnemonic GIGO (garbage in, garbage out) but in general, better accuracy encourages increased productivity. Typists can use spellcheckers and correct errors, improving their rates of letter correction and production. Accounts staff can be confident that day books and ledgers will be correctly cast and will balance, and users of stock control systems can have confidence that stock balances reflects receipts and despatches input to the system.

The volume of transactions now processed in many organisations is too great for clerical manpower to deal with. In industries like banking, for example, huge volumes of transactions are processed daily. Examples include the encoding of cheques in the cheque clearing process and the processing of credit card transactions at card services centres.

The speed of processing is improved. Computers can, for practical purposes, work 24 hours a day and batches of transactions that are not time-critical can be processed overnight and at weekends. Real-time processing allows instantaneous updating of records. Thus a travel agent making a booking for a client in Plymouth can update booking files in Nottingham so that a second agent in Glasgow can see, instantly, that the reservation has been made.

This leads into a related benefit: that electronic information can be transmitted hundreds of miles with no apparent delay, using electronic data interchange, voice mail or electronic mail. Video technology saves travelling time with video phones or computer conferencing.

Information can be made available to more people. Databases implemented on local area networks or wide area networks allow staff in different offices to work on data together.

(b) The use of IT can also harm a business's performance. As noted above, the use of IT must be carefully evaluated prior to any decision to invest. Many organisations spent huge sums of money on IT in the 1980s and 1990s only to find that the investment was not well directed or did not fit in with corporate strategy.

End-user computing has become prevalent. Broadly spreading, this is the concept of placing PCs, perhaps in a network configuration, on everyone's desks. This can damage productivity. Some software products are too sophisticated for the average user. Thus a manager who wishes to use a spreadsheet to log employee hours, or an employee who wishes to use a word processor to produce an internal newsletter, might get carried away experimenting with the features of the system.

If proper training is not provided much time will be wasted. Tasks may take longer than the old manual way of working.

Other problems include failure to back up files resulting in the loss of data and inconsistent file naming and filing techniques making information hard to locate.

Viruses present another risk. These may be carried on program or data files and can spread via floppy disk, e-mail attachments or across network links. They can be very destructive - to the extent of to wiping hard disks clean. All files (whether on disk or via e-mail or other links) coming into an organisation should be checked using proprietary anti-virus software.

The use of telecommunications links across, and between, large organisations makes them vulnerable to hackers. The risk ranges from 'nuisance value' to potential loss of commercially sensitive material. On-line banks have been attacked in this way.

Computer breakdown, whether through malfunction or natural disaster can disrupt operations. The use of back ups, coupled with a full contingency plan, is essential. Many organisations now depend on IT for product delivery and many more have 'back office' functions that are entirely reliant on IT for continual operation.

# Index

# ORDER FORM

Any books from our Business Basics range can be ordered in one of the following ways:

- Telephone us on **020 8740 2211**

- Send this page to our **Freepost** address

- Fax this page on **020 8740 1184**

- Email us at **publishing@bpp.com**

- Go to our website: **www.bpp.com**

We aim to deliver to all UK addresses inside 5 working days. Orders to all EU addresses should be delivered within 6 working days. All other orders to overseas addresses should be delivered within 8 working days.

**BPP Publishing Ltd**
**Aldine House**
**Aldine Place**
**London W12 8AW**
**Tel: 020 8740 2211**
**Fax: 020 8740 1184**
**Email: publishing@bpp.com**

Full name: _____

Day-time delivery address: _____

_____

_____ Postcode _____

Day-time telephone (for queries only): _____

Please send me the following quantities of books:

| | No. of copies | Price | Total |
|---|---|---|---|
| Accounting | | £13.95 | |
| Law | | £13.95 | |
| Quantitative Methods | | £13.95 | |
| Information Technology | | £13.95 | |
| Economics | | £13.95 | |
| Marketing | | £13.95 | |
| Human Resource Management | | £13.95 | |
| Organisational Behaviour | | £13.95 | |

| | Sub Total | £ |
|---|---|---|

**Postage & Packaging**

| | |
|---|---|
| **UK** : £3.00 for first plus £2.00 for each extra | £ |
| **Europe** : (inc. ROI)  £5.00 for first plus £4.00 for each extra | £ |
| **Rest of the world** : £20.00 for first plus £10.00 for each extra | £ |

| | Grand Total | £ |
|---|---|---|

I enclose a cheque for £_____ (cheque to BPP Publishing Ltd) or charge to Access/VISA/Switch

Card number: ☐☐☐☐☐☐☐☐☐☐☐☐☐☐☐☐☐☐☐

Issues number (Switch only): _____

Start date: _____ Expiry date: _____

Signature _____

# REVIEW FORM & FREE PRIZE DRAW

We are constantly reviewing, updating and improving our publications. We would be grateful for any comments or thoughts you have on this book. Cut out and send this page to our Freepost address and you will be automatically entered in a £50 prize draw.

**Jed Cope**
**Business Basics Range Manager**
**BPP Publishing Ltd, FREEPOST, London W12 8BR**

Full name: _____

Address: _____

_____

_____ Postcode _____

Where are you studying?

Where did you find out about BPP books?

Why did you decide to buy this book?

Have you used any other BPP products in your studies?

What thoughts do you have on our:

- Introductory pages

- Topic coverage

- Summary diagrams, icons, chapter roundups and quick quizzes

- Activities, case studies and questions

The other side of this form is left blank for any further comments you wish to make.

Please give any further comments and suggestions (with page number if necessary) below.

**FREE PRIZE DRAW RULES**

1    Closing date for 31 January 2001 draw is 31 December 2000. Closing date for 31 July 2001 draw is 30 June 2001.

2    Restricted to entries with UK and Eire addresses only. BPP employees, their families and business associates are excluded.

3    No purchase necessary. Entry forms are available upon request from BPP Publishing. No more than one entry per title, per person. Draw restricted to persons aged 16 and over.

4    Winners will be notified by post and receive their cheques not later than 6 weeks after the relevant draw date.

5    The decision of the promoter in all matters is final and binding. No correspondence will be entered into.